Legal Research and Education Abridgment

Legal Research and Education Abridgment

Edward J. Bander
with the assistance of David F. Bander

"Abridgments of the law are brief digests
of the law, arranged alphabetically."
1 Steph. Comm. 51

Ballinger Publishing Company • Cambridge, Mass.
A Subsidiary of J. B. Lippincott Company

This book is printed on recycled paper.

International Standard Book Number: 0-88410-794-9

Library of Congress Catalog Card Number: 78-2408

Printed in the United States of America

Library of Congress Cataloging in Publication Data

Bander, Edward J.
Legal research and education abridgment.

Includes bibliographies.
1. Legal research—United States. I. Bander, David F., joint author. II. Title.
KF240.B26 340'.07'2073 78-2408
ISBN 0-88410-794-9

TO MY WIFE — The genius in the family

I would like to thank David Bander for taking on a good deal of the drudgery of this book and Sid Bander for pitching in when I needed him.

Contents

Preface

The purpose of this book is to simplify the researching of law. Part I presents the major tools of the trade that will enable the law student, lawyer, paralegal, and layman to understand and apply legal research methods to the solution of legal problems.

The reader is urged to learn by doing. The proper use of legal materials such as annotations, digests, and encyclopedias become obvious when they are diligently used and remains an enigma when read about in exhaustive detail. This volume provides sufficient information on how to use legal material effectively. However, while legal material per se may be relatively easy to use, legal problem solving can be time consuming, laborious, and intricate. No legal research treatise can teach the user how to conceptualize, analyze, analogize, or rationalize conflicting precedents or how to reduce a mountain of facts into a manageable legal equation.

We have tried, in Part II, to add a new dimension to this book on research and to further assist the reader by introducing him to the experts. We have broken the law down into its major components and, under each, listed all the leading texts, journals, treatises, and bibliographies. As an additional feature, leading New York texts have been appended to the subject listings (see Part II: BIBLIOGRAPHIES for the Henke and Jacobs books that do the same for California and Illinois), but readers in other states are advised to write or call local law librarians to determine whether texts pertinent to their subject needs are available. To expedite and update research, we have included specific references to encyclopedias and the West Digest key number. This material will enable the researcher to determine to what extent his problem has already been researched; if so, he need only bring the information up to date.

Law school course descriptions are also included in Part II, as they succinctly circumscribe particular areas covered so that the researcher can determine if he is looking into the correct legal areas. Descriptions of courses have been taken from a number of law school catalogs—particularly the catalog of New York University School of Law, whose offerings are more diversified than other law schools because of its unique location, large graduate program in law, and an enrollment that is the largest in the country. Finally, frequent reference is made to more compendious books on research so that the librarian and scholar may have ready access to all available sources.

As a reference consultant on law for twenty-five years, the author has constantly made the point that the law is available to those who want it. This book is dedicated to those who have made use of my suggestions in the past, whose inquiries contributed much to the organization of this book, and who have waited patiently for this book to be published.

Edward J. Bander

Part I

Legal Research Techniques

LEGAL RESEARCH BOOKS

This volume differs from the selected legal research texts listed below. This volume is designed to provide quick access to legal information. Part I can be read in an afternoon. It will enable a researcher to commence his research. The theory behind this book is that one learns to do research by using the material rather than reading about it. References are made to more extended discussions in the books listed below for those who desire it. Moreover, Part II of this volume is designed to bypass the legal research component by referring the reader to treatises, reports, encyclopedias, and so forth directly. The author can only emphasize that it is not the ability to research that counts; it is what you do with what you have in the time available.

Andrews et al. *The Law in the United States of America; A Selective Bibliographical Guide* (New York University Press 1965).

A dated bibliographic guide that is geared to indicate to the law librarian a basic American law collection. More conveniently than elsewhere, you get a bird's-eye view of just which sets are in a standard law library. There is an annotated listing of books by subject from accounting to zoning.

Cohen. *Legal Research in a Nutshell.* 3d ed. (West 1978).

Chapters on judicial reports, case finding, statutes, legislative history, administrative law, loose leaf services, treaties, secondary materials (encyclopedias, restatements, periodicals, citators, etc.), foreign and international law. A 415 page summary of the more complete texts, such as *How to Find the Law*, Price and Bitner, and so forth. Referred to as *Cohen* in this book.

Cohen. ed. *How to Find the Law*. 7th ed. (West 1976).

The chapter on analysis of the problem effectively describes how a factual problem can be solved with legal research tools. There are also chapters on legal encyclopedias, digests, American court reports, statutes, administrative and executive publications, loose leaf services, periodical literature, treatises, restatements, uniform laws, dictionaries, citators, English and Canadian materials, nonlegal materials (government documents, biography, etc.), the writing of letters, opinions, memoranda, and appellate briefs. Each chapter is written by a law librarian. There are also chapters on multimedia (microforms, computers, etc.); research in the social sciences; and international, foreign, and comparative law. Referred to as *How to* in this book.

Farnsworth. *An Introduction to the Legal System of the United States* (Oceana 1963; rpt. 1975).

A brief introductory text on the legal system. Its chapters on the judicial system, case law, the legislative system, statutes, and secondary authority form a cohesive and well-written commentary for an American student, as well as for the foreign student for whom it was designed. There are also bibliographical essays on civil procedure, criminal procedure, evidence, conflict of laws, contracts, torts, property, family law, commercial law, business enterprises, constitutional law, trade regulation, labor law, tax law, and criminal law. While the book is dated, particularly as to current texts, it is superior in insight to the other texts.

Jacobstein and Mersky. *Fundamentals of Legal Research* (Foundation Press 1977).

Chapters on glossary of terms used in legal research, the legal process, preliminary procedure in legal research, court reports, federal court decisions, state court decisions and the National reporter system, digests, annotated law reports, constitutions, federal legislation, legislative history, state and municipal legislation, court procedure, administrative practice, citations, encyclopedias, legal periodicals and indexes, treaties, restatements, model codes, uniform laws, international law, English legal research, Canadian law, computers and microforms, summary of research procedure, citation style, abbreviations. Referred to as *Jacobstein* in text.

Lloyd. *Finding the Law; A Guide to Legal Research* (Oceana (1974).

Chapters on researching the common law, using the statutes, persuasive authority, researching in specific fields of law (environmental law, consumer law, bankruptcy, criminal law, constitutional law, commercial law, family law, taxation, business organizations, natural resources law, international law, torts, trade regulation, property law, estate planning), citation style, abbreviations, citators. An inexpensive beginner's text that has some excellent features.

New York University School of Law. *Moot Court Handbook; Introduction to Legal Research, Brief Writing and Oral Argument.* 5th ed. (New York University Moot Court Board 1978).

The chapter on researching the brief presupposes a knowledge of legal research, but nevertheless is a fine summary of legal research materials and citation style. Although designed to assist students in writing a brief, it can be helpful to the neophyte, particularly as the entire book is offset from typewritten copy and the student can observe the form in typed copy rather than printed copy. There is also a bibliography of books on legal writing and oral argument.

Price and Bitner. *Effective Legal Research; A Practical Manual of Law Books and their Use* (Prentice-Hall 1953).

Also published in a 1962 student edition (Little, Brown). Chapters on legislation, federal legislation, treaties, legislative histories, indexes and tables, work with federal statutes, state legislation, rules of courts and administrative agencies, law reports, administrative law, index and search books, digests, encyclopedias, treatises, legal periodicals, restatements, dictionaries, words and phrases, maxims, form books, loose leaf services, citators, English and Canadian materials, tables of cases, citation style. The appendixes include lists of American, British, and Canadian material; standard form of appellate brief; memorandum of law; and a list of commonly used Anglo-American abbreviations. While both editions are obviously dated, this is a standard text in the field and indispensable in any legal reference collection. Referred to as *Price* in this book.

Research Group, Inc. *Basic Legal Research Techniques* (American Law Pub. Service, [1976].

An innovative text on legal research by an organization engaged in legal research for lawyers with offices in Charlottesville, Va., Cambridge, Mass., Ann Arbor, Mich., and Berkeley, Calif. The discussion of the "back door approach" is a novel and satisfactory way of leading into secondary sources. This organization also published "Researchers," which they claim provides digests of cases more recent than West. Appendixes include legal writing information, citation form and spacing guide, citation style for state codifications, an extensive list of abbreviations, footnote terms such as "cf.," general abbreviations, and a short list of treatises by subject. Referred to as *Research Group* in this book.

Rombauer. *Legal Problem Solving: Analysis, Research and Writing.* 3d ed. (West 1978).

Chapters on how to brief a case, how to analyze an opinion, how to interpret legislation, how to use legal research material, how to write a memorandum (sample memorandum), how to argue orally (sample oral argument), how to do computer research. While not as exhaustive as books such as *Pollack* or *Price*, this is basically a book on how to do legal research.

Werner. *Manual for Prison Law Libraries* (Rothman 1976).

Chapters on the prison law library, library quarters and equipment, law books and their use, library acquisitions and records, cataloging and shelving books, lending and borrowing books, and so forth. While designed for a specialized clientele, with the emphasis on criminal law, the information on legal research is concise and informative (see also LAW FOR THE LAYMAN in Part II).

ABBREVIATIONS

The *Uniform System of Citation* (12th ed. 1976) lists abbreviations of frequently used words, states, reports, statutes, legal actions, and so forth. It has recommended abbreviations for law reviews, loose leaf services, and other materials published periodically. It also has abbreviations for English, United Nations, Common Market, and international and foreign law materials. A convenient list of citation abbreviations is in *Lloyd*. Abbreviations of reports and legal terms can be found in current editions of *Black's Law Dictionary* (West); *Ballantine's Law Dictionary* (LCP); and in *Price*, *Research Group*, and *Jacobstein*. Mary Chapman, *Bibliographical Index to the State Reports Prior to the National Reporter System* (Trans Media 1977), has the most accurate and complete listing of early American reports. *American Jurisprudence* and *Corpus Juris Secundum* also list abbreviations.

For acronyms (ERISA for Employment Retirement Income Security Act) consult Ellen T. Crowley, ed. *Acronyms, Initialisms, and Abbreviations Dictionary* (Gale 1976).

Shepard's citation abbreviations are unique to the publisher. Many publishers have preferred abbreviations. They need not be followed.

ADVANCE SHEETS (see SLIP DECISIONS)

AMERICAN DIGEST SYSTEM (see DIGESTS)

AMERICAN JURISPRUDENCE 2d (see also ENCYCLOPEDIAS)

"A modern comprehensive text statement of American Law—State and Federal" (*Am. Jur. 2d* title page). Arranged alphabetically by legal word or phrase. There is a General Index to the entire set and indexes in each volume. One volume is "Table of Statutes and Rules Cited." A "Words and Phrases" volume extracts definitions from the set and includes citations to *Am. Jur. 2d* and the publisher's annotated sets. The publisher also issues New Topic Service titles. A loose leaf volume contains the following titles with a 1977 update:

Comparative Negligence, Consumer Credit Protection, Consumer Products Safety Acts, No Fault Divorce, No Fault Insurance, Occupational Safety and Health Acts, Uniform Probate Code. Also separate volumes for Federal Rules of Evidence, Pension Reform Act, 1976 Tax Reform Law.

The *Am. Jur. 2d* "Desk Book" contains "historical and legal documents, facts, tables, charts, and statistics of special interest to attorneys" with 1977 update (documents include ancient statutes; also professional responsibility code, law school enrollment, and so forth).

AMERICAN LAW REPORTS (see ANNOTATIONS)

ANNOTATIONS

The most comprehensive set of annotations is published by the Lawyers Cooperative Publishing Company (LCP). Their *American Law Reports* (*A.L.R.*, *A.L.R. 2d*, *A.L.R. 3d* and *A.L.R. Federal*) are organized as follows: significant cases are reprinted with headnotes and also a summary of briefs of counsel. This is followed by a signed annotation that explores thoroughly an issue raised in the reprinted case. The editors provide an index to the annotation, a breakdown by jurisdiction (state or federal), and a checklist of LCP publications that treat aspects of the annotation (such as forms, encyclopedic references, practice, etc.) *A.L.R.* is updated by the *Blue Book of Supplemental Decisions*. *A.L.R. 2d* is updated by the *Later Case Service*, and a pocket part updates *A.L.R. 3d* and *A.L.R. Fed.* (see Appendix for chart). There are *Quick Index* volumes that lead to annotations in these sets as well as a table of cases reprinted and a list of annotations that have been superseded. The *Federal Quick Index* leads to references in United State Code Service as well as annotations. Many publications, including *American Jurisprudence, Second Series* (*Am. Jur. 2d*), law review articles, treatises, and *Shepard's Citations*, will refer one to these annotations.

LCP also published the *Lawyers' Edition*, Supreme Court Reporter (L.Ed.), which reprints United States Supreme Court Reports and also annotates them. Marginal markings provide parallel citations to the *United States Reports* (U.S.), making it unnecessary to cite to anything but the official *United States Reports.* There is also a *Lawyers' Edition Digest* (similar to the *West Supreme Court Digest*), which has a volume that indexes all the annotations as well as the usual table of cases and topic index.

An annotation "in point" can save the researcher a good deal of work. It will not only provide an overview of a narrow legal topic but cite one to precedents in all jurisdictions, including the jurisdiction he or she is researching.

One research approach to locate annotations is as follows: if one reads the *Bowling case* (see Appendix for text of case), one will find that the court cites (not as authority but to illustrate its position) 27 *Am. Jur.* Infants, Section 17. *Am. Jur.* has been superseded by *Am. Jur. 2d*, and a table in front of the volume containing the topic Infants advises the user that 42 *Am. Jur. 2d* Infants, Section 70 now covers this topic. By consulting this citation and the pocket part, one will have cases bearing on the rule as to disaffirmance by infants when motor vehicles are involved. One is also told that there is an annotation in 56 *A.L.R. 3d* 1335 (1974) on "Automobile or Motorcycle as Necessary for Infant." The *Bowling* case is discussed and distinguished at 56 *A.L.R. 3d* 1350 (1974). In effect, one has brought the 1962 *Bowling* case up to date. The lesson to be learned is that research tools complement each other, particularly if issued by the same publisher.

For explanatory pamphlets, write to the Lawyers Cooperative Publishing Co. See also *Cohen*, pp. 89–90; *How to*, pp. 39–48; *Jacobstein*, p. 96; *Price*, p. 143; *Research Group*, p. 11.

AUTHORITY (see also COMMON LAW)

Legal materials are designed to inform the user where to locate and how to apply authority—that is, what the courts believe they are obligated to obey in deciding a case before them. In general, this means researching for applicable laws, regulations, decisions of courts (also called cases, opinions, reports), and, obviously, state and federal constitutions.

This authority can be a law (National Labor Relations Act), the United States Constitution (Fifth Amendment on the right against involuntary self-incrimination), a regulation (tax deductions for moving expenses), and cases interpreting the above. Cases have assumed such an important part of our legal system that it can safely be said that no one knows what a law means until the courts interpret it through decided cases.

What about cases in such areas of the law as contracts and torts that are not generally based on the passage of a law (which involves approval by a legislature and signing by the executive)? The long answer is to read a treatise on the common law (the heartbeat of our legal system), consult the American Law Institute Restatements (see RESTATEMENT), and find a good treatise on the topic (see Part II). The short answer is to find the relevant cases.

The previous paragraph may mislead the reader into believing that all legal research leads to litigation. Most research, in fact, safeguards the individual from litigation. It is called preventive law. Also, most litigation ends at trial (that is, an appeal is not taken), and it may be heartening to know that for the myriad cases that come before the courts, comparatively few are recorded in the official reports.

As you read this book, keep in mind that our system of jurisprudence is determined to a great extent by what courts have written in the past. We are guided by precedent (see PRECEDENT). All the material pertaining to legal research is designed to lead one to precedent (unless the situation is governed by statute) or to try and establish a precedent. For a fuller explanation of this concept (and such related terms as *stare decisis, res judicata, ratio decidendi*), consult the texts mentioned earlier and the following:

Comment. Diverse Views of What Constitutes the Principle of Law of a Case. 36 *Colo. L. Rev.* 377 (1964).

Cross. *Precedent in English Law*. 3d ed. (Clarendon Press 1977).

It may also be instructive as you read about legal research in this book to keep in mind the order of research that one law professor recommended for state law: (1) local encyclopedia, (2) annotated statutes, (3) state digest, (4) *American Jurisprudence 2d*, (5) *American Law Reports* series, (6) *Corpus Juris Secundum*, (7) treatises, (8) *Words and Phrases*, (9) loose leaf services, (10) *Restatements*, (11) law reviews, (12) *Shepard's Citators.* See Emery, *A Streamlined Briefing Technique for States with Encyclopedias* (A.B.A. Law Student Division, 1970), p. 10.

BRIEFS AND RECORDS (see also Part II: LEGAL WRITING

Official papers submitted to a court in a pending case. All briefs and records are a matter of public record and must be made available by the court that required them. The usual practice is for courts to appoint depositories for their briefs. Briefs are also available from private publishers. For instance, Information Handling Services and Law Reprints sell briefs and records for the United States Supreme Court on microfiche. Hein sells them on microfilm for the New York Court of Appeals, beginning with 36 N.Y. 2d. *Lawyers Edition*, the *American Law Reports*, and the *New York Reports* include summaries of briefs of cases they print. *Preview of United States Supreme Court Cases* (Association of American Law Schools) summarizes and distinguishes cases pending before the United States

Supreme Court. *United States Law Week* has oral arguments in selected cases. Kurland and Casper, *Landmark Briefs and Arguments of the Supreme Court of the United States*, has briefs on constitutional law, tax law, and so forth in bound volume form.

Briefs and oral arguments, it should be mentioned, have no precedent value. Most student and scholarly research can limit itself to the opinion of the court without delving into the labyrinth of points made and considered unworthy of incorporation into the opinion of the court. The constipated strain for citation usually evidences a lack of self-confidence in reasoning power.

New York

New York State Law Library (Albany 12224) has records and briefs for the New York Court of Appeals; the Appellate Division, 1st–4th Depts.; and the United States Supreme Court. The Supreme Court Library (Brooklyn 11201) has records and briefs for the New York Court of Appeals and the Appellate Division, 1st–4th Depts. The Association of the Bar of the City of New York has the records and briefs for the New York Court of Appeals; the Appellate Division, 1st–4th Depts.; the United States Court of Appeals for the Second Circuit; and the United States Supreme Court. This information is from *Union List of Cases and Points/Records and Briefs in New York State Law Libraries* compiled by Gibson and Spencer (Charles B. Sears Law Library, 1977).

CANADA (see ENGLISH AND CANADIAN MATERIAL)

CASE LAW—HOW TO FIND A CASE (see also REPORTS, UNITED STATES SUPREME COURT

1. If you have the name of the case and no idea as to where it is published, use the Table of Cases to each unit of the *American Digest System* (see DIGESTS). This will take you from the earliest reported cases to the latest reports as listed in the latest issue of the *General Digest*.

2. If you know the jurisdiction, follow these simple rules: (a) If it is a federal case, use the Table of Cases to the *Modern Federal Practice Digest* (1939 to date) and *Federal Digest* (to 1939), which will give you every opinion that has appeared in *Federal Supplement* (district courts), *Federal Reporter* (courts of appeals), *Federal Rules Decisions*, and the United States Supreme Court Reports (more on

this later). Most federal district court cases do not result in a reported opinion (you can go to the court and inspect the docket). The *Federal Supplement* publishes, in general, only those opinions submitted by the federal district courts. Some publishers (in tax, labor, securities, environment, etc.) include opinions in their sets that were not approved for publication in *Federal Supplement.* If your case is followed by "Civ. No. 10701" or "Cr. No. 70922," the chances are that it is, at most, an unreported case. There is a trend not to report court of appeals cases that lack precedent value (see 50 *Cal. L. Rev.* 1181 [1977]). (b) If it is a state case, check the state digest or the regional digest that includes the state (see DIGESTS) for its Table of Cases. State digests have plaintiff-defendant tables and defendant-plaintiff tables.

3. For United States Supreme Court cases (see also UNITED STATES SUPREME COURT), the *Lawyers Edition Digest* (LCP) and the *United States Supreme Court Digest* (West) have tables of cases volumes that are alphabetical by plaintiff and defendant. For current cases, check *United States Law Week* and Commerce Clearing House *Supreme Court Bulletin* for their tables of cases.

4. Caveat: Always check for a pocket part at the back of a volume or a cumulative bound supplement to make sure you have checked from earliest cases to latest (or work in reverse if it is a recent case). These sets will always tell you up to what current volume they have covered on the verso of the title page of the pocket supplement. It is a simple matter to check subsequently received material to bring your research up to date (for instance, the *United States Supreme Court Digest* [West]), at this writing, covers all volumes of the *United States Reports* up to volume 425; the library has *United States Reports* up to volume 432. Volumes 426 to 432 have tables of cases. One more item, if you are trying to convert a *Supreme Court Reporter* or *Lawyers Ed.* citation to the *United States Reports* and nothing else works, the date of decisions runs chronologically in both, thereby making it easy to go from one to the other.

CITATION STYLE

The following is a guide to commonly used footnote citations as adapted from *A Uniform System of Citation* (commonly known as the "Blue Book"). The 12th edition of this publication was published in 1976. For capitalization, spacing, and type styles when preparing a manuscript for law review publication consult the Blue Book.

NEW YORK CITATIONS

Constitution

N.Y. CONST. art. 1, sec. 6
Note: A symbol for section (§) is required by Blue Book.

Code

N.Y. CIV. PRAC. sec 302(a) (1) (McKinney 1972).
N.Y. BUS. CORP. sec. 1314 (Consolidated Law Service Supp. 1975).
Note: The Blue Book cites only to McKinney, but either set will do.

Session Laws

Ch. 167, [1975] N.Y. Sess. Laws sec. 100–601.

Bills

S.2824, N.Y. State Senate (1975); A.2543, N.Y. State Assembly (1975). See 1 N.Y. LEGISLATIVE RECORD AND INDEX S274, A237 (1975).

Court of Appeals

pre-1956

People v. Manfredi, 309 N.Y. 898, 131 N.E. 2d 576 (1955).

post-1955

Cohen v. Boyland, 1 N.Y. 2d 8, 132 N.E. 2d 890, 150 N.Y.S. 2nd 5 (1956).

use of *id* and citing to page when context is clear

68. People v. Sandoval, 34 N.Y. 2d 371, 314 N.E. 2d 413, 357 N.Y.S. 2d 849, aff'g 337 N.Y.S. 2d 994 (2d Dep't 1972) (mem.).
69. . . .
70. The record shows otherwise. 34 N.Y. 2d at 373, 314 N.E. 2d at 415, 357 N.Y.S. 2d at 852.
71. *id.* at 375, 314 N.E. 2d at 417, 357 N.Y.S. 2d at 853.

. . .

74. 34 N.Y. 2d at 375, 314 N.E. 2d at 416, 357 N.Y.S. 2d at 854.

Appellate Division

Brown v. Lavine, 45 App. Div. 2d 858, 358 N.Y.S. 2d 530 (1974) (mem.).
Tappis v. New York State Racing and Wagering Bd., 46 App. Div. 2d 613, 359 N.Y.S. 2d 780 (per curiam), *rev'd*, 36 N.Y. 2d 862, 331 N.E. 2d 697, 370 N.Y.S 2d 922 (1975).

Miscellaneous

Heath v. Diamond, 82 Misc. 2d 217, 368 N.Y.S. 2d 440 (Sup. Ct. 1975).

FEDERAL AND OTHER CITATIONS

Federal Reports

Baird v. Day & Zimmerman, 390 F. Supp. 883 (S.D.N.Y. 1974), *aff'd mem.*, 510 F 2d 968 (2d Cir. 1975).

United States Reports

Jenkins v. Delaware, 395 U.S. 213 (1969).

Law Reviews

vom Bauer, Some Fundamentals of Looking Up Law, 18 Prac. Law 63 (1972).

Books

W. PROSSER, LAW OF TORTS sec. 47 (4th ed. 1971).

Annotations

Annot., 12 A.L.R. 2d 382 (1950).

Signals

For the use of signals (cf., see also), see N.Y.U. School of Law, *Moot Court Handbook* (1978), p. 59-60.

For critiques of *A Uniform System of Citation*, see 3 *J. Contemp. Law* 133, 140 (1976); 12 *Harv. Civil Rights-Civil Liberties Law Rev.* 507 (1977); 44 *Univ. of Chicago Law Rev.* 695 (1977); and 86 *Yale Law J.* 197 (1966).

CITATORS

Shepard Case Citators

Basically, and with qualifications, this set will tell one every time a case he is researching has been subsequently cited. In the publisher's language, "The case divisions. . .is to make available to the lawyer every instance in which a reported decision has been cited in a subsequent case." (From *How to Use Shepard's Case Citations*, available from the publisher.)

By using the state citation (193 Mass. 364), the researcher can locate every case in a state that has cited his or her case; by using the regional citation (79 N.E. 745), the researcher can also locate every citation to his or her case thoughout the fifty states. If your case is not listed, it has never been cited.

By adding symbols to this simple compilation of cases by citation of the case, the publisher can quickly let the reader know whether his case has been overruled, distinguished, followed, or in any way characterized. It is imperative that one check the prefatory pages to the citator so that all the abbreviations are understood. By use of the superscript, the user can also determine which headnote in the cited case is being considered in the citing case (see sample pages from a Shepard citator in Appendix).

There is a Shepard citator for every state. Besides providing the above information, the user can get parallel citations (i.e., to the unofficial National Reporter), references to the cited case in selected law reviews, annotations, *Restatement* references, federal citations, and other information. As with all secondary sources, Shepard's is neither final nor infallible. The researcher must read the cases.

Shepard's regional citators provide a means of determining if one's state case has been cited in other jurisdictions as well as in the jurisdiction of the cited case.

Besides the state and regional citators, there are federal citators for the United States Supreme Court and other federal couts (including administrative courts such as the Securities and Exchange Commission), and a labor citator.

This does not exhaust the Shepard repertoire. There is also a law review citator and there are statutory citators, basically arranged by sections of the state code or *United States Code*, that will inform the user if the statute cited has been amended by the legislature or cited by a court. If you write to Shepard's Citations (see PUBLISHERS for a list of addresses), they will send you a lengthy pamphlet that gets into all ramifications of this unique and useful (and expensive) set. Pages from that pamphlet are reproduced in the appendix.

The advantage and disadvantage of Shepard's is that it indiscriminately tells you every time "your" case is subsequently cited. Librarians are often asked, "Do I have to check each citation?"—to which one facetious answer is, "Only if your client can afford it." The nonfacetious answer is, "Yes." The practical answer is to apportion your time for research, cite checking, and writing.

Shepard's is not the only publisher who provides a citation service. Prentice-Hall and Commerce Clearing House tax services include a citator factor in their table of cases. Any analysis of a case, your own included, updates a case, particularly if it is accepted by the court to which the analysis is given. And Lexis, a computer research tool, can perform a citator function that is particularly useful for current updating.

You must also remember that in doing your research you are your own citator. There is no law stating that a case that does not expressly consider a cited case does not affect it. If that were so, the law could well be a static system of jurisprudence. There are times when the power of reasoning before a court is far more persuasive than research by rote. Even more important, courts can overrule precedents—examples can be given for every court in the land.

The previous paragraph cannot pass without a mention of Louis Brandeis, a great Justice of the United States Supreme Court and a magnificient lawyer. Prior to 1890, no English or American court had ever granted relief based expressly on a right to privacy. After Warren and Brandeis wrote an article on the subject (4 *Harv. L. Rev.* 193 [1890]), this right came to be accepted in many jurisdictions (see Prosser on *Torts* § 117 4th ed. 1971). Another example of this justice's ability to fashion the law is "the Brandeis brief." In *Muller v. Oregon*, 208 U.S. 412 (1908), he submitted a brief containing two pages of legal argument and over 100 pages of sociological data. It was the latter that won the day. Mason, *Brandeis* (Viking, 1946). The significant point to be made is that all books on legal research and finding the law suffer from the fatal flaw of equipping the researcher to locate the illusive, while it is the artist who discerns the obvious.

CHECKLIST OF SHEPARD'S CITATORS

State

There is a citator for each state—cases and statutes (also District of Columbia and Puerto Rico).

Federal

United States Citations (Cases; Statutes and Court Rules)
United States Administrative Citations (Attorney General, F.C.C., Customs, Interior, Internal Revenue, I.C.C., Maritime Cases, F.P.C., S.E.C., Tax Court, F.T.C.)
United States Patents and Trademark Citations
Federal Citations (Part 1: Federal Reporter, Federal Cases; Part 2: Federal Supplement, Federal Rules Decisions, Court of Claims)
Federal Circuit Table
Federal Law Citations in Selected Law Reviews
Federal Labor Citations

New York

Court of Appeals (Common Law, Chancery)
Supreme Court (A.D.)

Miscellaneous
New York Supplement
Statutes (U.S. Constitution, Federal Court Rules as cited in N.Y., N.Y. Constitution, Consolidated Law. Table of N.Y. Acts by Popular Name, Court Acts, Court Rules, Ordinances, Pattern Jury Instructions, etc.)

Others

Acts and Cases by Popular Name
Criminal Justice Citations
Law Review Citations
Restatements of the Law

See also *Cohen*, pp. 97–104 ff.; *How to*, pp. 160–83; *Jacobstein*, p. 261; *Research Group*, p. 64.

CODE OF FEDERAL REGULATIONS (see also FEDERAL REGISTER)

Citation style: 11 C.F.R. § 37 (1975).
A compilation of all regulations by title (similar to United States Code) that have appeared in the *Federal Register.* Title 3 accumulates all executive orders, and the set has an index to each title and an index to the set. It is currently being recompiled each year on a staggered basis.

The regulations are promulgated by administrative agencies to implement the law. They have the effect of law. Federal regulations are not easy to fathom, cannot be Shepardized, and in certain subject areas, such as tax and labor, are more accessible in loose leaf services.

The following publication attempts to explain how to use the *Federal Register* and the *Code of Federal Regulations* with explicit details as to the finding lists and tables that make it possible to follow a regulation to a current date: *The Federal Register: What It Is and How to Use it—A Guide for the User of the Federal Register–Code of Federal Regulations System.* (GPO, 1977).

It should be noted that President Carter has made it one of his goals to cut down on the volume and clear up the language of this publication.

See also *Cohen*, pp. 211–22; *How to*, pp. 156–59; *Jacobstein*, p. 214.

COMMON LAW

"The common law of England is that body of law which has been judicially evolved from the general custom of the realm." *Stroud's*

Judicial Dictionary (Sweet & Maxwell 1971). Some further quotations from Justice Holmes' Supreme Court opinions may be enlightening: "[The law of the states] does issue and has been recognized by this court as issuing from the state courts as well as from the state legislatures. When we know what the source of the law has said that it shall be, our authority is at an end. The law of a State does not become something outside of the state court and independent of it by being called the common law. Whatever it is called it is the law as declared by the state judges and nothing else." *Kuhn v. Fairmount Coal Co.*, 215 U.S. 349, 370–72 (1910). "The common law is not a brooding omnipresence in the sky but the articulate voice of some sovereign or quasi-sovereign that can be identified; . . ." *Southern Pacific Co. v. Jensen*, 244 U.S. 205, 221–22 (1917). "If there were no statute the common law of Massachusetts would supplement the Constitution as it would supplement the statutes of the State. But the common law of Massachusetts is not superior to its statutes and may be modified by them at the pleasure of the State, at least until in some substantial sense it impairs substantive constitutional rights, . . . " *Burrill v. Locomobile Co.*, 258 U.S. 34, 38–39 (1922). "Books written about any branch of the common law treat it as a unit, cite cases from this Court [U.S. Supreme Court], from the Circuit Courts of Appeals, from the State Courts, from England, the Colonies of England indiscriminately, and criticise them as right or wrong according to the writer's notions of a single theory. It is very hard to resist the impression that there is one august corpus, to understand which clearly is the only task of any Court concerned. If there were such a transcendental body of law outside of any particular State but obligatory within it unless and until changed by statute, the Courts of the United States might be right in using their independent judgment as to what it was. But there is no such body of law. The fallacy and illusion that I think exist consist in supposing that there is this outside thing to be found. Law is a word used with different meanings, but law in the sense in which courts speak of it today does not exist without some definite authority behind it. The common law so far as it is enforced in a State, whether called common law or not, is not the common law generally but the law of that State existing by the authority of that State without regard to what it may have been in England or anywhere else. It may be adopted by statute in place of another system previously in force. But a general adoption of it does not prevent the State Courts from refusing to follow the English decisions upon a matter where the local conditions are different. It may be changed by statute, as is done every day. It may be departed from deliberately by judicial decisions. . . .Whether and how far and in what sense a rule shall be adopted whether called common law or Kentucky law is for the State alone to decide. *Black & White Taxicab Co. v. Brown & Yellow Taxicab Co.*, 276 U.S. 518, 532–36 (1928).

It should be noted at this point that Justice Holmes is considered one of the great justices of all time. His book on the *Common Law* (Harvard University Press, 1963), published in 1881, is still in print. For a reverent look at Holmes, see Bander, *Justice Holmes Ex Cathedra* (Michie 1966).

For a fuller treatment of the common law, particularly as it relates to precedent, *stare decisis, ratio decidendi, dictum*, see Cross, *Precedent in English Law*, 3d ed. (Clarendon Press 1977); Levi, *An Introduction to Legal Reasoning* (University of Chicago 1949, 1963). For historical treatment see Holdsworth, *A History of English Law*, 7th ed. (Little Brown 1964), 16 v.; and Plucknett, *A Concise History of the Common Law*, 5th ed. (Little, Brown 1956).

Checklist: 15A *C.J.S.* Common Law
15A *Am. Jur. 2d* Common Law
8 *N.Y. Jur.* Common Law
West Digest key number topic: Common Law

CONGRESSIONAL RECORD (see also LEGISLATIVE HISTORY)

This is allegedly a verbatim account of congressional proceedings that appears in a daily edition and, some months after the session is over, in a set of bound volumes. The pagination differs in the bound volume. There is an appendix section that permits members of Congress to insert material, at taxpayer's expense, that is not included in the bound volume. There is also a daily digest of floor and committee action. There are biweekly indexes and a cumulative index in the bound volume. For excellent background information on the *Record*, see *Guide to Congress* (Congressional Quarterly 1976), p. 495.

See also *Cohen*, p. 173; *Price*, p. 61; *How to*, pp. 199, 204.

CONSTITUTIONS (see also Part II: CONSTITUTIONAL LAW)

Probably every state code carries a copy of the United States Constitution as well as its state constitution. If it is an annotated set, the state constitution will carry all state and federal cases interpreting the state constitution.

CORPUS JURIS SECUNDUM (see also, in general, ENCYCLOPEDIAS)

"A complete restatement of the entire body of American Law. . ." (1 *C.J.S.* v). Arranged alphabetically by subject. Arrangement includes words, phrases, and maxims. *American Jurisprudence 2d* is limited to legal topics. The Part II subject arrangement, has references to *Corpus Juris Secundum.*

DICTIONARIES (see also ABBREVIATIONS)

Ballantine's Law Dictionary. 3d ed. by William S. Anderson (LCP 1969).

Bander. *Law Dictionary of Practical Definitions* (Oceana 1966).

Black's Law Dictionary. Rev. 4th ed. (West 1968).

Maloy. *The Simplified Medical Dictionary for Lawyers.* 3d ed. (Callaghan 1960).

Oran. *Law Dictionary for Non-Lawyers* (West 1975).
Includes abbreviations, current terms ("plea bargaining" is in Oran but not in Black or Ballantine).

Stedman. *Stedman's Medical Dictionary.* 23d ed. (Williams and Wilkins 1976).

Stroud. *Judicial Dictionary of Words and Phrases.* 4th ed. by J.S. James (Sweet and Maxwell 1971-).
An English publication, multivolume.

Words and Phrases (West).
A set of over one hundred volumes that extracts direct quotes from National Reporter System cases. The state digests include a volume that performs a similar function. Annual pocket parts. *N.Y. Jurisprudence* also has a words and phrases volume, and see ENCYCLOPEDIAS, generally.

For a bibliography, see Association of American Law Schools, *Law Books Recommended for Libraries*, No. 16 Dictionaries (Rothman 1968; 1974 supp.).

See also *How to*, pp. 296, 198; *Cohen*, pp. 304-305; *Jacobstein*, p. 369.

DIGESTS

The headnotes in the National Reporters System (see REPORTS) are the reason that West has a virtual monopoly on unofficial reporting. The headnote(s) or abstract(s) that precede the opinion refer to points of law or factual situations discussed in the case. The headnotes are numbered consecutively, and when this number appears in the opinion in brackets, it relates to that portion of the opinion that is summarized in the headnote (the order of headnotes also has use when Shepardizing cases). The topic-key number is not only relevant to the case at hand but will also lead you to other cases in the entire National Reporter System.

For instance, a headnote in the *Bowling* case (see Appendix) reads as follows:

1. Infants, key number 47
   Contracts of minors are voidable and may be disaffirmed.

That proposition is obviously applicable to the *Bowling* case, but by consulting any West Digest unit, you can find other cases holding similar propositions. And remember that while an Indiana court cannot consider the reports of other states as precedent, it can use their reasoning to set its own precedent.

Obviously these topics and key numbers do not tell us enough. The topic and key number lead to cases that must be read to determine their relevance.

The overall method West uses to assemble these headnotes is the American Digest System. Theoretically (there are always qualifying factors to every legal proposition), we can find every federal and state case on the proposition that "contracts of minors are voidable and may be disaffirmed" by utilizing "Infants, key number 47" in the following units of the American Digest System:

Century Digest (to 1896)
Decennial Digests (1896–1976: seven units)
General Digest, Fifth Series (1976 to date: 6 units to date)

This translates into 33 units that will have to be consulted to locate every case that West has on any topic-key number. Usually, the researcher works backward, beginning with the latest volumes first.

If you wish to localize your search, consult a state digest (*Indiana Digest* in the *Bowling* case) or the *Federal Digest*, *Modern Federal Practice Digest*, and *Federal Practice Digest 2d* for all federal material in the National Reporter System. For United States Supreme Court cases, consult the *Supreme Court Digest*. There are also regional digests corresponding to the National Reporter System.

The advantage of a state digest is that you can completely research the topic and key number in one volume and the pocket part to that volume (at times it can be a separate volume—each volume or pocket part will tell you what reports have been digested). Remember that each volume of the regional reporter and each weekly pamphlet has the same key number breakdown as the digest units. There are no state digests for Delaware, Nevada and Utah.

There are three methods of search that can be utilized to locate a desired key number, which will lead one to cases (this analysis is abstracted from West's *Law Finder*, available from the publisher):

1. Descriptive Word Index: Each digest unit has an exhaustive listing of terms that includes parties (infants), places and things (automobiles), basis of action or issue (contract), defense (infancy), relief sought (disaffirmance of contract).
2. Topic Method: There are 400 topical breakdowns in the digests, from Abandonment to Zoning. By going directly to the topic (if one is certain regarding the basis of the cause of action), consulting the scope note and then the key number breakdown to that topic, one can bypass the Descriptive Word Index.
3. Table of Cases: If one has the name of a case said to be in point, each digest unit has a table of cases, arranged alphabetically, that provides the citation to the case, the history of the case, and the topics and key numbers used to digest the case. There are also defendant-plaintiff (the reverse of the general order of case name) listings for units other than the American Digest.

The first method is the most practical, the second comes with experience, and the third gives the citation and parallel citation to the case whose name you have.

The critical thing to remember is that digests lead to cases. Digests cannot be cited, they cannot be relied on for precedent and only constitute a beginning point in one's research. The cases must be read, briefed, and analyzed in the context of the problem.

The West key number system is copyrighted by West; however, digests are a common device for a subject breakdown of material by law publishers. Other publishers who employ this device (using their own logical subject breakdown of the material) are *United States Patent Quarterly* (BNA), *Uniform Commercial Code Reporting Service* (Callaghan), *Negligence and Compensation Cases Annotated* (Callaghan), and all the annotated codes.

One last comment, Gilmore, in the *Ages of American Law* (Yale University Press, 1977), believes that the West system of publishing all reported cases of courts of last resort (and some intermediate appellate decisions) has created a chaotic condition remedied only by the diligence of law reviews to isolate and expound on cases that have made a significant contribution to American law. He failed to comment that the proliferation of law reviews closely parallels the increased number of published reports. Efforts by courts to selectively publish have not been met with joy by the bar (see Unreported Decisions in the United States Court of Appeals, 63 *Corn L. Rev.* 128 [1977]). If there is anything to be learned from all this, it is that precedent, whatever it is, is not a license to forage for silly cases. Students and researchers would be well advised not to search antiquity for a similar set of facts or a desirable grouping of words. The law is reason, and any judge who will cling to a hoary precedent, or an approximation of such, in the face of a well-reasoned argument demeans his authority and disgraces the law.

See also *Cohen*, pp. 66–88; *How to*, pp. 51–84; *Jacobstein* p, 66; *Price*, pp. 158, 183. For a critque of digests, see *Research Group*, p. 41. In general, see *Martindale-Hubbell Law Directory* for another type of digest of all fifty states, foreign countries, and so forth.

DIRECTORIES (see also Part II: BIOGRAPHY)

The Bar List of the United Kingdom 1977 (Stevens).

Congressional Directory 1977 (GPO).

Information on House and Senate members, committees, international organizations, judiciary, independent agencies, names and addresses. Judiciary is limited to Washington, D.C., courts.

Directory of Law Libraries (AALL 1976).

Directory of Law Teachers (West 1976).

Also revised list of teachers by subject (1976).

Dow Jones-Irwin Business Almanac. Ed by Levine. (Dow Jones-Irwin 1977).

International Bar Association. *Directory of Members* as of 1st February 1977.

Martindale-Hubbell Law Directory. 7 v (1978).

Arranged alphabetically by state and then by city for lawyer listings. There are two listing for each state. The first listing is open to all lawyers; the second is solicited by the publisher. Volume 7 is a digest of the fifty states, D.C., P.R., and V.I. The digest includes citations to statutes and cases. Also a digest of copyright, patent, and trademark laws. Also Canadian law digest. Also foreign law digest (fifty-two countries). The U.S. Court section lists judges, clerks, and term for Washington, D.C., courts. For state and federal district courts, there is a category for courts and another for reports. The former gives the official name of all the courts in the state; the latter lists what reports are currently published and where they are digested. See also *Am. Jur. Pleading and Practice Forms* for state statutory references by subject. Volume 7 also has the Uniform and Model Act in full, a selected number of International Conventions to which the U.S. is a party, directories, and the like of the American Bar Association (including legal aid and defender offices, public interest firms).

Rhyne. *Law and Judicial Systems of Nations.* 3rd ed. (World Peace Through Law (1978).

Tseng. *The Law Schools of the World* (Hein 1977).

U.S. Government Manual (GPO 1977–78).

Annual. Federal agencies and personnel (names and addresses), publications, "for further information" listed after most entries.

New York

New York Lawyers Diary and Manual (1978).

Personnel of all state, city, and federal courts in New York state; term information, forms of pleading. Also directory of New York's city and state governments; also lists of marshals, tax appraisers, corporation counsel, telephone directory, legal aid offices. Also directory of N.Y. bar associations and law libraries. Also directory of New York City attorneys, followed by state attorneys listed alphabetically by name of city. Also telephone area code directory, medical charts, charts for marriage and divorce laws, directory of vital statistics offices, and solicited directory of attorneys by specialty.

New York City. Official Directory (1976 ed.).

City, state, and federal agencies and personnel. Telephone numbers and addresses.

The New York Red Book 1977 (Williams Press).

Information concerning New York State, its departments and political subdivisions, and the officials who administer its affairs.

ENCYCLOPEDIAS

Legal encyclopedias, in many ways, perform the same function as treatises. The advantage of the encyclopedia is that it attempts to be a complete compendium on the law, it is exhaustively indexed, and it is supplemented annually. The major encyclopedias are *Corpus Juris Secundum* (*CJS*) and *American Jurisprudence* (*Am. Jur. 2d*). There are also state encyclopedias such as *New York Jurisprudence* (also *California Jurisprudence 2nd* and *3d*, *Florida Jurisprudence*, *Florida Law and Practice*, *Michigan Law and Practice*, *Ohio Jurisprudence*, *Summary of Pennsylvania Jurisprudence*, *Texas Jurisprudence*, *Michie's Jurisprudence of Virginia and West Virginia*) and multivolume treatises such as White on *New York Corporations*, Wigmore on *Evidence*, and Wright and Miller on *Federal Practice and Procedure* (see Part II: BUSINESS ORGANIZATIONS, EVIDENCE,

AND CIVIL PROCEDURE respectively, for bibliographic information) that treat their subject matter in encyclopedic fashion.

Shepard's Inc. has recently published a spinoff on encyclopedias that they call "Law Locators." They are multivolume sets arranged alphabetically by "Legal Concept, Fact Word, or the Popular Name." Sets have been published for Illinois, New Jersey (also has five volume text with it), New York, and Texas. Digests follow most items and refer the reader to the state's constitution, statutes, cases, court rules, administrative regulations, and law reviews. There is also a *Federal Tax Locator* and a *Securities Law Locator.* The sets are a sort of Shepard's Citator in reverse.

A few caveats about encyclopedias. They will generally give you the law on all sides of an issue. You will not find them opinionated as you will a law review article or treatise. The reason is that their primary purpose is to provide the researcher with cases—and encylopedias have copious footnotes citing the user to cases, usually by jurisdiction. Encyclopedias are case finders; they are not authorities. No research should be limited to encyclopedias, and it is a weak researcher who cites an encyclopedia.

One further word about encyclopedias that applies to all legal research tools. Legal research texts of necessity go to interminable lengths to describe the features of legal tools. A careful inspection of each tool can be more productive. Peruse a subject in an encyclopedia. Is there an index to the subject as well as to the set? Is there a table of cases? (There is none.) Is it supplemented? (Practically all law material is supplemented or promised as such.) You will learn more about research by using the material than by reading about it.

See also *Cohen*, p. 92–94, 288–90; *How to*, pp. 264–84; *Jacobstein*, p. 290; *Price*, p. 213; *Research Group*, p. 14.

ENGLISH AND CANADIAN MATERIAL

Consult books listed in introduction, particularly *How to*, pp. 366–88.

Murphy, P.T. *Canadian Legal Research Guide* (University of Windsor 1976).

The following chart is reproduced from this concise and gifted author, Paul T. Murphy and the Community Law Program, with their kind permission:

	CANADA	GREAT BRITAIN	AUSTRALIA	NEW ZEALAND
ENCYCLOPEDIA	1. C.E.D. (Ontario) 2. C.E.D. (Western) 3. Halsbury's Laws of England: Canadian Converter	Halsbury's Laws of England	Halsbury's Laws: Australian Pilot	Halsbury's Laws: New Zealand Pilot
DIGEST	1. Canadian Abridgment & Canadian Current Law 2. Butterworth's Ontario Digest 3. C.C.H. Dominion Report Service, 1958–	1. English & Empire Digest 2. Mew's Digest 3. Current Law	1. Australian Digest 2. Australian Current Law	Abridgment of New Zealand Case Law
CASES JUDICIALLY NOTICED	1. Canadian Abridgment volumes & Canadian Current Law OR 2. D.L.R. Annotation Service 3. Index Gagnon	1. Current Law Citator OR 2. All E.R. Index & Noter-Up	Australian Digest Volumes	Current Law (New Zealand)
STATUTES	R.S.C. 1970 & Citator or Annual Statute Volumes R.S.O. 1970 & Citator or Annual Statute Citators	1. Halsbury's Statutes of England 2. Law Report Statutes	Federal and Various State Volumes	1. New Zealand Statutes 2. Recent Law
STATUTES JUDICIALLY NOTICED	Canada Statute Citators Ontario Statute Citators	1. Notes in Halsbury's Statutes of England 2. Current Law Statutes Annotated	Australian Current Law	1. Butterworth's Cases Annotations to the New Zealand Statutes, 1908– 2. Current Law (New Zealand)
REGULATIONS	*Canada*: Canada Gazette Part 2 (with cumulative index) *Ontario*: Revised Regulations of Ontario 1970 & Ontario Gazette	Halsbury's Statutory Instruments		
PERIODICAL INDICES	1. Index to Canadian Legal Periodical Literature, 1961– 2. Canadian Bar Review Index, vol. 1 to 50 (1923–1972)	Index to Legal Periodicals (I.L.P.)	Current Australian and New Zealand Legal Index	Current Australian and New Zealand Legal Index

EXECUTIVE ORDERS

Code of Federal Regulations (see also as topic).
Title 3 has a compilation of executive orders.
Federal Register (see also as topic).
Executive orders can be located through indexes.
Loose leaf services (see also as topic).
Presidential Papers. A Weekly Compilation of Presidential Documents, 1965–.
United States Code Annotated (see STATUTES AND REGULATIONS).
The tables volume lists executive orders as cited by U.S.C.A. section.
U.S.C.C.A.N. (see STATUTES AND REGULATIONS).
Tables list orders for the period covered.
See also *Cohen*, p. 226; *Jacobstein*, p. 226; *How to*, pp. 241–42; *Price*, p. 144.

FEDERAL CASES

A thirty volume set of federal district court and circuit court cases arranged alphabetically. It covers the years from 1789 to 1880 and effectively replaces the many reports put out by the individual federal courts during those years. The *Federal Reporter* begins where this set leaves off.

Citation style: *Salmon v. Burgess*, 21 F. Cas. 254 (No. 13, 262) (C.C.E.D. Va. 1875).

See also *Cohen*, p. 32; *How to*, pp. 37–38; *Jacobstein*, p. 40; *Price*, p. 108.

FEDERAL REGISTER (see also CODE OF FEDERAL REGULATIONS)

Citation style: 22 *Fed. Reg.* 8910 (1964).

Published five times a week, this is the official receptacle for all agency regulations, cease and desist orders, proposed regulations, and so forth. It is indexed monthly and annually and has tables that indicate which sections of the *Code of Federal Regulations* have been affected by current regulations. Includes Presidential Documents (proclamations and executive orders), Rules and Regulations, Proposed Rules, and Notices (hearings and investigations, committee meetings, agency decisions and rules, deadlines for filing petitions and applications, and agency statements of organization and function).

See also *Cohen*, p. 32; *How to*, pp. 35–38; *Jacobstein*, p. 40; *Price*, p. 109.

FEDERAL REPORTER (For a full perspective of reports, see REPORTS)

First series, v. 1–300 (West 1880–1925)
2d series, v. 1–556 (West 1924–1977)

The *Federal Reporter* succeeded *Federal Cases* and contains the decisions of the U.S. courts of appeals, court of claims, court of customs and patent appeals, and temporary emergency court of appeals. Until 1932 it published the opinions of the federal district courts (see FEDERAL SUPPLEMENT). The *Modern Federal Practice Digest* Table of Cases includes all *Federal Reporter* cases. Court of appeals opinions are issued first as a slip opinion and are available for a fee from the clerk's office (see DIRECTORIES: *Martindale-Hubbell* for addresses). The preferable cite is to the *Federal Reporter*, although they can be found in loose leaf services, in full or in edited form. The opinions are digested (see DIGESTS), annotated (see ANNOTATIONS), and Shepardized (see CITATIONS).

See also *Cohen*, p. 32; *How to*, p. 35–38; *Jacobstein*, p. 40; *Price*, p. 109.

FEDERAL RULES DECISIONS (see REPORTS; see also Part II: CIVIL PROCEDURE)

A competitor to this set is Pike and Fischer, *Federal Rules Service* (Callaghan). Both these sets report the opinions interpreting the Federal Rules of Civil and Criminal Procedure.

See also *Cohen*, p. 35, *Jacobstein*, p. 207; *Price*, p. 110.

FEDERAL SUPPLEMENT (see also REPORTS)

The *Federal Supplement* publishes only those opinions submitted to it by federal district court judges. Many loose leaf services (particularly tax and labor) publish opinions that do not appear in the *Federal Supplement*. There is an average two month lag between the date a court hands down an opinion and the date West publishes the opinion in its National Reporter series (except for the *Supreme Court Reporter*).

See also *Cohen*, p. 33; *How to*, pp. 37–38; *Jacobstein*, p. 40; *Price*, p. 109.

FOREIGN STUDENTS STUDYING LAW IN AMERICA

See Legal Research books at the beginning of Part I, particularly Andrews, Farnsworth, and New York University *Moot Court*

Handbook; see also *Uniform System of Citations* 12th ed. (Harvard 1976); also Hay, *An Introduction to United States Law* (North-Holland 1976).

FORMS

Forms are also included in Part II by subject.

The following is only a sampling, as most states are inundated with practice books that contain forms (see, for instance, *California County Law Library Basic List*, issued by California State Library, May 1976).

Am. Jur. Legal Forms Annotated 2d. (LCP).
23 v. 1977 pocket parts. Federal tax guide to forms included.
Jones. *Legal Forms Annotated.* 10th ed. 3 v. (Bobbs-Merrill 1962).
Modern Legal Forms. (West).
17 v. 1977 pocket parts.
New York Forms. 5 v. (LCP).
1977 pocket parts.
Nichols. *Cyclopedia of Legal Forms Annotated.* 16 v. (Callaghan).
1977 pocket parts.
Rabkin and Johnson. *Current Legal Forms with Tax Analysis.* 22 v. (M. Bender).
Loose leaf. 1977 update.
See also *Jacobstein*, p. 375.

LAW REVIEWS

Most law schools publish at least one law review. Law reviews are student run publications that feature lead articles by law professors and practitioners, comments, student notes, case notes on current significant cases, and book reviews. Although this characterization may not be strictly accurate, a comment is narrower in scope than an article and usually concerned with an issue just emerging rather than one ready to be laid to rest. A student note can range from a full investigation by the law reviewers of state court jurisdiction to a discussion of right to counsel in a particular jurisdiction. Case notes are abbreviated comments on current cases of significance. Many reviews publish annual surveys of the law in a particular jurisdiction (for instance, New York University School of Law publishes *Annual Survey of American Law*, *Harvard Law Review* publishes a survey of the work of the United States Supreme Court, *Syracuse Law Review* publishes a review of New York law, and *St. John's Law Review* publishes a review of New York practice). The articles can provide valuable information on burgeoning legal topics, and the case notes may provide fresh perspective on current cases. It takes a degree of sophistication in research to determine whether an article should be cited in a finished piece of legal research or in a court opinion.

Many law reviews are indexed in the *Index to Legal Periodicals* by subject and author, case comments (by name of case), and book reviews. This index is published nine times a year (with cumulations) and is cumulated annually and triannually. It also contains subscription information for all reviews it indexes. References to law review articles can be found in treatises, loose leaf services, annotated codifications, and Shepard's citators. Readers should be cautioned that the *Index to Legal Periodicals* has its limitations. Not all law reviews are included, few bar journals are included, and the indexing is too broad for effective use (See 69 *Law Lib. J.* 125 [1976] for a rationale for this). Wypyski, *Legal Periodicals in English* (Glanville 1976) is a loose leaf volume that lists periodicals and indicates whether they appear in the *Index to Legal Periodicals*, as well as providing other information.

There are other legal periodicals besides the law reviews published by law schools. Private publishers offer them in the following areas: securities, criminal law, corporation law, real estate, banking, and so forth (see the subject listings). Bar associations (federal, state, county, and city) publish periodicals that vary in content. The *American Bar Association Journal* is the best known of this genre. Associations of the trial bar, the defense bar, the insurance bar, law professors, and law librarians also publish periodicals dedicated to the perpetuation of their interest in the law.

Another source of related information is provided in legal newspapers. The *New York Law Journal*, for instance, besides covering current legal events, reporting docket information, and being the only source for many lower New York court opinions, carries an array of articles by members of the legal profession. The *New York Law Journal's* reported cases are digested in *Clark's Digest-Annotator*, which also includes an index of the articles published in the *New York Law Journal* as well as other features. Announced for publication in 1978 is the *National Law Journal*, designed for national distribution to attorneys and emanating from the same address as the *New York Law Journal.* See Who Says a Newspaper has to be Dull, *Corpus Juris* (16 February 1978).

The role of law reviews can be appraised by reading Gilmore, *Ages of American Law* (Yale University Press 1977); Merryman, Toward a Theory of Citations. . . , 50 *So. Calif. L. Rev.* 381 (1977); Maru,

Measuring the Impact of Legal Periodicals, 1 *ABA Research J.* 227 (1976); and the incomparable Rodell, Goodbye to Law Reviews—Revisited, 48 *Va. L. Rev.* 179 (1962). The latter article was printed originally in 23 *Va. L. Rev.* 38 (1936), along with other perceptive comments on this genre.

Additionally there are:

Contents of Current Legal Periodicals (CSC).
V. 6 in 1977.
Current Index to Legal Periodicals (University of Washington Law Library).
Published weekly and disposed of after entries appear in *Index to Legal Periodicals.*
Index to Periodical Articles Related to Law (Oceana 1958–).
Law Review Digest (Kimball-Clark 1950–).
Ulrich's *International Periodicals Directory* 17th ed. (Bowker 1977), see "Law" pp. 851–82.

Citation style: Bander, How to Protect Yourself from Legal Experts, 1 *Obiter Dictum* 24 (Fall 1975).

See also *Cohen*, pp. 297–301; *How to*, pp. 306–26; *Jacobstein*, p. 307.

LEGISLATIVE HISTORY (see also Part II: LEGISLATION)

Sutherland on *Statutes and Statutory Construction* is a multivolume set that exhaustively covers the vagaries and intracies of legislative history.

Constitutional Provisions and Amendments

The Constitution of the United States of America (1973) is a one volume, indispensable source. The *U.S.C.*, *U.S.C.A.*, and *U.S.C.S.* provide annotations to the legislation and the amendments. Classical sources such as the *Federalist Papers* and *Farrand's Records of the Federal Constitution* are compelling.

Federal Legislation

Legislative histories for important federal enactments have been compiled in the tax, labor, atomic energy, and securities areas. Check the card catalog in law libraries by subject or under "Legislative Histories" to determine what legislative histories are available. *The Monthly Catalog of United States Government Publications* is another good source. A good deal of this material is being compiled on microfilm and microfiche (the Securities Acts of 1933 and 1934 are available in this form).

The *United States Code Congressional and Administrative News* (see STATUTES AND REGULATIONS) is an invaluable aid in legislative history, despite the fact that the material it reprints is available elsewhere. It selectively publishes presidential messages, proclamations, executive orders, administrative regulations, the Statutes at Large, House and Senate reports. All public laws are printed, but only selected House and Senate reports. It does provide information as to legislative history which it does not reprint. It is published monthly while Congress is in session and is usually the first available source for the material it publishes. This publication does not contain hearings of the various House and Senate committees, which are available through the Government Printing Office, through the committee holding the hearing, or at depository libraries, which are required to provide the general public access to all government documents.

The last volume of the *Congressional Record* (for each session of Congress) has a history of bills and resolutions that will also assist one in compiling legislative histories. *U.S.C.A.* and *U.S.C.S.* may provide you with citations or actual text of legislative material such as committee reports and, in a few instances, of debates from the *Congressional Record* and testimony given at congressional hearings (compare their treatment of the Federal Rules of Evidence). The *CCH Congressional Index* loose leaf service is a complete index for current bills in that it will provide information as to the status of bills and tell whether committee reports and hearings have been held. It does not print the material. Many large libraries and universities have the bills on file for the current session of Congress. This is a vast and complicated field, which is covered more fully in the *Cohen*, *Jacobstein*, *Price*, and *How to Find the Law* books.

State Legislation

There is no uniform method of collecting legislative histories of state enactments. There are research books on California, Florida, Pennsylvania, and Texas law that provide detailed information for those states. In New York, legislative documents are published by commissions, but they are generally related to the work of the commission rather than to specific legislation. These legislative documents are available at the State Law Library in Albany and in designated depository libraries throughout the state. Transcripts of hearings are usually not available; application for information as to hearings must be made to the commission conducting the hearing. *McKinneys' Session Laws of New York* publishes the Law Revision Commission Report and the governor's covering memoranda for certain pieces of legislation. The New York Judicial Conference *Reports* does discuss pending legislation relating to its function. The *Empire State Report* (January 1975, p. 40) contains an excellent summary of material published relative to legislation in New York.

Commerce Clearing House. *Congressional Index.*

Indexes all congressional bills and resolutions and lists their current status. There is a section summarizing the week in Congress and indexes to legislation and treaties by subject, bill number, author and "headline" legislation. Loose leaf; weekly during session.

CIS Index. Index to publications of the U.S. Congress (Congressional Information Service).

Brief abstracts of committee hearings and prints, House and Senate documents and reports, House and Senate miscellaneous publications, and Senate executive reports and executive documents. Includes a detailed index of subjects and names plus an index of bills, reports, and document numbers; and one of committee and subcommittee chairmen. CIS microfilms all documents cited in the index. Monthly, with quarterly and annual cumulations.

Congressional Quarterly. *Almanac.*

A survey of legislation arranged by topic, and so forth. Annual.

_______, *Congress and the Nation.* 4 v. (1945–76).

_______, *Guide to Congress.* 2d ed. (1976).

_______, *Weekly Report.*

Cumulates into *Almanac.*

Congressional Record (GPO).

Daily edition during period Congress sitting; subsequent bound volumes provide an edited transcript of what goes on on the floor of the House and Senate. Daily digest of floor and committee actions. Indexes published biweekly and cumulated into bound volume. Many Senate bills are reproduced in *Record.* Voluminous appendix contains some valuable material such as reprints of law review articles, studies, and the like.

Daily Report for Executives (BNA).

Provides broad coverage of governmental developments affecting business. Gives full texts of important bills and committee reports in Congress (many loose leaf services provide this feature; see LOOSE LEAF SERVICES), and so forth.

Digest of Public General Bills and Selected Resolutions with Index (GPO).

Summarizes public bills and resolutions and gives current status. Normally published each session in five cumulative issues with biweekly supplements.

Federal Index (Predicasts).

Abstracts the *Congressional Record*, *Federal Register*, *Weekly Compilation of Presidential Documents*, and so forth. Monthly.

Folsom. *Legislative History—Research for the Interpretation of Law* (University Press of Virginia 1972).

Evaluation of types of legislative history, finding guides, special needs for tax, constitutions, and treaties.

Information Handling Service. Legislative Histories Indexed Guide. (1978).

Part A — General Acts and Internal Revenue Acts (82–93 Cong.); Part B — Internal Revenue Acts (61–81 Cong.). Histories on agriculture, aviation, finance, civil rights, communications, consumer protection, copyright, criminal law, environment, H.E.W., labor, taxation, etc.

Law Librarian's Society of the District of Columbia. *Union List of Legislative Histories*. 4th ed. 1881–1972 (Ruthman, 1976).

Listed by Public Law, bill, *Statutes at Large* citation, and library compiling material. Unfortunately it does not list what they have compiled.

Serial Set (GPO).

Contains Senate and House journals, documents, and reports. There is a *Numerical List* that will locate the volume of the serial that contains the specific Senate or House report or document, although this can also be done by scanning the volumes. The *Serial Set* contains a mishmash of government trivia, and it is a disgrace that Senate and House reports do not have a set of their own.

Sloane. Federal Legislative History. *N.Y.L.J.*, January 26 and October 12, 1976.

New York Law

Breuer (1977 rev. by Carter). *Source Material Relating to Legislation in the State of New York and Annotated Bibliography of Legislative History and Legislative Intent* (1977).

Discusses *N.Y. State Legislative Annual*, Governor's Bill Jackets (1905, 1921–1958 available at N.Y. Public Library; 1959–1974 available at Legislative Reference Library in Albany;

1974 to date available only through Governor Carey's office), *N.Y. State Legislative Documents, New York State Law Revision Commission, New York State Legislative Record and Index and New York Legislative Service* (the latter two index and provide summaries of pending bills).

Podell. Writing Your Own Bill. *N.Y.L.J.*, January 13, 1975.
Sloane. State Legislative History. *N.Y.L.J.*, November 12, 1974.

LOOSE LEAF SERVICES

This term is applied to publishers who supply a weekly, biweekly, or monthly service that involves updating by means of adding and removing pages. Commerce Clearing House (CCH), Prentice-Hall (P-H), and the Bureau of National Affairs (BNA) are the best known of this genre. An example is the *CCH Standard Federal Tax Reporter.* The publisher supplies the subscriber with the following: (1) relevant statutory material; (2) a reprinting of each section of the code followed by regulations, digests of cases, an annotation or explanation of key sections of the code; (3) full text of cases, some of which are not included in the *National Reporter System*; (4) finding lists; (5) special releases containing new laws and bills, explanations of new laws, committee reports, and studies; (6) a short review of significant developments since the last release; and (7) instructions as to what pages to remove and what pages to insert.

These services are made available in fields where the subscriptions can support the service, such as criminal law, tax, labor, environment, trade regulation, patents, and so forth.

Some loose leaf services, such as the *BNA Criminal Law Reporter*, provide analysis but limit themselves to full text only of pertinent United State Supreme Court cases and significant lower federal court and state cases. Other services, such as *Standard and Poor's Review of Securities Regulation*, limit themselves to a thirty or forty page monthly review of the field.

The BNA *United States Law Week* (*U.S.L.W.*), deserves special mention. It publishes all United States Supreme Court cases (CCH *Supreme Court Bulletin* also does this) within a week of decision day and provides a calendar of all activity of the Supreme Court, such as a list of pending cases, certiorari matters, and so forth. In its general section, it quotes selectively from significant state and lower federal court opinions. It also reviews the work of the court each summer, prints significant new laws, and on occasion prints oral arguments before the court.

Although they are not strictly loose leaf services, a word should be included here about those sets that provide for loose leaf updating.

Many publishers put out loose leaf treatises that are updated annually (more frequently if the occasion warrants) by providing instructions for removing and replacing pages.

Loose leaf services and loose leaf treatises are listed by subject and type in Part II.

See also *Cohen*, pp. 236–59, 373–82 (list of services by subject); *Jacobstein*, p. 238; *How to*, pp. 248-63.

MICROFORMS

Microforms come in reels, microcard, and microfiche. All the state reports prior to the National Reporter System are on microfilm (Oceana). West has issued its first series of the National Reporter System on ultrafiche. Many legislative histories are available in this form. Law reviews, United National material, government documents, and theses are among the materials available through University Microfilms, Fred Rothman, Government Printing Office, and other publishers (check their catalogs for material and prices). See Part II: PUBLISHERS. Microforms make it possible for law libraries to expand without building additional stack space. See Tseng, *Complete Guide to Legal Materials in Microform* (University Publications 1976, 1977 supp.).

See also BRIEFS AND RECORDS; *How to*, pp. 447–56; *Jacobstein*, p. 476.

NATIONAL REPORTER SYSTEM

A product of the West Publishing Co., it is the unofficial reporter for some states and the official reporter for others. The first series of the set reported opinions to about 1880 and is also available on ultrafiche. *Martindale-Hubbell*, vol. 7, lists the available reports for each state under the caption Reports. *A Uniform System of Citation*, 12th ed. (1976) does the same. See REPORTS for a complete analysis of the American reporting system.

See also *Cohen*, pp. 35–53; *How to*, pp. 21–39; *Jacobstein*, p. 476; also write to West for a brochure.

PARALLEL CITATIONS

It is proper citation style to cite to the official state report and to the West regional reporter. All the *Digests* have case tables that provide this information, if available. *Shepard's Citators* can be used for this purpose. The West *Blue Books* and *Blue and White Books* have tables for this purpose. There is also a Shepard's *Acts and Cases by Popular Names—Federal and State* that can be useful. If you know the subject matter, try the case tables to treatises and case books.

See CITATION STYLE for examples and *Uniform System of Citation*, 12th ed, for rules applicable to law review style. Caveat: New York rules require only citation to official reports for brief writing, so check local rules for style.

See also *Cohen* pp. 58-63; *How to*, pp. 25-29.

PERIODICALS (see LAW REVIEWS)

PRECEDENT (see also AUTHORITY)

The common law requires courts to follow the reasoning of their prior decisions. One must therefore expose the court to its past. Cases, like fingerprints, are never the same, and one must balance fact patterns, analogous situations (which digests do not reveal), the temper of the times, and even the temper of the judge with the agility of a juggler. For a collection of writings, see Aldisert, *The Judicial Process* (West 1976). See also *Cohen*, pp. 10, 11; *How to*, pp. 4–11.

Students of law stymied by precedent should take a leaf from Rufus Choate, who, when asked by a court for a precedent for his legal argument, responded, "I will look, your Honor and endeavor to find a precedent if you require it; though it would seem a pity that the Court should lose the distinction of being the first to establish so just a rule." Fuess, *Rufus Choate* (Minton, Balch and Co., 1928), p. 177.

REPORTS

Official Reports

Most states publish official reports of their cases, including the reports of the highest court of the state and its intermediate appellate court. For example, Massachusetts publishes the *Massachusetts Reports* and *Appellate Decisions.* The former contains the opinions of the Supreme Judicial Court, the highest court in Massachusetts; the latter contains the reports of the intermediate court—that is, the court that is appealed to from the trial court. About a third of the states have made the West Publishing Company the official reporter for their decisions. For example, *Oklahoma Decisions*, although published by West, is certified as the official reporter for that state. The units of the *National Reporter System* (see Unofficial Reports, below) are unofficial reports and provide a parallel citation, except for states like Oklahoma that have contracted with West to do their printing. In fact, *Oklahoma Decisions* are taken directly from the *Pacific Reporter*, a unit of the National Reporter System. The significance of official and unofficial reports has become blurred with current practice. Legally, if a discrepancy occurs between the official and unofficial report, the former holds; practically, the only difference is in the order of citation (official citation first). *Martindale-Hubbell Law Directory*, published every year, has a law digest volume that conveniently keeps abreast of this information. For each state digest there is a category for courts and another for reports. The former gives the official name of all the courts in the state, including federal courts; the latter lists what reports are currently published for that state and where they are digested. This volume also digests the substantive law of all states and many foreign countries by subject.

The federal government publishes the official United States Supreme Court Reports (*United States Reports*). Lower federal court decisions are published by West: *Federal Reporter*, *Federal Supplement*, *Federal Rules Decisions.* It is imperative that you cite this material properly (see CITATION STYLE).

Most libraries get advance sheets of official reports only for their own state and the United States Supreme Court. These reports are mailed within a week of the date of decision. For other jurisdictions they rely on the unofficial reports that take about two months from the date of decision. Lexis, a legal research computer system, is proving to be an excellent, albeit expensive, source for obtaining opinions in advance of publication.

Unofficial Reports

The Uniform System of Citation (12th ed. 1977), is a valuable research tool, as well as setting the style for legal footnoting. It requires that official state citations be complemented by the National Reporter citation, if both are available. The *National Reporter System* is published by West, and it reprints (or prints, in a state that has designated West as its official reporter) the highest court decision in all fifty states, as well as the aforementioned federal material.

The complete West system is as follows:

Atlantic Reporter (A.)
(Conn., Del., Me., Md., N.H., N.J., Pa., R.I., Vt.)
North Eastern Reporter (N.E.)
(Ill., Ind., Mass., N.Y., Ohio)
North Western Reporter (N.W.)
(Iowa, Mich., Minn., Neb., N. Dak., S. Dak., Wis.)
Pacific Reporter (P.)
(Alaska, Ariz., Cal., Colo., Hawaii, Idaho, Kan., Mont., Nev., N.M., Okla., Ore., Utah, Wash., Wyo.)

South Eastern Reporter (S.E.)
(Ga., N.C., S.C., Va., W. Va.)
South Western Reporter (S.W.)
(Ark., Ky., Mo., Tenn., Tex.)
Southern Reporter (So.)
(Ala., Fla., La., Miss.)

These reports encompass all fifty states' highest court opinions and some intermediate court opinions. Other state units are:

California Reporter (Cal. Rptr.)
New York Supplement (N.Y.S.)

These units accommodate the needs of attorneys who want all the reported opinions of California and New York. The *North Eastern Reporter* and the *Pacific Reporter* presently have only the opinions of the highest courts of New York and California respectively.

The federal units of the *National Reporter System* are as follows:

Supreme Court Reporter (S. Ct.)
(United States Supreme Court reports beginning with 106 U.S.)
Federal Reporter (F.)
(Opinions of the United States Courts of Appeals).
lst Circuit (1st Cir.)
(Me., Mass., N.H., P.R., R.I.)
2d Cir.
(Conn., N.Y., Vt.)
3d Cir.
(Del., N.J., Penn., V.I.)
4th Cir.
(N. Car., S. Car., Va., W. Va.)
5th Cir.
(Ala., Canal Zone, Fla., Ga., La., Miss., Tex.)
6th Cir.
(Ken., Mich., Ohio, Tenn.)
7th Cir.
(Ill., Ind., Wis.)
8th Cir.
(Ark., Iowa, Minn., Miss., Neb., N. Dak., S. Dak.)
9th Cir.
(Alaska, Ariz., Cal., Guam, Hawaii, Idaho, Mont., Nev., Ore., Wash.)
10th Cir.
(Colo., Kan., N. Mex., Okla., Utah., Wyo.)

D.C. Cir.
U.S. Court of Claims
U.S. Court of Customs and Patent Appeals

Federal Supplement (F. Supp.)
(United States District Courts, United States Customs Court, Special Court–Regional Rail Reorganization Act, and Rules of the Judicial Panel on Multidistrict Litigation.)

Federal Rules Decisions (F.R.D.)
(Opinions, decisions, and ruling involving the Federal Rules of Civil and Criminal Procedure. Also contains articles on these topics.)

Military Justice Reporter

It is important to note that a "2d" after any unit (this applies to all legal publications) means a new series of volumes. For example, volumes 1–200 of the *North Eastern Reporter* covers cases from 1885–1936; volume one of the *North Eastern Reporter 2d Series* (N.E.2d) began in 1936 and continues to the present day. It is the publisher's prerogative to designate the volumes as he pleases (the British practice of emphasizing the year is much preferable as it eliminates the need for the cumbersome "2d".

All West Reports are published as follows: a weekly pamphlet for each unit (200–300 pages) that contain (1) the opinions, (2) headnotes, (3) an alphabetical arrangement by topic and key number of these headnotes, (4) special features that can easily be understood by checking the pamphlet. These pamphlets are eventually replaced by bound volumes containing the same pagination (thus the pamphlet can be cited).

The Lawyers Cooperative Publishing Company (LCP) is another printer of reports. *Lawyers' Edition* reprints the reports of the United States Supreme Court and includes notations to indicate precisely where each page of the official *United States Reports* begins and ends (the *Supreme Court Reporter* also does this). The accepted and logical practice is to cite only to the *United States Reports.* Example: *In re Winship* 397 U.S. 358 (1970). If you question the need for these unofficial reporters, remember that *Lawyers' Edition* provides annotations and the *Supreme Court Reporter* is keyed into West's *National Reporter System.* The unofficial reports also reach the user before the official reports.

Let us discuss an actual case before we go to the digests. Larry Bowling, a teenager, purchased a car from Sperry Ford, a dealer. He disaffirmed the contract ostensibly because of his infancy and refused to make further payments. Mr. Sperry sued for the balance due and won the case. On appeal to the Indiana Appellate Court, the trial court was reversed, and Mr. Bowling now has no legal obligations to Mr. Sperry. This court held that a minor can disaffirm a contract unless an exception can be found to this rule, such as that the purchase was a necessity (which the court did not find after reviewing the facts). For this principle of law or precedent, the Indiana Appellate Court cited the highest court of Indiana, the Indiana Supreme Court (theoretically only the highest court of a state can establish precedent in that state).

How is this information made available? Information on the trial can be found only in the archives for the trial court under the name of the case: *Sperry v. Bowling.* Sperry was the plaintiff or person seeking redress at law, and Bowling the defendant (a much misspelled word) or the person being sued. The appellate opinion can be found in *Bowling v. Sperry*, 133 Ind. App. 692, 184 N.E.2d 901 (1962). Bowling, who lost at trial and is appealing, is now the appellant; Sperry is the appellee. 133 stands for volume 133 of the *Indiana Appellate Reports.* 692 is the page where the case begins. 184 is the volume of the *North Eastern Report, 2d Series*, and 901 is the page where this case is reprinted verbatim, but with the West headnotes that make up their digests. 1962 is the year the case was decided. (This case is reprinted in the Appendix.)

RESTATEMENTS

The *Restatement* is an attempt to "codify" case law in those areas where case law rather than state statutes predominate: agency, conflict of laws, contracts, judgments, property, restitution, security, torts, and trusts (there is also a *Restatement* for *Foreign Relations Law*). It is the work of a prestigious body of scholars and practitioners under the aegis of the American Law Institute. The set is constantly being reappraised, and there is an *Agency 2d*, *Torts 2d*, as well as tentative drafts currently being published to *Contracts 2d* and *Torts 2d.* While the *Restatement* is a secondary authority, it is most persuasive and cited frequently by the courts. *Restatement in the Courts* provides annotations to cases that have cited the *Restatement.* Each *Restatement* is indexed, and there is an index for *Restatement I. Restatements* have been published for individual states; they can be Shepardized and are not neglected by authors of treatises and law review articles.

But see Merryman, Toward a Theory of Citations. . .50 *So. Calif. L. Rev.* 381 (1977). The comments following the *restatements* are particularly useful, and the recent *Landlord and Tenant Restatement* (part of Property 2d) contains a table of secondary authorities and cross references to annotations and key numbers. Specific *Restatements* are also listed by subject in this monograph.

See also *Cohen*, pp. 295–97; *How to*, pp. 290–95; *Jacobstein*, pp. 342–49.

SECONDARY MATERIAL

Basically, all that is not a primary source, such as laws, regulations, and court opinions. Secondary material includes treatises, restatements, law review articles, and, in this century, social science studies. Secondary sources are to be confused with finding tools, which some librarians characterize as legal encyclopedias, law dictionaries, loose leaf services. The distinction is not significant. If a secondary source is brought to the attention of the court, it is not obligated to accept it as a mandate. In Justice Holmes's time it was thought improper to refer to a law review article in a court opinion, and it was a rash judge who cited a living authority. For further information on secondary authorities, see ANNOTATIONS, ENCYCLOPEDIAS, LAW REVIEWS, LOOSE LEAF SERVICES, RESTATEMENTS, and TREATISES.

See also *Cohen*, pp. 4–7; *How to*, pp. 286-305; see also Part II of this volume.

SHEPARD'S CITATORS (see CITATORS)

SLIP DECISIONS (see, in general, REPORTS)

This is the first official record of a court decision. As a practical matter, reprints of these decisions are more readily available from private publishers. West, loose leaf services, U.S.L.W., legal computers, are examples of publishers that provide opinions in lieu of the general unavailability and awkwardness of maintaining slip opinions.

See also *Cohen*, pp. 30, 56.

STATE REPORTS (see REPORTS)

See also *Cohen*, pp. 35, 54, 363-69; *How to*, pp. 21–35; *Jacobstein*, p. 54.

STATE STATUTORY MATERIAL (see STATUTES AND REGULATIONS; see Part II: LEGISLATION)

See also *Cohen*, pp. 134–40; *How to*, pp. 140–53; *Jacobstein*, p. 188; *Research Group*, pp. 49, 55.

STATUTES AND REGULATIONS

United States

Statutes at Large. Sample Citation: 84 *Stat.* 1943 (1971). A chronological arrangement of laws and resolutions as promulgated by Congress and signed by the president (when necessary). This is the primary source of all law unless Congress enacts certain titles of the *United States Code* into positive law (such as the Internal Revenue Code).

United States Code Congressional and Administrative News (West) is published monthly while Congress is in session and contains all current laws, selected regulations and committee reports, and other primary material. It publishes the laws in the same form as the *Statutes at Large*, and its pamphlets are usually the earliest source for current legislation.

United States Code. Sample Citation: 15 *U.S.C.* § 13 (1970). The official compilation of all laws in force, arranged by title (approximately fifty: the Internal Revenue Code is Title 26). This code is derived from the *Statutes at Large*, and the appropriate citation is provided after each section. A cumulative supplement is provided after each session of Congress to keep the set up to date. *Supplement IV* brings the 1970 edition up to January 2, 1975. A new edition is published every six years. The set includes a popular name table (Taft-Hartley Act) and a conversion table from a *Statute at Large* citation to the *United States Code*; also an index.

United States Code Annotated (*U.S.C.A.*). Basically the same as the *United States Code* except that it contains extensive case annotations following each section. It is not published in an edition (which is why it should not be cited as authority), but volumes are supplemented with pocket parts or recompiled when warranted. There are also pamphlet supplementations to the pocket parts. *U.S.C.A.* contains a popular name table, a conversion table from the *Statutes at Large* to the *United States Code*, plus additional features.

United States Code Service. Basically the same as the *U.S.C.A.*, but this set provides citations to Lawyers Cooperative Publishing Company and occasionally prints committee reports and excerpts from the Congressional Record (see the volume on the Federal Rules of Evidence).

Administrative Law. When Franklin D. Roosevelt introduced the New Deal to the American society, he advertently revolutionized legal research. The executive branch of government undertook the onerous task of policing the business community so as to prevent such abuses as monopolies, impure foods, antiunion practices, and a host of other relationships between the powerful and the weak. To implement President Roosevelt's program, administrative agencies proliferated (Federal Communication Commission, National Labor Relations Board—see the *United States Government Manual* for a complete listing), which naturally resulted in regulations to carry out the laws that created these agencies, decisions of administrative courts to resolve differences between the agency and those they sought to regulate, and many reports and studies issued by these agencies. Once the pride of reformers, these agencies are now being given second thoughts by a new breed represented by Ralph Nader.

Under EXECUTIVE ORDERS, there are references that fully explore the ramifications of this development. It should be kept in mind that most agencies issue decisions, that there is a *Shepard's United States Administrative Citations* that Shepardizes many of them, and that the agencies themselves put out helpful publications. Most important, loose leaf services, in many instances, reprint administrative materials (check Part II: COMMERCIAL LAW and TRADE REGULATION, for example, for specific mention of applicable services.

Federal Register. Citation style: 22 *Fed. Reg.* 8910 (1964). Published five times a week, this is the official receptacle for all agency regulations, cease and desist orders, proposed regulations, and so forth. It is indexed monthly and annually and has tables that indicate which sections of the *Code of Federal Regulations* have been affected by current regulations.

Code of Federal Regulations. Citation style: 11 *C.F.R.* § 37 (1975). A compilation of all regulations by title (similar to *U.S.C.)* titles) that have appeared in the *Federal Register.* Title 3 accumulates all executive orders, and the set has an index to each title and an index to the set. It is currently being recompiled each year on a staggered basis.

The regulations are promulgated by administrative agencies to implement the laws. They have the effect of law. Federal regulations are not easy to fathom, cannot be Shepardized, and in certain subject areas, such as tax and labor, are more easily accessible in loose leaf services.

States

Codes and Session Laws. Each state publishes session laws (public laws, acts, and so forth) that are the equivalent of the *Statutes at Large* (see above). Codifications are published by the states and also by publishers with the permission of the states. The latter are extensively annotated and contain features as dictated by the publisher.

While all provide annotations, a West publication will invariably refer you to key numbers, and a Lawyers Cooperative publication will refer you to annotations. On occasion, law review articles are also provided. All codifications refer the reader to where the codification section originally appeared in the session laws (or whatever nomenclature the state uses for its laws). The sets are indexed, usually contain numerous tables, and are supplemented by pocket parts and for some states, by monthly pamphlets. There is a *Shepard Citator* for each codification. The *Uniform System of Citation* provides the recommended style of citation. Always put the name of the state first in any citation to a codification. Another safe rule is to ignore all publishers' recommended styles of citation.

In New York, *New York Jurisprudence* has a volume called "Citation Table to Consolidated Laws, Constitution, C.P.L.R." that will direct you to textual matter. The *New York Law Locator* (*Shepard's Citations*) is an alphabetical listing of words and phrases followed by citations to the New York Constitution, Statutes, Court Rules, Codes, Rules, Regulations, Cases, Attorney General's Opinions, New York law reviews, and so forth.

Not all state laws are part of the code. In New York, for instance, rent control legislation is not part of the consolidated code but is included under the title of Unconsolidated Laws. Appropriations are not part of the *United States Code* and can only be found in the *Statutes at Large.*

Rules of Court. The West codification include the state rules of court with their subscriptions. Local publishers also publish them, usually with their practice volumes (see Part II: CIVIL PROCEDURE).

State Administrative Agencies. New York, Florida, and California are three states that publish administrative regulations in a formal manner. If not available in a formal publication, it is suggested that the particular state agency be written to.

Cities and Towns. There is no consistent pattern for the publication of laws, rules, and regulations for cities and towns. In New York City there is an eight volume *Charter and Code* as well as the *City Record.* For a citator to city and town material consult: *Ordinance Law Annotations; A comprehensive Digest of American Cases that Interpret or Apply City and County Ordinances* (Shepard's Citations 1969 to date), 6 v. This set is arranged by subject with references to case law.

Case Research for Statutes. All that we have said about research in case law applies to statutes and constitutions (see CITATORS). State digests will provide cases interpreting statutory material; the

Federal Digest, *Modern Federal Practice Digest*, and *Federal Practice Digest 2d*, while overlapping, provide case coverage for all federal statutory material; the *Supreme Court Digest* and *Lawyers Edition Digest* does the same for United States Supreme Court cases.

STATUTES AT LARGE (see also STATUTES AND REGULATIONS

A session of Congress lasts two years. Laws passed during these sessions are first published as slip laws and then cumulated into a bound volume called the *Statutes at Large*. The slip laws contain the same pagination that appears in the bound volume. Laws begin as bill numbers preceded by a designation of "S" or "H," depending upon which chamber introduced the bill. When passed into law, they are numbered as follows: 92-109, which means 92d Congress, one hundred and ninth law passed. These laws can also be found in the *United States Code Congressional and Administrative News*, loose leaf services, and elsewhere. *United States Law Week* publishes selective legislation.

See also *Cohen*, p. 118; *How to*, pp. 120-24; *Jacobstein*, p. 138.

Volume 89 of the *Statutes at Large* contains the following enactments of the 94th Congress, 1st Session (1975): Public Laws 91-696, 93-650, 93-651, 94-1 to 94-205; Private Laws 94-1 to 94-27; Concurrent Resolutions; and Proclamations. Joint Resolutions are tabulated with the Public Laws. Each law is followed by a legislative history (previously listed at the end of the volume): House and Senate reports, congressional action, presidential documents. To physically locate legislative history is a problem that the government could easily solve by publishing the material as a unit, as follows: Part I: the bills; Part II: *Congressional Record*; Part III: House and Senate Reports; Part IV: *Statutes at Large*. At present, the public must flounder for results, pay exorbitant amounts for publishers who do publish the material logically, or hire lawyers to do it for them.

TREATIES

Treaties appear in the *Statutes at Large* up to 1949. Since 1949, they appear in slip form as *Treaties and Other International Acts Series* (T.I.A.S.) and in bound form as *United States Treaties and Other International Agreements* (U.S.T.). *Treaties in Force*, published annually, is an index to this material that is arranged alphabetically by country and subject. It provides citations to the material listed. CCH *Congressional Index* can be used to unearth legislative history on pending treaties (see, in general, LEGISLATIVE HISTORY), and *International Legal Materials* publishes the more significant materials on a current basis. CCH and P-H have services on tax treaties, and there is also Diamond and Diamond, *International Tax Treaties of all Nations* (Oceana). United States treaties can be Shepardized in the Shepard's for United States and also for each state.

See also *Cohen*, pp. 260-85; *How to*, pp. 136–40, 418–25; *Jacobstein*, pp. 380–403.

Folsom, *Legislative History* (University Press of Virginia 1972).
Henkin, *Foreign Affairs and the Constitution* (Foundation 1973).

Checklist: 87 *C.J.S.* Treaties
74 *Am. Jur. 2d* Treaties
60 *N.Y. Jur.* Treaties and Interstate Compacts
West Digest key number topic: Treaties

TREATISES

Treatises and hornbooks can be good secondary authorities. Prosser on *Torts* is a reliable and opinionated text, but it is dated. Wigmore on *Evidence* is a venerated name in law, but Mr.Wigmore died long ago and the set is kept up to date by many others.

A West treatise is called a hornbook; West has also recently been publishing minitreatises or "nutshell" volumes.

Akin to treatises are casebooks, which are designed specifically for classroom use but can be helpful to the researcher as they include the text of opinions, author's notes, references to other material, and so forth.

In recent years, there has been a growth of continuing legal education among lawyers. Organizations providing this service publish many books that vary from authentic texts through how to try it manuals to compilations of various legal materials and outlines.

Current issues of the *Harvard Law Review* contain an alphabetical arrangement of current casebooks and treatises. Sloane, *Recommended Law Books* (American Bar Association 1969), contains a listing designed for law firms. The Farnsworth, Lloyd, and *How to Find the Law* books listed in the beginning of this volume have selective listings, and this book lists this material by subject in Part II.

Additional perspective can come from the following: "Many law professors' reputations—indeed the most eminent reputations—are built on a casebook, a treatise that only elliptically or intermittently advances original ideas, or an article that canvasses a narrow problem. . .[footnote 11] Treatises have also absorbed much of the profession, but this form of writing is now so much in decline that I shall avoid reference to it. A more comprehensive account would dwell also on the intellectual energy dissipated first in Restatements of the Law and now in re-Restatements of the Law." Danzig, The Death of Contract. . . 29 *Stanford Law Rev.* 1125 (1977).

See also *Cohen*, pp. 291-94; and for an excellent, though unpublished, list of treatises, see Schanck, *Secondary Legal Sources: A Selected Bibliography of Treatises, Looseleaf Services and Form Books (Michigan Law Library 1977*); see also Part II: BIBLIOGRAPHIES.

UNIFORM LAWS ANNOTATED

Uniform laws are not laws until adopted by some state. The National Conference of Commissioners on the Uniform State Laws publishes these laws in areas where states impinge upon one another and reciprocal treatment is advisable, such as the Uniform Support Act. In 1968, West began publishing a new annotated set of these laws as adopted by the conference, beginning with the Uniform Commercial Code. The laws are annotated, and the states adopting the laws are listed along with notes as to any changes that may have been made by the adopting state. The *Handbook* of the conference has a chart of all uniform laws and also includes a good deal of information as to the work of the conference and prints verbatim uniform laws that are presently being considered.

See also *Cohen*, pp. 138-39; *How to*, pp. 146–49; *Jacobstein*, p. 342.

UNITED STATES CODE (see STATUTES AND REGULATIONS)

See also *Cohen*, pp. 138-39; *How to*, pp. 126–35; *Jacobstein*, p. 139.

UNITED STATES CONSTITUTION (see Part II. CONSTITUTIONAL LAW)

See also *Cohen*, pp. 132–33; *How to*, pp. 116–17; *Jacobstein*, p. 117.

UNITED STATES REPORTS (see REPORTS)

See also *Cohen*, pp. 16-19; *How to*, pp. 35-37; *Jacobstein*, p. 35.

UNITED STATE SUPREME COURT (see also Part II: CONSTITUTIONAL LAW and specific subject matter, such as LABOR LAW)

Note: to locate a specific case, see also Part I: CASE LAW—HOW TO FIND A CASE.

Abraham. *The Judicial Process; An Introductory Analysis of the Courts of the United States, England, and France.* 3d ed. (Oxford 1975).

Chapter V—Supreme Court; Appendix A—list of all justices; Appendix B—succession table of justices; Bibliography—judges and justices (pp. 406–407; the law (pp. 412–16); legal profession (pp. 416–17); biographical by justice (pp. 428–38); famous cases (pp. 512–15); and so forth.

American Bar Association J.

"Supreme Court Report" on current Supreme Court cases. this feature has appeared since v. 6, p. 2 (1920).

American Enterprise Institute for Public Policy Research (Washington, D.C.).

A conservative organization that comments frequently on the work of the court. See Fein, *Significant Decisions of the Supreme Court, 1974-75 Term* (1976). Also *1975–76 Term* (1977).

Annual Survey of American Law (N.Y.U. School of Law).

1977 issues—weighted with work of Supreme Court.

Books in Print (Bowker)

Subject Guide to Books in Print 1977–78 lists books under category "U.S.-Supreme Court."

Briefs and Records

Published in fiche by Information Handling Services and Law Reprints. The fiche appears about forty-five days after oral argument. Hard copy is available at selected depository libraries (Association of the Bar of the City of New York and Columbia Law School in New York City area). Law Reprints also publishes hard copy in tax, labor, trade regulation, and so forth. *Kurland and Casper, Landmark Briefs and Arguments of the Supreme Court of the U.S.: Constitutional Law* (University Publications) is an eighty volume set. Note: *Lawyers Ed.* publishes capsule briefs along with the court opinions and their annotations. Some briefs are commercially sold as separates, such as *DeFunis* and *Bakke* (Oceana).

Christian Science Monitor

Daily; excellent analytical items on work of court.

Commerce Clearing House. *Supreme Court Bulletin.*

Loose leaf opinions of court received within five days of release. Also contains information as to pending cases, index, and related matters.

Congressional Quarterly. *Congress and the Nation 1945–1976.* 4 v.

Each volume has capsule descriptions of significant cases of the court; v. 4, pp. 658-59, has chart of all court appointments with dates and so forth. Kept up to date with weekly and annual publications. Valuable for research for all branches of government.

The Constitution of the United States of America, Analysis and Interpretation. . .to June 29, 1972 (GPO 1973).

Contains clause-by-clause analysis of Constitution and Amendments with copious citation to cases; Appendixes: Acts of Congress held unconstitutional, state acts held unconstitutional, ordinances held unconstitutional, Supreme Court decisions overruled, table of cases, index.

Cushman. *Cases in Constitutional Law.* 4th ed. (P-H 1975).

Excellent source for quickly locating citations to leading Supreme Court cases.

Equal Justice Under Law, The Supreme Court in American Life. Rev. ed. (Federal Bar Assn. 1975).

Excellent photography; text on the court and its landmark cases. See also Schwartz, B., *Law in America* (McGraw-Hill 1974), for similar, but more comprehensive treatment. Ideal for high school and college students.

Freidel. *Harvard Guide to American History.* 2 v. (Harvard University Press 1974). Pp. 368–73: judicial branch; pp. 374–76; law—includes selected articles and books.

Friedman, L., and Israel. *The Justices of the United State Supreme Court.* 4 v. (Chelsea 1969).

Lives of the justices, including bibliographical essay plus padding of reprinted cases.

Harvard Law Review

An annual survey of the court's work is included in one of its issues each year. Major breakdowns are constitutional law, federal jurisdiction and procedure, federal statutes and regulations, statistics. Began in 1935 with v. 51.

History of the Supreme Court of the United States (Macmillan).

v. 1—Goebel, *Antecedents and Beginning to 1801* (1971);

v. 5--Swisher, *The Taney Period 1836–64* (1974);

v. 6—Fairman, *Reconstruction and Reunion 1864–88* Part One (1971).

Index to Legal Periodicals (Wilson).

Nine times a year, plus annual and three year cumulations, in subject arrangement. Check under "United States Supreme Court" for surveys of the Court's work; see also under specific subject matter. Table of Cases index provides entries by name of case (limited to cases contemporary with issue; see LAW REVIEWS).

Law Books in Print. 4 v. (Glanville 1976).

V. 3 is a subject list, check under "United States—Supreme Court." 1975, 1976 update volumes.

Lawyers' Edition. U.S. Supreme Court Reports (LCP)

Contains text of all Supreme Court decisions. Bound volumes incorporate pagination of official *U.S. Reports.* Annotations to decisions in vols. 1-31 (352 U.S. to 406 U.S.) are updated in Later Case Service; v. 32 to date are updated with pocket part; pamphlets, with cumulative table of cases keep set up to date. Total Client-Service Library provides access to related material published by LCP: *L.Ed.* v. 1–100 covers 1 U.S. to 351 U.S., continued by *L.Ed.* 2d; complete table of cases in *L.Ed. Digest,* which is alphabetical by plaintiff, defendant, popular name, and so forth (v. 15 to 15C). Desk Book (1978) contains table of cases, index to annotations, and other material.

Lewis. *Gideon's Trumpet* (Random 1964).

A narrative of the famed *Gideon* case that painlessly explains the working of the Supreme Court; also in paperback.

New York Law Journal.

Five times a week. Publishes a review of the work of the court each summer, with feature articles, occasional printing of opinion, and news items on Court.

New York Times

Daily. Occasionally publishes complete text of Court decision, oral arguments. Has legal reporters who write analysis on Court's decisions as well as news articles and roundup of work of Court while in session. Magazine section and book review section also contain material. Consult Index to *New York Times* for material.

New York University.

See subject catalog: Constitutional Law, United States—Supreme Court; see also under author and title and specific subject. See also Marke, *Catalogue of the Law Collection of New York University. . .*(1975), pp. 172–75.

Preview of United States Supreme Court Cases (Association of American Law Schools).

Published six times a month September–May; "is devoted to

memoranda authored by law school professors, describing the background, the significance, and the issues in all cases pending before the U.S. Supreme Court" (publisher's flyer).

Public Affairs Information Service Bulletin (PAIS) (N.Y. Public Library).

Weekly; cumulated. Excellent source for periodicals, pamphlets, government documents, and so forth.

Readers Guide to Periodical Literature.

For undergraduate research, this is probably the best place to begin for background information on cases that have stirred the realm. Provides references to articles about the court and its work that appear in hundreds of periodicals, such as *The Nation, National Review,* and the like.

Rodell. *Nine Men* (Random House 1955).

An iconoclastic view of the Court.

Rohde. *Supreme Court Decision Making* (W.H. Freeman 1976).

Rules of the U. S. Supreme Court

Available in many places, such as *U.S.C., U.S.C.A., U.S.C.S., Lawyers' Ed. Digest.*

Stern and Gressman. *Supreme Court Practice.* 4th ed. (BNA 1969).

A manual for practitioners.

Supreme Court Historical Society (1511 K St. N.W. #333, Washington, D.C. 20005).

Yearbook 1977; *Newsletter* 1977.

Supreme Court Reporter (West).

Covers from 106 U.S. to date; bound volumes incorporate pagination of official *U.S. Reports.* Features West key number system that exhaustively lists cases by a complex subject arrangement that is rarely helpful for nonlegal research (see DIGESTS). Pamphlets, with cumulative table of cases for each term, keep set up to date. The bound volume has a summary of the work of the court for each term since volume 73 (1953).

United States Government Manual 1977-1978 (GPO).

Pertinent information on court, its personnel, phone numbers; court of appeals judges; listing of district courts, legislative courts, and Administrative Office of the United States Courts.

United States Law Week. 2 v. (BNA).

Opinions within five days of release. Supreme Court volume contains text of Court opinions, table of cases, status of cases before the Court, index; during Court hiatus it reviews the work of the previous term, and so forth. Note: indexes are not cumulated each issues, but it is a simple matter to update your research by going over issues not as yet covered by index.

United States Reports (GPO).

Official. Issued first as slip opinion, then in a temporary pamphlet (pagination in bound volume remains the same as in pamphlet), finally in bound volume. Citation style: *Brown v. Illinois*, 422 U.S. 590 (1975). The first set of numbers is the volume, the second represents the page in the volume, and within the parenthesis is the decision date.

United States Supreme Court Digest (West).

Complete table of cases to U. S. Reports: v. 14 is alphabetical by plaintiff; v. 15 alphabetical by defendant. Descriptive Word Index in v. 1, 1A, 1B. For use of this digest, see, in general, DIGESTS. Caveat: Always check pocket part for update and information as to inclusive volumes covered by pocket part. It is then an easy task to check the few subsequent current volumes to update the digest.

Warren. *The Supreme Court in United States History*. Rev. ed. 2 v. (Little, Brown 1937).

WORDS AND PHRASES (see also DICTIONARIES)

An alphabetical arrangement of judicially considered words and phrases. It is published by West and supplemented annually. Each definition is followed by a citation to the case from which the quotation comes. Thus it can be a case finder as well as a key number finder. Do not cite. West also includes a words and phrases section with its state and federal digests in a less inclusive format. See *Cohen*, pp. 95-96; *Jacobstein*, pp. 76, 369.

Part II

Subject and Topic Research

ACCOUNTING

Course description: It is designed for students having no previous business knowledge of bookkeeping, and the principles of double entry bookkeeping are briefly studied. An analytical study of the basic pattern of business accounting, giving special attention to the problems of matching costs and revenues, valuation of tangible and intangible assets, depreciation and amortization, inventory methods, surplus and reserves, and the meaning of business figures in the light of accounting conventions and practices. Emphasis is on the accounting problems involved in the work of the financial lawyer. An advanced section covers consolidated financial statements and accounting for business combinations.

American Institute of Certified Public Accountants. *AICPA Professional Standards.* 3 v. (Commerce Clearing House 1977).
Commerce Clearing House. *Accountancy Law Reporter.*
Looseleaf.
Faris. *Accounting for Lawyers.* 3d ed. (Bobbs-Merrill 1975).
Ferst. *Basic Accounting for Lawyers.* 3d ed. (ALI-ABA 1975).
Fiflis and Kripke. *Accounting for Business Lawyers.* 2d ed. (West 1977).
Casebook.
Journal of Accountancy (AICPA).
Sellin. *Attorney's Handbook of Accounting.* Rev. ed. (M. Bender 1971).

For a bibliography on accounting, see Association of American Law Schools, *Law Books Recommended for Libraries*, No. 2: Accounting (Rothman 1968; 1974 supp.).

Checklist: 1 *C.J.S.* Accounting
1 *Am. Jur. 2d* Accountants, Accounts, and Accounting
1 *N.Y. Jur.* Accountants, Accounts, and Accounting

ADMINISTRATIVE LAW

When Franklin D. Roosevelt introduced the New Deal to American society, he inadvertently revolutionized legal research. The executive branch of government undertook the onerous task of policing the business community so as to prevent such abuses as monopolies, impure foods, antiunion practices, and a host of other relationships between the powerful and the weak. To implement President

Roosevelt's program, administrative agencies proliferated (Federal Communications Commission, National Labor Relations Board—see the *United States Government Manual*, issued annually, for a complete listing), which naturally resulted in regulations to carry out the laws that created these agencies, decisions of administrative courts to resolve differences between the agency and those they sought to regulate, and many reports and studies issued by these agencies. Once the pride of reformers, these agencies are now being given second thoughts by a new breed represented by Ralph Nader.

The material listed below fully explores the ramifications of this development. It should be kept in mind that most agencies issue decisions, that there is a *Shepard's United States Administrative Citations* that Shepardizes many of them, and that the agencies themselves put out helpful publications. Most important, loose leaf services provide ready access to the intricacies of dealing with these agencies by efficiently packaging the laws, regulations, decisions, reports and other material issued by the agency. They provide interpretation, annotation, and update; and, most importantly, they put the material at hand so as to save the researcher time and money. See COMMERCIAL LAW, TAXATION AND ESTATE PLANNING, and TRADE REGULATION for examples of loose leaf services.

Course description: The administrative agency; administrative rulemaking, adjudicatory and investigatory powers; the problem of delegation; right to be heard; administration procedure, emphasizing Administrative Procedure Act; freedom of information, administrative courts, and ombudsmen.

Administrative Law Review (ABA).
V. 29 published in 1977.

Davis. *Administrative Law Text.* 3d ed. (West 1972).

Davis. *Administrative Law Treatise.* 4 v. (West 1958, 1970).
1976 bound supplement (*Administrative Law of the 70's*).

Gellhorn. *Administrative Law and Process in a Nutshell* (West 1972).

Pike and Fischer. *Administrative Law.*
4 volumes loose leaf; 39 volumes of cases.

Schwartz, B. *Administrative Law* (Little, Brown 1976).

United States Government Manual 1977–1978 (GPO).

Volz, et al. *West's Federal Practice Manual.* 2d ed. 7 v. West 1970).
Provides text and forms for federal actions, particularly as regards federal agencies. 1977 pocket parts.

See also *Cohen*, pp. 160–200; *How to*, pp. 219–47; *Jacobstein*, p. 212.

For a bibliography on administrative law, see Association of American Law Schools, *Law Books Recommended for Libraries*, No. 3: Administrative Law (Rothman 1968), 1974 supp.

New York

Benjamin. *Administrative Adjudication in the State of New York Report. . .*1942.
City of New York *Official Directory* (1977).
Codes, Rules and Regulations of the State of New York.
Loose leaf. 22 titles; 33 v.
New York Red Book.
New York Legislative Manual.
Reports and opinions. Attorney General's Reports and Opinions, Public Employment Relations Board Decisions, and so forth. Legislative Document series publishes annual reports.
Smith, T. *Guide to the Municipal Government of the City of New York.* 10th ed. (Meilen Press 1973).

Note: The Municipal Reference Library (212 566–4284) is a viable source for state and city information. For a treatise on state administrative law, generally, see: Cooper. *State Administrative Law.* 2 v. (Bobbs-Merrill 1965).

Checklist: 73 *C.J.S.* Public administrative Bodies and Procedure
1, 2 *Am. Jur. 2d* Administrative Law
1 *N. Y. Jur.* Administrative Law
Note: see also specific topics, such as Labor Relations
West Digest key number topic: Administrative Law and Procedure

ADMIRALTY

Course description: Admiralty practice and jurisdiction; limitation of shipowners' liability; maritime liens and ship mortgages; maritime personal injury and wrongful death; carriage of goods by water under charter parties and bills of lading; salvage; general average; marine collision; towage and pilotage; marine pollution liability.

American Maritime Cases.
V. 54 publihsed in 1977.
Baer. *Admiralty Law of the Supreme Court.* 2d ed. (Michie 1969).
Pocket part.
Benedict. *Admiralty.* 7th rev. ed. 13 v. (M. Bender 1958).
Loose leaf.

Gilmore and Black. *The Law of Admiralty.* 2d ed. (Foundation 1975).
Casebook.
Journal of Maritime Law and Commerce. (Jefferson).
V. 9 published in 1977.
Lloyd's Maritime and Commercial Law Q.
Norris. *Law of Maritime Personal Injuries.* 3d ed. 2 v. (LCP 1975).
Pocket part.
Norris. *Law of Seamen.* 3d ed. 3 v. (LCP 1970).
Pocket part.
Robertson. *Admiralty and Federalism.* (Foundation Press 1970).
Casebook.
Sea Grant Law J.
V. 2 published in 1977.

For a bibliography on admiralty law, see Association of American Law Schools. *Law Books Recommended for Libraries,* no. 4: Admiralty (Rothman 1967; 1974 supp.).

Checklist: 2 *C.J.S.* Admiralty
2 *Am. Jur. 2d* Admiralty
70 *Am. Jur. 2d* Shipping
54 *N.Y. Jur.* Ships and Shipping
West Digest key number topic: Admiralty

ADMISSION TO THE BAR (see also LEGAL EDUCATION)

American Bar Association. Section of Legal Education and Admissions to the Bar. *Law Schools and Bar Admission Requirements.*
Fall 1976 published in 1977.
Bar Examiner (National Conference of the Bar Examiners).
V. 45 published in 1977.
The Bar Examiners' Handbook (National Conference of the Bar Examiners 1968).
Klein, ed. *Bar Admission Rules and Student Practice Rules* (Ballinger 1977).
Los Angeles County Law Library. *Admission to the Bar; An Annotated Bibliography of Law Review Articles,* 1966–1976 comp. by Houdek (December 1976).

Note: see also *Index to Legal Periodicals* for update.

Checklist: 7 *C.J.S.* secs. 4–16 Attorney and Client
West Digest key number topic: Attorney and Client

AGENCY

Course description: The relations between principal and agent, and the rights and duties of persons with whom the agent deals or comes into contact. Usually taught as part of a business organizations course.

American Law Institute. *Restatement of the Law, Second: Agency 2d.* (ALI 1958).
Seavey. *Handbook of the Law of Agency* (West 1964).
Seavey. *Studies in Agency* (West 1949).
Sell. *Agency* (Foundation 1975).
Casebook.
Steffen. *Agency-Partnership in a Nutshell* (West 1977).
The author also has a casebook on this topic.

Checklist: 2A, 3 *C.J.S.* Agency
3 *Am. Jur. 2d* Agency
2 *N.Y. Jur.* Agency
West Digest key number topic: Principal and Agent

AIR POLLUTION (see ENVIRONMENT LAW)

ANTITRUST (see TRADE REGULATION)

APPELLATE PRACTICE (see CIVIL PROCEDURE, LEGAL WRITING)

ARBITRATION (see also LABOR LAW)

Course description (arbitration): Deals with the law and the practice of public and private arbitration in the United States and its place in the legal system as an alternative method of dispute settlement. Included is a study of commencing arbitrations; notice; choosing arbitrators; the hearings; enforceability of agreement and awards; the relationship of federal and state arbitration laws; and selected problems in compulsory, labor, international, commercial, and uninsured motorist arbitration. (International trade arbitration): The settlement of controversies, through arbitration, in private international trade and in economic relations with governments. Various types of arbitration clauses in foreign trade, rules of procedure in international commercial arbitration, international trade arbitration, international arrangements, and the role of the specialized agencies of the United Nations.

Arbitration J. (AAA).
V. 31 published in 1977.
Bernstein, *Private Dispute Settlement, Cases and Materials on Arbitration* (Free Press 1968).
Includes a collection of primary material.
Bureau of National Affairs. Annual Meeting of National Academy of Arbitrators. 29th meeting in 1976 published.
Commerce Clearing House. *Labor Arbitration Awards.*
Loose Leaf.
Domke. *Commercial Arbitration* (P-H 1965).
______. *Handbook of Institutional Arbitration in International Trade* (North-Holland 1977).
______. *The Law and Practice of Commercial Arbitration* (Callaghan 1968; 1977 cum. supp.).
Elkouri. *How Arbitration Works.* 3d ed. (BNA 1973).
Schmitthoff. *International Commercial Arbitration* (Oceana 1974).
Loose leaf.
Updegraff. *Arbitration and Labor Relations.* 3d ed. (BNA 1970).
Wehringer. *Arbitration Precepts and Principles* (Oceana 1969).

Write to the American Arbitration Association for their publication list and a description of their services. For a bibliography, see Seide, *The Paul Felix Warburg Union Catalog of Arbitration. . .*(Rowman and Littlefield 1974).

Checklist: 6 *C.J.S.* Arbitration
5 *Am. Jur. 2d* Arbitration and Award
West Digest key number topic: Arbitration

ART LAW (see also PATENTS, TRADEMARKS, AND COPYRIGHT)

ALI-ABA. *Course of Study on Legal Problems of Museum Administration. . .*1973–1975. 4 v.
Art and the Law (N.Y. Volunteer Lawyers for the Arts) v. 1 (1976).
Associated Councils of the Arts. *The Visual Artist and the Law* (Association of the Bar of the City of New York. . .1971).

Berkowitz. Law and the Visual Arts: An Annotated Bibliography. 70 *Law Library J.* 5 (1977).
Crawford. *Legal Guide for the Visual Artist* (Hawthorn 1977).
DuBoff. *Art Law: Domestic and International* (Rothman 1975).
_____. *Desk Book of Art Law* (Federal Publications 1978).
Feldman, F. and Weil. *Art Works: Law, Policy, Practice.* (PLI 1974).
Feldman and Weil. *Legal and Business Problems of Artists, Art Galleries, and Museums. Sources and Materials* (PLI 1973).

Checklist: 86 *C.J.S.* Theaters and Shows
45 *N.Y. Jur.* Photography
West Digest key number topic: Theaters and Shows

ATOMIC ENERGY

Atomic Energy L.J. (Warren, Gorham and Lamont).
V. 17 published in 1976.
Commerce Clearing House. *Nuclear Regulation Reporter* (1975).
1977 update; loose leaf.
United States Government Manual (1977-1978).
For information on the U.S. Nuclear Regulatory Commission, see this publication, pp. 595-600. Publications are listed on pp. 599-600.

For a bibliography, see Association of American Law Schools, *Law Books Recommended for Libraries* No. 6: Atomic Energy (Rothman 1968; 1974).

Checklist: 6 *Am. Jr. 2d* Atomic Energy
3 *N.Y. Jur.* Atomic Energy

AUTOMOBILES (see also TORTS)

Blashfield. *Automobile Law and Practice.* 3d ed. 17 v. (West 1965-1970).
Pocket parts.
Erwin. *Defense of Drunk Driving Cases: Criminal-Civil.* 3d ed. 2 v. (M. Bender 1974).
Loose leaf.
Schwartz. *Trial of Automobile Accident Cases.* 3d ed. 6 v. (M. Bender).
Loose leaf.

New York Law

Encyclopedia of New York Law—Automobiles and Other Vehicles. 6 v. (West 1957).
1977 pocket parts.

Checklist: 60, 61A *C.J.S.* Motor Vehicles
7, 8 *Am. Jur. 2d* Automobiles and Highway Traffic
4, 4A *N.Y. Jur.* Automobiles and other Motor Vehicles
West Digest key number topic: Automobiles

AVIATION LAW

Course description: An exploration of selected topics in domestic and international air transport, including control of air space, the award of routes, setting of rates, the role of trade associations, interpretation of international agreements, the place of supplemental and charter carriers, jurisdiction aboard aircraft, liability to passengers, and aircraft hijacking.

Air Law (Kluwer).
V. 2 published in 1977.
Commerce Clearing House. *Aviation Law Reporter.*
Loose leaf.
Fizel. *The Law of Aviation.* 4th ed. (Michie 1967).
Journal of Air Law and Commerce (S. Methodist U. Law School).
V. 42 published in 1976.
Kreindler. *Aviation Accident Law.* 2 v. (M. Bender).
Loose leaf.
Lowenfeld. *Aviation Law.* (M. Bender 1972; 1974 cum. supp.).
Casebook. 1972 document supplement.

For a bibliography on aviation law, see Association of American Law Schools, *Law Books Recommended for Libraries*, No. 5: Aeronautics and Space Law (Rothman 1967; 1974 supp.).

Checklist: 2A *C.J.S.* Aeronautics and Aerospace
8 *Am. Jur. 2d* Aviation
2 *N.Y. Jur.* Aircraft and Airports
West Digest key number topic: Aviation

BANKRUPTCY

Course description (creditors' rights and debtors' protection I): Unilateral action by the individual creditor, including his remedies, such as attachment, execution, and enforcement of judgments; creation of judicial liens; statutory governmental liens and priorities; supplementary proceedings; and fraudulent conveyances and preferential transfers under federal and state laws; collective action by creditors in compositions and extension agreements and through receivers and assignees for the benefit of creditors; and protection of debtors by exemptions, social legislation, consumer protection statutes, and limitations of rights and remedies of creditors. (Creditors' rights and debtors' protection II): All proceedings under the Bankruptcy Act except corporate reorganization under Chapter X. The subject matter includes voluntary (ordinary bankruptcy and wage earner plans under Chapter XIII) and involuntary petitions, venue, jurisdiction of the bankruptcy court, summary and plenary proceedings, receivers and trustees, allowable exemptions, discharge of the bankrupt and dischargeable debt, assets of the bankrupt estate and the collection thereof, avoidance powers of the trustee, provability and allowability of claims and liquidations of assets and distribution of the proceeds, and priorities under the Bankruptcy Act.

Collier. *Bankruptcy.* 14th ed. (M. Bender), 21 v. text; 13 v. decisions.

Loose leaf 1977. Bender also publishes a five volume *Bankruptcy Manual*, a two volume. *Forms Manual*, and a two volume pamphlet containing the act and rules. Paskay, *Handbook for Trustees and Receivers in Bankruptcy*, is part of Collier and the manual.

Commerce Clearing House. *Bankruptcy Law Reporter*, 2 v.

Loose leaf 1977. Transfer binders for court decisions. Has "Bankruptcy Articles" tab for bibliographic material.

Corporation Reorganization Reporter, Inc. *Bankruptcy Court Decisions.* 3 v. (1974-to date).

Plus current news, comments, cases, and index.

Cowans. *Brankruptcy Law and Practice.* 3 v. (West 1978).

Includes forms.

Epstein. *Debtor-Creditor Relations in a Nutshell* (West 1978).

Forman. *Compositions, Bankruptcy and Arrangements.* 5th ed. 2 v. (ALI-ABA 1971).

Glenn. *Fraudulent Conveyances and Preferences.* rev. ed. 2 v. (Baker, Voorhis 1940, 1950).

Goldman, W.M. A Practitioner's Guide to Bankruptcy, 83 *Commercial L.J.* 86 (1978).

Herzog. *Bankruptcy Forms and Practice.* 5th ed. 2 v. (Boardman (1974).

MacLachlan. *Handbook of the Law of Bankruptcy.* (West 1956).

Newton. *Bankruptcy and Insolvency Accounting: Practice & Procedure* (Ronald 1975).
Remington. *Bankruptcy Law of the U.S., 5th and 6th ed.* 15 v. (LCP 1939).

Checklist: 8–8B *C.J.S.* Bankruptcy
9, 9A *Am. Jur. 2d* Bankruptcy (Rules, Forms)
28 *N.Y. Jur.* Insolvency
West Digest key number topic: Bankruptcy

BANKS AND BANKING

American Bankers Association. *State Banking Law Service.* 1 v.
Bailey. *Encyclopedia of Banking Laws* (Warren, Gorham & Lamont 1964).
Loose leaf.
Bailey. *Law of Bank Checks.* 4th ed. (Banking Law Journal 1969).
Banking L.J.
V. 93 published in 1977.
Blaine. *Federal Regulation of Bank Holding Companies* (BNA (1973).
Loose leaf.
Beutel. *Bank Officer's Handbook of Commercial Banking Law.* 4th ed. (Warren, Gorham & Lamont 1974).
Clark and Squillante. *The Law of Bank Deposits, Collections and Credit Cards* (Warren, Gorham & Lamont 1970).
Clarke. *Bank Deposits and Collections.* 4th ed. (ALI-ABA 1972).
Commerce Clearing House. *Federal Banking Law Reporter.* 5 v.
Loose leaf.
Federal Income Taxation of Banks and Financial Institutions (Warren, Gorham & Lamont 1971).
Loose leaf.
Heller. *Handbook of Federal Bank Holding Company Law* (Law Journal Press 1976).
Mandell. *Laws Governing Banks and Their Customers.* (Occana 1975).
Michie. *Banks and Banking.* 11 v. supp. (1956).
Prentice-Hall. *Banking* (Control of Banking, Federal Aids to Financing).
Loose leaf.

Checklist: 9 *C.J.S.* Banks and Banking
10 *Am. Jr. 2d* Banks

5, 5A *N.Y. Jur.* Banks and Trust Companies
West Digest key number topic: Banks and Banking

BIBLIOGRAPHIES

A.B.A. *Recommended Law Books* ed. by R. Sloane (1969).
ALI-ABA. *Catalog of Continuing Legal Education Program in the United States.*
Vol. 21 (1975–1976) includes continuing legal education programs listed by state and a subject index to publications issued in conjunction with these programs. This particular volume also includes a state-by-state breakdown of specialization practices of lawyers.
Association of American Law Schools. *Law Books Recommended for Libraries* (Rothman 1968; 1974 supp.), 6 v.
Loose leaf.
Current Publications in Legal and Related Fields (Rothman 1952 to 1977).
Published nine times a year.
Harvard Law School Library. *Annual Legal Bibliography.*
V. 17 published in 1977. Includes books, articles, and so forth.
Henke. *California Law Guide.* 2d ed. (Parker 1976).
Bibliography: pp. 483–612.
Jacobs. *Illinois Legal Research Sourcebook* (ICLE 1977).
Bibliography: pp. 5–114 to 161.
Law Books in Print. 4 v. (Glanville 1976).
Books published through 1974. Annual volumes for 1975, 1976, and 1977 current issues.
Marke, ed. *A Catalogue of the Law Collection at New York University with Selected Annotations* (N.Y.U. 1953).
Raistrick and Rees. *Lawyers' Law Books, A practical Index to Legal Literature* (Professional Books 1977).
A Bibliography of basically United Kingdom law texts broken down by subject and author and title.
Tate. *Treatises for Judges: A Selected Bibliography.* 3d ed. (Louisiana State University Law School 1977).

Bibliographies are also listed by topic.
See also *How to*, pp. 203, 205; *Research Group*, pp. 47–53.

BILLS AND NOTES

Course description: Negotiable instruments law under Articles 3 and 4 of the Uniform Commercial Code: requisites of negotiability;

transfer; legal effect of endorsement; value, maturity, and good faith; defenses, real and personal; acceptance and certification of checks; liability of parties secondarily liable on endorsement and on warranties; discharge; bank collections and relationship between bank and customer.

For bibliography, see COMMERCIAL LAW.

Checklist: 10, 11, *C.J.S.* Bills
11, 12 *Am. Jur.* 2d Bills and Notes
West Digest key number topic: Bills and Notes

BIOGRAPHY

The following items will provide bibliographical information on judges and lawyers:

The American Bench; Judges of the Nation (Forster 1977).
Association of American Law Schools. *Law Books Recommended for Libraries*, No. 7: Biography (Rothman 1968; 1974 supp.)
Friedman. *The Justice of the United States Supreme Court* 1789–1969. . . 4 v. (Chelsea 1969).
Index to Periodical Articles Related to Law (Oceana).
Index to Legal Periodicals (Wilson).
Law Books in Print (Glanville).
Martindale-Hubbell Law Directory.
Annual; note dual arrangement in volumes by state.
New York Times Index.
Tompkins. *The Supreme Court of the United States: A Bibliography* (University of California 1959).
Who's Who in American Law (Marquis 1977).

New York

New York Lawyers Diary and Manual 1978.

BUSINESS ORGANIZATIONS (see also AGENCY, SECURITIES)

Aranow and Einhorn. *Proxy Contests for Corporate Control.* 2d ed. (Columbia University Press 1968).
_____. *Tender Offers for Corporate Control* (Columbia University Press 1973).
_____. *Development in Tender Offers. . .*(Columbia University Press 1977).

Arnold and Sparrow. *Modern Corporation Checklists* (Warren, Gorham & Lamont 1972; 1977 cum. supp.).

Ballantine. *Corporations.* Rev. ed. (Callaghan 1946).

Bromberg. *Crane and Bromberg on Partnership* (West 1968).

Brown. *Franchising: Realities and Remedies* (Law Journal 1973).

Business Lawyer (ABA).

V. 32 published in 1977.

Cavitch. *Business Organizations with Tax Planning* (M. Bender).

1977 upkeep loose leaf. V. 1–10 covers corporations, partnerships; v. 11 series securities; v. 12 series trade secrets; v. 13 series corporate acquisitions and mergers; v. 14 series patent licensing transactions; v. 15 series franchising; v. 16 series antitrust and trade regulation; v. 17 series professional corporations and associations; v. 18 series labor law.

Christy. *Transfer of Stock; Law and Practice.* 5th ed. 2 v. (LCP (1975).

Commerce Clearing House. *Capital Changes Reporter.* 5 v.

Loose leaf.

_____. *Corporation Law Guide.* 2 v.

Loose leaf.

_____. *Professional Corporations Handbook* (1973).

Conard. *Corporations in Perspective* (Foundation 1976).

Corporate Counsel's Annual (M. Bender).

1976 is latest volume—collection of articles.

Corporate Practice Commentator (Callaghan).

V. 19 published in 1977.

Corporation J. (CT Corp. System).

V. 27 published in 1977.

Corporation Law Rev. (Warren, Gorham & Lamont).

V. 1 published in 1978.

Corporation Manual 1977 (U.S. Corp. Co.).

Contains uniform arrangement of the laws of all states as they relate to corporations.

Delaware J. of Corporate Law (Delaware Law School).

V. 2 published in 1977.

Deutsch and Bianco. *The Law of Corporations—What Corporate Lawyers Do* (Foundation 1976).

Casebook.

Eisenberg. *The Structure of the Corporation; A Legal Analysis* (Little, Brown 1976).

Encyclopedia of Corporate Meetings, Minutes and Resolution. 3 v. (P-H 1972).

Feuer. *Personal Liabilities of Corporate Officers and Directors.* 2d ed. (P-H 1974).

Fletcher. *Corporation Forms Annotated.* 4th ed. 10 v. (Callaghan 1972).

1977 pocket parts.

______. *Cyclopedia of the Law of Private Corporations* (Callaghan).

1977 pocket parts.

Fordham Corporate Law Institute (M. Bender).

1974—International antitrust; 1975—International project finance; 1976—International taxation and transfer pricing.

Henn. *Law of Corporations.* 2d ed. (West 1970).

Hornstein. *Corporation Law and Practice.* 2 v. (West 1959).

International Business Lawyer (International Bar Association).

V. 5 published in 1977.

Israels. *Corporate Practice.* 2d ed. (PLI 1969).

Journal of Corporation Law (University of Iowa Law).

V. 2 published in 1977.

Knepper. *Liability of Corporate Officers and Directors.* 2d ed. (Allen Smith 1973).

Pocket parts.

Lattin. *The Law of Corporations.* 2d ed. (Foundation 1971).

McCord. *Course Materials on Buying, Selling and Merging Business* (ALI-ABA 1975).

Model Business Corporation Act Annotated. 2d ed. 3 v. (West 1971).

______. 1974 revisions (ALI-ABA).

Model Nonprofit Corporation Act (ALI-ABA 1964).

Oleck. *Non-Profit Corporations, Organizations and Associations.* 3d ed. (P-H 1974).

O'Neal. *Close Corporations* (Callaghan 1971; 1977 cum. supp.).

______. *"Squeeze-Outs" of Minority Shareholders: Expulsion or Oppression of Business Associations* (Callaghan 1975).

Painter. *Corporate and Tax Aspects of Closely Held Corporations* (Little, Brown 1971; 1976 pocket supp.).

Pantzer and O'Neal. *The Drafting of Corporate Charters and By-laws.* 2d ed. (ALI-ABA 1968).

Prentice-Hall. *Corporations.* 6 v.

Loose leaf.

______. *Professional Corporation Guide.*

Loose leaf.

RADCO. *Protecting Corporate Officers and Directors Against Liability* (1971).

Collection of articles.

Rohrlich. *Organizing Corporate and Other Business Enterprises.* 5th ed. (M. Bender 1975).

Rowley Partnership. 2d ed. 2 v. (Bobbs-Merrill 1960).
Seward and Nauss. *Basic Corporate Practice*. 2d ed. (ALI-ABA 1977).
Sobeloff. *Tax and Business Organization Aspects of Small Business* (ALI-ABA 1974).
Strong. *Professional Corporations* (ALI-ABA 1971).
Volz and Berger. *The Drafting of Partnership Agreements*. 6th ed. (ALI-ABA 1976).
Webster. *The Law of Associations* (M. Bender 1975).
Loose leaf.

New York Law

Kessler. *New York Close Corporations* (Callaghan 1968; 1977 cum. supp.).
Marks. *Corporation Forms for New York* (Acme 1963).
White. *New York Corporations*. 8 v. (M. Bender).
1977 loose leaf supplement.

For a bibliography, see Association of American Law Schools. *Law Books Recommended for Libraries*, No. 8: Business Enterprises (Rothman 1968; 1974 supp.).

Checklist: 7 *C.J.S.* Associations
18,19 *C.J.S.* Corporations
18 *Am. Jur. 2d* Cooperative Associations
18,19 *Am. Jur. 2d* Corporations
36 *Am. Jur. 2d* Franchises
24 *N.Y. Jur.* Franchises
West Digest key number topic: Associatons

CIVIL LAW (see also COMPARATIVE LAW, ROMAN LAW)

Course description: Designed to give the practicing attorney and the student of comparative law a basic knowledge of the civil law. The general approach of the foreign lawyer and foreign courts to legal problems as well as the structure and essential topics of the civil law are considered and illustrated by reference to the civil codes of Western European and Latin-American countries.

DeVries. *Civil Law and the Anglo-American Lawyer; A Case-Illustrated Introduction to Civil Law Institutions and Methods* (Oceana 1975).
Keeton. *Venturing to do Justice: Reforming Private Law* (Harvard University Press 1969).

Lawson. *A Common Lawyer Looks at Civil Law* (University of Michigan Law School 1955).
Merryman. *The Civil Law Tradition; An Introduction to the Legal Systems of Western Europe and Latin America* (Stanford University Press 1969).
von Mehren and Gordley. *The Civil Law System; An Introduction to the Comparative Study of Law.* 2d ed. (Little Brown 1977).
Yiannopoulos, ed. *Civil Law in the Modern World* (Louisiana State University Press 1965).

CIVIL PROCEDURE (see also TRIAL PRACTICE)

Course description (procedure I and II): Considers the history of a lawsuit up to the point of trial. Jurisdiction, pleadings, motions, discovery, and pretrial conferences are discussed. Procedure from the time the case goes to trial includes a consideration of the right of trial by jury, the relationship of judge and jury, the trial process, posttrial motions, and judgment and appellate review. (federal practice I): A study of the civil jurisdiction of, and related practice in, the federal courts under the Judicial Code. The basis of original, removal, interpleader, and ancillary jurisdiction (cases arising under the Constitution and laws of the United States, diversity of citizenship and jurisdictional amount), the venue of actions and the law applied by federal courts (the Rules of Decision Act) are considered. (federal practice II): A study of civil procedure and practice in the United States courts. The Federal Rules of Civil Procedure with emphasis on commencement of actions, process, joinder of parties and claims, pleadings, pretrial devices (depositions and other discovery), motions, jury trial, trial procedure, and judgments. Appellate procedure and practice of the courts of appeal are considered incidentally.

Am. Jur. *Pleading and Practice Forms* 25 v. (LCP).
1976 pocket parts. Includes state statutory references by subject.
Bender's Federal Practice Forms. 13 v.
Loose leaf.
Bender's Forms of Discovery. 20 v. (1963).
Loose leaf.
Casad. *Res Judicata in a Nutshell* (West 1976).
Currie. *Federal Jurisdiction in a Nutshell* (West 1976).
Cyclopedia of Federal Procedure. 3d ed. 23 v. (Callaghan 1951).
Pocket parts.

Federal Procedural Forms (LCP 1975).
V. 12 published in 1977 (chs. 45–48 of projected 68 chapters).
Federal Rules Service (Callaghan).
Loose leaf. 23 F.R.S. 2d published in 1977 (compilation of cases). This material is digested in *Federal Rules Digest* 3d ed. 8 v. (Callaghan). 1977 pocket parts.
Hunter. *Federal Trial Handbook* (LCP 1974).
1977 pocket part.
James and Hazard. *Civil Procedure.* 2d ed. (Little, Brown 1977).
John Marshall Journal of Practice and Procedure (John Marshall Law School).
V. 9 published in 1976.
Koffler and Reppy. *Common Law Pleading* (West 1969).
Kooman. *Federal Civil Practice.* 3 v. (Harrison 1970).
Lavine, R.A., and Horning. *Manual of Federal Practice* (McGraw-Hill; 1973 supp.).
Millar. *Civil Procedure of the Trial Court in Historical Perspective* (N.Y.U. School of Law 1952).
Moore's *Federal Practice.* 2d ed. 25 v. (M. Bender).
Loose leaf.
Moore's *Manual—Federal Practice and Procedure.* 2 v. (M. Bender; 1976 update).
Stern and Gressman. *Supreme Court Practice.* 4th ed. (BNA 1969).
West's *Federal Forms.* 10 v.
Loose leaf. 1976 pocket parts.
West's *Federal Practice Manual.* 2d ed. 7 v. (1970).
Pocket parts.
Wright. *Handbook of the Law of Federal Courts.* 3d ed. (West (1976).
Wright et al. *Federal Practice and Procedure.* 15 v. (West 1969).
1976 pocket parts.

New York Law

Cahill-Parsons New York Civil Practice. 6th ed.
Text of Civil Practice Law and Rules, Court Acts, official forms, and so forth. This information is also available in *Mc-Kinneys Consolidated Laws.*
New York. Advisory Committee on Practice and Procedure.

1957 N.Y. Leg. Doc. No.	6(b)
1958	13
1959	17
1960	120
1960	Final Report

New York Civil Practice Series (M. Bender).
Loose leaf 1977 update.
Cox et al. *Surrogate Court Practice Act.* v. 10 series 7 v.
Rohan. *Estates Powers and Trusts Law.* v. 9 series 5 v.
Peterfreund and McLaughlin. *New York Practice—Cases and Other Materials.* 4th ed. (Foundation 1978).
Siegel. *New York Practice* (West 1978).
Survey of New York Practice. 51 *St. John's Law Rev.* 632 (1977).
Issued annually.
Wachtell. *New York Practice under CPLR.* 5th ed. (PLI 1976).
Weinstein et al. *New York Civil Practice.* 31 v. (M. Bender).
Loose leaf 1976 supplement.

For a bibliography, see Association of American Law Schools, *Law Books Recommended for Libraries*, No. 9: Civil Procedure (Rothman 1968; 1974 supp.)

Court Rules

Court rules are to be distinguished from rules of civil and criminal procedure, which apply to practice before the courts. Court rules, in some respects, are the minutiae of rules of procedure. See Peterfreund, The Essentials of Modern Reform in the Litigative Process, 287 *Annals* 154 (1953). See also *How to*, p. 156. Court rules have to do with admission to the bar, judicial conduct, and professional responsibility and generally govern the conduct of the court as procedural rules govern the conduct of lawyers before the court. These rules appear in bar association journals, in addenda to the reports of the particular court, as separate pamphlets, as loose leaf services, and as part of West Publishing Company's service to subscribers to their annotated statutes. A selective list follows:

Alaska Rules of Court Procedure and Administration. 4 v. (Washington Book Publishing Co., 1974).
Loose leaf.
Arkansas Rules of Criminal Procedure (Bobbs-Merrill 1976).
Part of Arkansas Statutes Annotated.
California Rules of Court (West 1976).
Includes both California and federal court rules for 9th Circuit.
District of Columbia Courts. Court Rules (West 1976).
Part of District of Columbia Code Encyclopedia.
______. United States Courts (West 1976).
Part of District of Columbia Code Encyclopedia.

Florida Rules of Court (West 1976).

Includes both Florida and federal court rules for 5th Circuit.

Illinois Practice Act and Rules (West 1976).

Includes both Illinois and federal court rules for 7th Circuit.

Louisiana Court Rules (West 1976).

Includes both Louisiana and federal court rules for 5th Circuit.

Maine Rules of Court (West 1976).

Includes both Maine and federal court rules for 1st Circuit.

Massachusetts Rules of Court (West 1976).

Includes both Massachusetts and federal court rules for 1st Circuit.

New Jersey. *Rules Governing the Courts of the State of New Jersey.* (West 1975).

Includes both New Jersey and federal court rules for 3d Circuit.

New York Court Rules (West 1975).

Includes both New York and federal court rules for 2d Circuit. It should be kept in mind that in New York, the New York Civil Practice Law and Rules are enacted by the legislature, whereas the New York courts are limited to supplementary rulemaking power to create court rules. (The legislature can, at any time, step in and change the court rules.)

Ohio. *Rules Governing the Courts of Ohio* (W.H. Anderson 1975).

Part of Page's Ohio Revised Code.

Oklahoma Court Rules and Procedure (West 1975).

Includes both Oklahoma and federal court rules for 10th Circuit.

Pennsylvania Rules of Court (West 1976).

United States. *Federal Local Court Rules.* 2 v. (Callaghan).

Loose leaf. An up to date collection of rules for all federal district courts.

United States Code Annotated (West).

Title 28 carries the court rules for the United States Supreme Court, Bankruptcy, Court of Claims, Court of Customs, Federal Rules of Appellate Procedure, United States Court of Appeals, and Federal Rules of Evidence. It does not contain the rules for the federal district courts. It should be added that Title 28 also carries the Federal Rules of Civil Procedure and Title 18 carries the Federal Rules of Criminal Procedure. The *United States Code Service* and *L. Ed. Digest* carry basically the same material.

See also Researching a Federal Rules Problem, in *Research Group*, op. 58-62; *Jacobstein*, p. 206-11.

Checklist: 4-5B *C.J.S.* Appeal and Error
35A, B *C.J.S.* Federal Civil Procedure
32 *Am. Jur. 2d* Federal Practice and Procedure
West Digest key number topics: Appeal and Error, Federal Civil Procedure

CIVIL RIGHTS (see CONSTITUTIONAL LAW)

CLASS ACTIONS (see also CIVIL PROCEDURE)

Federal Class Action Digest (PLI 1971).

1974, 1976 ed. by McLaughlin. Arranged by subject: antitrust, civil rights, copyright, environment, labor, prisoners, torts, and so forth.

Fuchsberg; ed. *Class Actions Primer* (N.Y.L.J. 1973).

Newberg. *Newberg on Class Actions; A Manual for Group Litigation of Federal and State Levels.* 6 v. (McGraw-Hill 1977).

Checklist: See General Index in *C.J.S.* for entries under various topics.

CLINICAL PROGRAMS

Course description (clinical program in criminal law): Designed to expose law students to the practice of criminal law. Students represent indigent defendents in nonfelony cases, conducting all formal and informal proceedings under the guidance of supervising attorneys, whom they also assist in felony cases. In the seminar sessions, students obtain additional training in advocacy skills through simulation. Students also attend a weekly advanced criminal procedure seminar, in which the underlying problems of the system are analyzed. The course is open to third year students only.

Other types of clinical programs are: consumer law clinic, employment law, environmental law, government civil litigation, juvenile rights clinic, law and psychiatry, legislation clinic, public interest law clinic, urban law clinic, women's prison project clinic, women's rights clinic.

The Council on Legal Education for Professional Responsibility supports and encourages clinical education. See their *Newsletter*, reports, and surveys.

Freeman and Weihofen. *Clinical Law Training—Interviewing and Counseling* (West 1972).
Meltsner and Schrag, ed. *Public Interest Advocacy: Materials for Clinical Legal Education* (Little, Brown 1974).
Bibliographies.

COMMERCIAL LAW (see also BILLS AND NOTES)

Course description (secured transactions): An integrated treatment of modern security transactions in tangible and intangible personal property under the Uniform Commercial Code, and preference and voidable transfers under the Federal Bankruptcy Act as related to secured transactions. (sales): Coverage of Article 2 of the Uniform Commercial Code, dealing with the sale of goods, including contract formation, enforcement, warranty, passage of title, and remedies. (commercial law I): An integrated course dealing mainly with the sales, secured transactions, and commercial paper articles of the Uniform Commercial Code. Examples of topics covered are various aspects of the sale of goods, the use of credit and collateral in sale and loan transactions, bankruptcy, consumer credit, the check as a means of payment, and the check collection process. The course focuses on problems of statutory analysis and policy in meeting the needs and reconciling the interests of the various parties to business transactions—manufacturers, lenders, dealers, insurers, consumers, and the government. (commercial law II): An in-depth analysis of several problems in commercial paper, such as adverse claim, discharge, and suretyship; and some specialized procedures in selling, storing, and shipping goods, such as documents of title, letters of credit, documentary sales, and bulk sales.

American Business L.J. (American Business Law Association).
V. 15 published in 1977.
Anderson. *Uniform Commercial Code.* 2d ed. 7 v. (LCP 1970).
Pocket part.
______. *Legal Forms.* 2d ed. 2 v. (LCP 1974).
Pocket part.
Bailey. *The Law of Bank Checks.* 4th ed. (Warren, Gorham & Lamont 1969; 1978 cum. supp.).
______. *Modern Uniform Commercial Code Forms* (Warren, Gorham & Lamont 1963).
Bender's *Uniform Commercial Code Service.*
Loose leaf 1977 update. Secured transactions, commercial paper, sales, forms, reporter-digest, index.

Betsos. *Modern U.C.C. Litigation Forms* (Bender 1969).
Loose leaf.

Boston College Industrial and Commercial Law Review.
V. 17 published in 1976.

Braucher. *Documents of Title Under the UCC* (ALI-ABA 1955).

Braucher and Riegert. *Introduction to Commercial Transactions* (Foundation 1977).
Research and bibliography, pp. 40–48, 59–60.

Business Lawyer (A.B.A.).
V. 33 published in 1977.

Casey. *Forms of Business Agreements with Tax Ideas, Annotated* (Institute for Business Planning, 1974).

Clark. *Handling Consumer Credit Cases* (LCP 1972).
Pocket part.

Commerce Clearing House. *Consumer Credit Guide.* 5 v.
Loose leaf. 1977 update.

______. *Secured Transactions Guide.* 4 v.
Loose leaf. 1977 update.

Commercial Law J. (Commercial Law League of America).
V. 82 published in 1977. Includes bibliographies by Professor Squillante. See 83 *Commercial L.J.* 96 (1978).

Epstein. *Consumer Protection in a Nutshell* (West 1976).

Ezer. *UCC Bibliography* (ALI-ABA 1972; 1975 update).

Gilmore. *Security Interests in Personal Property.* 2 v. (Little, Brown 1965).

Hawkland. *A Transactional Guide to the Uniform Commercial Code.* 2 v. (ALI-ABA 1964).

Kripke. *Consumer Credit* (West 1970).
Casebook.

Marke and Bander. *Commercial Law Information Sources* (Gale (1971).

Nordstrom. *Law of Sales* (West 1970).

Stone. *Uniform Commercial Code in a Nutshell* (West 1975).

Uniform Commercial Code J. (Warren, Gorham & Lamont).
V. 9 published in 1977.

Uniform Commercial Code Reporting Service (Callaghan).
2 v. of loose leaf current commentary and case index; 21 v. of reported cases; 8 v. case digest.

Uniform Laws Annotated (West 1973).
Pocket parts. V. 1–3 UCC; v. 4, 5 UCC forms. This set also includes v. 6 Uniform Partnership Act, Uniform Limited Partnership Act; v. 7 Business and Financial Laws; v. 8 Estate, Probate, etc.; v. 9 Matrimonial, Family and Health Laws; v. 10

Criminal Procedure and Model Penal Code; v. 11 Criminal Law and Procedure; v. 12, 13 Civil Procedural and Remedial Laws.

Weber, *Commercial Paper in a Nutshell* (West 1975).

White and Summers. *Handbook of the Law under the Uniform Commercial Code* (West 1972).

Williston. *Sales* (by Squillante and Fonseca) 4th ed. (LCP).

Pocket parts.

New York Law

Bender's Forms for the Consolidated Laws.

1977 pocket parts. Forms for the UCC, arranged by section of the law, are in v. 8B pt. 1, 8B, pt. 2, 8C.

New York Forms (LCP).

1977 pocket parts. V. 5 contains the following: ch. 33 Sales, ch. 34 Commercial Paper, ch. 35 Bank Deposits and Collections, ch. 36 Letters of Credit, ch. 37 Bulk Transfers, ch. 38 Documents of Title, ch. 39 Investment Securities, ch. 40 Secured Transactions.

Note: Each chapter contains a concise statement of the law, references to relevant N.Y. and federal statutes, New York court decisions, tax notes, *A.L.R.* and *L. Ed.* annotations, *New York Jurisprudence*, law review articles, and so forth. For convenience, a listing of all chapters is included here: 1: Sales and Exchanges; 2: Conveyances; 3: Security Transactions; 4: Easements and Profits; 5: Boundaries; 6: Contracts; 7: Mechanics' Liens; 8: Real Property; 9: Personal Property; 10: Employment Contracts; 11: Indemnity; 12: Powers of Attorney; 13: Suretyship and Guaranty; 14: Rescission and Modification; 15: Compromises, Settlements, and Releases; 16: Bailments and Deposits; 17: Corporations; 18: Partnerships; 19: Joint Adventures; 20: Franchises; 21: Assumed Business Names; 22: Rights and Interests; 23: Notice; 24: Wills; 25: Trusts; 26: Gifts; 27: Husband and Wife; 28: Parent and Child; 29: Minors; 30: Social, Business, and Recreation; 31: Charities; 32: Cooperatives; 33: Sales; 34: Commercial Paper; 35: Bank Deposits and Collections; 36: Letters of Credit; 37: Bulk Transfers; 38: Documents of Title; 39: Investment Securities; 40: Secured Transactions; 41: Acquisition of Land for Development, Subdivision; 42: Condominiums; 43: Cooperative Apartments; 44: Management of Real Property; 45: Syndication—Limited Partnerships; 46: Syndication—Investment Trusts; 47: Professional Corporations, 48: Sales of Businesses.

McKinney's Consolidated Law of New York Annotated (West).

1977 pocket parts. V. 62½ pts. 1, 2, 3, contains the Uniform Commercial Code. Sections of the UCC are followed by practice commentaries by practitioners, official comments of the American Law Institute, official comments of the Commissioners on Uniform State Law of the State of New York. The annotations include excerpts from N.Y. legislative documents, law review citations, and so forth.

New York Transaction Guide—with Forms (M. Bender).

1977 pocket parts. V. 1—General Financial Guide, Sale of Business, Equipment Leasing, Accounts Receivable; v. 2—Accounts Receivable (2), Advertising, Venture Capital; v. 3—Franchising, Small Business Administration Financing, UCC Sales; v. 4—UCC Sales (2), Export-Import Financing, Theatrical Production financing; v. 5—Oil, Gas and Mineral, Inventory Financing, Consumer Instalment Loans, Agricultural Financing, Local Development Company Financing; v. 6—Executive Employment and Compensation, Sales Representatives, Scientific and Educational Employment Contracts, Professional Services; v. 7—Service and Maintenance Contracts, Athletes and Entertainers, Government Contracts, Contracting and Subcontracting, Commission Brokers and Agents, Vending Machine Contracts and Operations; v. 8—Personal Investment Transactions, Educational and Health Financing, Credit Card Transactions, Matrimonial Agreements, Personal Property; v. 9—Intellectual Property, Immigration and Nationality, Retirement Planning, Minors and Parents; v. 10—Surviving Insolvency, Personal Bankruptcy, Third Party Undertakings, Assignments, Discharge of Obligations.

West's McKinney Forms. UCC. 2 v.

1977 pocket parts.

For a bibliography, see Association of American Law Schools, *Law Books Recommended for Libraries*, No. 10: Commercial Law (Rothman 1968; 1974 supp.).

Checklist: 77, 78 *C.J.S.* Sales (see also General Index to set)
79 *C.J.S.* Secured Transactions
11, 12 *Am. Jur. 2d* Bills and Notes
15A *Am. Jur. 2d* Commercial Code
62 *Am. Jur. 2d* Warehouse Receipts and Other Documents of Title
67 *Am. Jur. 2d* Sales
68, 69 *Am. Jur. 2d* Secured Transactions

77 *Am. Jur. 2d* Vendor and Purchaser
78 *Am. Jur. 2d* Warehouses
8 *N.Y. Jur.* Conditional Sales
41, 42 *N.Y. Jur.* Negotiable Instruments and Other Commercial Paper
50, 51 *N.Y. Jur.* Sales
53, 54 *N.Y. Jur.* Secured Transactions
62 *N.Y. Jur.* Uniform Commercial Code, Vendor and Purchaser
West Digest key number topics: Sales, Secured Transactions

COMMUNICATIONS

Course description (communications policy and law seminar): Examines the present and future policies and significant legal problems connected with the communications media, particularly broadcasting. Discussions cover development and regulation (including licensing) of American broadcasting: access to the media; the Fairness Doctrine; First Amendment problems as they relate to governmental regulation; and use of new technology, including cable TV and satellites.

Bureau of National Affairs. *Media Law Reporter.*
Loose leaf 1977 update.
Federal Communications Bar J.
V. 28 published in 1977.
Federal Communications Commission. Planning Conference, Washington, D.C., 1976. *Computers and Communications* (AFIPS Press 1976).
Jones, William K. *Cases and Materials on Electronic Mass Media—Radio, Television and Cable.* 2 v. (Foundation 1976).
J. of Broadcasting
V. 20 published in 1977.
Kahn. *Documents of American Broadcasting.* 2d ed. (Appleton 1973).
Legal Briefs for Editors, Publishers, and Writers (McGraw-Hill).
V. 1 in 1977.
The News Media and the Law (Reporters Committee for Freedom of the Press).
V. 1 published in 1977.
Pike and Fischer. *Radio Regulation.*
Loose leaf. 1977 update. Cases, 2d series, 41 v.; Current Service, 5 v.; Digest, 3 v.

Checklist: 66 *C.J.S.* Newspapers
58 *Am. Jur. 2d* Newspapers, Periodicals, and Press Associations
74 *Am. Jur. 2d* Telecommunications
42 *N.Y. Jur.* Newspapers
58A *N.Y. Jur.* Telecommunications
West Digest key number topic: Newspapers, Telecommunications

COMMUNITY PROPERTY (see also PROPERTY)

"Community of property between husband and wife is that system whereby the property which the husband and wife have is common property, that is, it belongs to both by halves." De Funiak and Vaughn, *Principles of Community Property.* 2d ed. (University of Arizona Press 1971) p. 1. The authors follow that definition with over 500 pages of text. The community property states are Arizona, California, Idaho, Louisiana, Nevada, New Mexico, Texas, and Washington. Community property is treated within family law and property courses.

2 *American Law of Property* (Little, Brown 1952).
1977 supplement § 7.1 *et seq.*
Community Property J. (Panel Publishers).
V. 4 published in 1977.
De Funiak and Vaughn. *Principles of Community Property.* 2d ed. (University of Arizona Press 1971).

Checklist: 41, 42 *C.J.S.* Husband and Wife, sec. 462–590 (see also General Index)
15A *Am. Jur. 2d* Community Property

COMPARATIVE LAW (see also CIVIL LAW, ROMAN LAW)

A comparison of one system of law with another. Israeli law, encompassing many cultures and embodying many systems of law, frequently results in the courts citing to common and civil law jurisdictions before deciding cases before it.

American J. of Comparative Law. (University of California).
V. 25 published in 1977.
David and Brierley. *Major Legal Systems in the World Today.* 2d. ed. (Carswell 1977).

Gutteridge. *Comparative Law.* 2d ed. (Cambridge University Press 1949).

Marke, ed. *A Catalogue of the Law Collection at New York University. . .*(N.Y.U. 1953) 889-898.

Schlesinger, *Comparative Law.* 3d ed. (Foundation 1970).
Casebook.

Szladits. *A Bibliography on Foreign and Comparative Law: Books and Articles in English* (Oceana 1790/1953–).
Updated annually in *American J. of Comparative Law.*

Zweigert and Kotz. *An Introduction to Comparative Law.* 2 v. (Elsevier North-Holland 1977).

For a bibliography, see Association of American Law Schools, *Law Books Recommended for Libraries,* No. 11: Comparative Law (Rothman 1968; 1974 supp.).

COMPUTERS

Course description: A study of the effects of the computer and computer applications on the law and the legal profession, including: (1) the impact on social and economic institutions and resulting legal developments, such as with respect to privacy and electronic funds transfer systems ("computer impact on law"); (2) special issues relating to essentially computer-oriented legal problems, such as software protection ("computer law"); (3) uses of the computer by the legal profession for administration, legal research, data retrieval, prediction, and decisionmaking ("computers in law"). Computer scientists and other professionals from the computer industry participate. No background or experience with computers is necessary.

There are two "working" computers for legal research. LEXIS is based on word retrieval (a method of feeding words such as "last clear chance" and "motor vehicles" into a bank of opinions (or laws, etc.) and locating opinions utilizing these words; it can also be used to retrieve the names of judges and lawyers as well as case names, which means that it can be an effective citator). To quote from an advertisement in the November 1977 American Bar Association Journal (comments in brackets are mine):

> a general [which means incomplete] Federal library containing the U.S. Code and decisions of the U.S. Supreme Court, Courts of Appeals and District Courts. Specialized Federal libraries in the areas of tax, securities [including material difficult to locate elsewhere], trade regulations, and patent, trademark and copyright law, and special library of Delaware corporation law. State libraries of Arizona, California, Florida, Illinois,

Kansas, Kentucky, Massachusetts, Michigan, Missouri, New York [also incomplete], Ohio, Pennsylvania and Texas law, with others being added soon [I suspect not too soon].

The distributor of LEXIS is MeadData Central. Westlaw, on the other hand, has a data bank of its headnotes. In 1977, West announced that it is going full text as LEXIS. While the field is presently confined to these two giants, there is no telling how the field will be split up in the future.

At present only large law firms and a number of law schools carry the equipment. Only continued experimentation will determine its true value. Until computers can think, until they can analogize, until they can create new law, they will be just another tool to contend with in legal research, along with the digests and annotations.

Adams. *Courts and Computers* (American Judicature Society 1972).
Bigelow and Nucum. *Your Computer and the Law* (P-H 1976).
Computer Law Service. 10 v. (Callaghan). 1977 supp.
Loose leaf.
Dee and Kessler. The Impact of Computerized Methods on Legal Research Courses. . . , 69 *Law Lib. J.* 164 (1976).
Freed. *Computers and the Law—A Reference Work.* 5th ed. (1976).
Jurimetrics J. (ABA).
V. 18 published in 1977.
Law and Computer Technology (World Peace through Law Center) 1977 v.
Rutgers J. of Computer Law.
V. 6 in 1977.
Sprowl. *A Manual for Computer-Assisted Legal Research* (ABF 1976).
Wessel. *Materials and Cases on Computers, Society and Law.* 2d. ed. 5 v. (Spring 1976—exclusive use of N.Y.U. School of Law).

See also *Cohen*, pp. 104-105; *How to*, pp. 459-64; *Jacobstein*, p. 456. For a humorous but ominous look at computers, see Ewing, The Robots are Coming! Is It Time for A Computer Court? *Juris Doctor* (December 1977) 18.

CONFLICT OF LAWS

Course description: Examination of legal problems with multistate or international aspects. Thorough inquiry into selected topics in the fields of torts, contracts, civil procedure (jurisdiction and judgments), trusts and estates, and family law, the course seeks to shed light on the aims and consequences of our federal system. Also, by presenting issues in situations where no single rule must govern according to statutes and precedent, the course seeks to probe the underlying and often inconsistent purposes of the law. In addition to the above topics, the spring course focuses on problems in conflict of laws in an international context.

American Law Institute. *Restatement of the Law, Second: Conflicts of Laws 2d.* 3 v. (1971).
Ehrenzweig. *Conflicts in a Nutshell.* 3d ed. (West 1974).
Leflar. *American Conflicts Law* (Bobbs-Merrill 1978).
Professor Leflar has an annual article on this topic in the *Annual Survey of American Law* (N.Y.U.).
Weintraub. *Commentary on the Conflict of Laws* (Foundation (1971).

For a bibliography, see Association of American Law Schools, *Law Books Recommended for Libraries,* No. 12: Conflict of Laws (Rothman 1968; 1974 supp.).

Checklist: 15 A *C.J.S.* Conflict of Laws
16 *Am. Jur. 2d* Conflict of Laws
8 *N.Y.Jur.* Conflict of Laws

CONSTITUTIONAL LAW (see also Part I; UNITED STATES SUPREME COURT)

Course description (constitutional law I): The judicial function in constitutional cases, with particular emphasis on the case and controversy limitation, ripeness, and standing to sue. The affirmative powers of Congress and the president, with special emphasis on the Commerce Clause and current issues of separation of power and federalism, limitations on the power of states to regulate interstate commerce, and intergovernmental immunities. (constitutional law II): The chief limitations on governmental power imposed by the Bill of Rights. Special attention is given to the varied problems involving freedom of expression and racial discrimination. Individual instructors give emphasis to particular topics, including other problems of equal protection of the law and freedom and establishment of religion. (Other courses in this area: racism and American law, women and the law, first amendment freedoms seminar, constitutional litigation, current constitutional issues seminar.)

In general: Probably every state code carries a copy of the United States Constitution as well as its state constitution. If it is an annotated set, there will be state and federal annotations pertinent to the state.

The United State Constitution can also be found in the official *United States Code* (see UNITED STATES CODE), *United States Code Annotated* (West) and the *United States Code Service* (LCP).

Antieau. *Modern Constitutional Law.* 2 v. (LCP 1969).
1976 Pocket part.

Civil Liberties Review (ACLU).
V. 4 published in 1977.

Cushman. *Cases in Constitutional Law.* 4th ed. (P-H 1975).

Emerson. Haber and Dorsen's *Political and Civil Rights in the United States.* 4th ed. v. 1 by Dorsen, Bender, and Neuborne (Little, Brown 1976; 1977 supp.).

Engdahl. *Constitutional Power: Federal and State—In a Nutshell* (West 1974).

Folsom. *Legislative History* (University Press of Virginia 1972).

Freund. *The Supreme Court of the United States* (World 1961, 1965).

Harvard Civil Rights-Civil Liberties Law Review.
V. 12 published in 1977.

Hastings Constitutional Law Q.
V. 4 published in 1977.

Henkin. *Foreign Affairs and the Constitution* (Foundation 1972).

Legislative Drafting Research Fund. *Constitutions of the United States: National and State.* 5 v. (Oceana 1974).

Millet. *A Selected Bibliography of American Constitutional History* (Clio 1975).

Nowak et al. *Handbook on Constitutional Law* (West 1978).

Schwartz, B. *Constitutional Law* (Macmillan 1972).
Professor Schwartz has also published a five volume commentary on the Constitution (Macmillan), documentary histories of the Bill of Rights (Chelsea) and Civil Rights (Chelsea), and *The Great Rights of Mankind—A History of the American Bill of Rights* (Oxford 1977).

Supreme Court Review (University of Chicago Press).
Published annually since 1960.

Swindler. *Sources and Documents of United States Constitutions* (Oceana 1973).
Up to Ohio in 1977.

Tribe. *A Treatise on American Constitutional Law* (Foundation (1977).

U.S. Constitution. *The Constitution of the U.S.A.: Analysis and Interpretation* (GPO 1973).

For a bibliography, See Association of American Law Schools, *Law Books Recommended for Libraries*, No. 13: Constitutional Law (Rothman 1968; 1974 supp.).

Checklist: 14, 14A *C.J.S.* Civil Rights
15A *C.J.S.* Constitution
16, 16A *C.J.S.* Constitutional Law
15 *Am. Jur. 2d* Civil Rights
16 *Am. Jur. 2d* Constitutional Law
8 *N.Y. Jur.* Civil Rights
8, 9 *N.Y. Jur.* Constitutional Law
West Digest key number topics: Civil Rights, Constitutional Law

CONSUMER LAW (see, in general, COMMERCIAL LAW)

Clark and Fonseca. *Handling Consumer Credit Cases* (LCP 1972).
Clontz. *Equal Credit Opportunity Manual* (Warren, Gorham and Lamont 1976).
Clontz. *Truth-In-Lending Manual.* 4th ed. 2 v. (Warren, Gorham and Lamont).
Loose leaf 1977 supp.
Commerce Clearing House. *Consumer Product Safety Guide.* 2 v.
Loose leaf 1977 update.
Epstein. *Consumer Protection in a Nutshell* (West 1976).
Feldman. *Consumer Protection: Problems and Prospects* (West 1976).
Fonseca. *Consumer Credit Compliance Manual* (LCP 1975).
Kimble. *Federal Consumer Product Safety Act* (West 1975).

CONTRACTS

Course description: The body of law concerned with the enforceability, by the parties or others, of "private agreements." Matters considered include capacity, contract formation, interpretation, conditions, excuse of performance, and remedies for breach. Attention is given to the Uniform Commercial Code and other relevant statutes as well as to principles of common law and equity.

Calamari and Perillo. *The Law of Contracts* 2d ed. (West 1977).

Corbin on Contracts. 8 v. (West).
1971 pocket parts. Also in one vol. ed. (1952).
Gilmore. *The Death of a Contract* (Ohio State University 1974).
Gordon & Kurzman. *Gordon's Modern Annotated Forms of Agreement* (P-H 1970).
Restatement of Contracts (1933).
Tentative drafts for *Contract 2d* currently being published.
Restatement of Restitution (1937).
Schaber and Rohwer. *Contracts in a Nutshell* (West 1975).
Simpson. *Handbook on the Law of Contracts.* 2d ed. (West 1965).
Warren et al. *Warren's Forms of Agreements—Business Forms.* 3 v. in 4. (M. Bender).
1976 update. Loose leaf.
Williston. *A Treatise on the Law of Contracts.* 3d ed. by Jaeger. 16 v. (LCP).
1975 pocket parts. Also in one vol. ed. (1938).

For a bibliography, see Association of American Law Schools, *Law Books Recommended for Libraries,* No. 14; Contracts (Rothman 1968; 1974 supp.).

New York Law

Encyclopedia of New York Law (West 1957-)

Contracts. v. 6-8. v. 1-5.
1975 pocket parts.

Checklist: 17, 17A *C.J.S.* Contracts
17 *Am. Jur. 2d* Contracts
9, 10 *N.Y. Jur.* Contracts
West Digest key number topic: Contracts

COPYRIGHT (see PATENTS, TRADEMARKS, AND COPYRIGHT)

CORPORATIONS (see also BUSINESS ORGANIZATIONS)

Course description (corporations): A basic course in business organizations, including choice of forms and procedures of formation; corporate privileges and powers; the role of corporate management and the rights of shareholders and creditors; consolidation, merger, reorganizations, and dissolution; the interaction of federal and state corporation law. (corporate finance): Problems in the issuance and reacquisition of corporate securities. Analysis of various types of securities. Study of mergers, acquisitions, voluntary recapitalizations, dissolutions, and liquidations. Consideration of problems involved in payment of corporate dividends.

Checklist: 18–20 *C.J.S.* Corporations
18, 19 *Am. Jur. 2d* Corporations
11, 12 *N.Y. Jur.* Corporations
12 *N.Y. Jur.* Corporations Not-For-Profit
23 *N.Y. Jur.* Foreign Corporations
West Digest key number topic: Corporations

COURT RULES (see CIVIL PROCEDURE)

COURTS (see Part I: DIRECTORIES, REPORTS; Part II: JUDICIAL ADMINISTRATION, and other topics)

Checklist: 21 *C.J.S.* Courts
20 *Am. Jur. 2d* Courts
West Digest key number topic: Federal Courts

CREDITORS' RIGHTS (see BANKRUPTCY)

CRIMINAL LAW (see also LAW FOR THE LAYMAN)

Course description (criminal law): The purpose of criminal law, the characteristics of particular crimes, the general principles of liability to punishment, the negation of punishability by reason of special defenses, and an introduction to some of the problems of criminal procedure. (criminal procedure): A study of fundamental aspects of criminal procedure. Emphasis will be given to judicial control of police practices by means of the exclusionary rule, including search and seizure, police interrogation, pretrial identification and entrapment. Consideration will also be given to fundamentals of procedural due process, including the right to counsel, the right to jury trial, and jeopardy. (Other courses are: liberty, responsibility, and punishment; introduction to criminology, international criminal law, the law of criminal correction, post conviction proceedings, criminal trials.)

American Bar Association. Project on Standards for Criminal Justice. Standards relating to: *The Urban Police Function*

(1973), *Electronic Surveillance* (1971), *The Prosecution Function and the Defense Function* (1971), *Providing Defense Services* (1965), *The Function of the Trial Judge* (1972), *Fair Trial and Free Press* (1968), *Pretrial Release* (1968), *Discovery and Procedure Before Trial* (1970), *Speedy Trial* (1968), *Joinder and Severance* (1968), *Pleas of Guilty* (1968), *Trial by Jury* (1968), *Sentencing Alternatives and Procedures* (1968), *Probation* (1970), *Appellate Review of Sentences* (1968), *Criminal Appeals* (1970), *Post-Conviction Remedies* (1968), *Compilation of all Standards with Index* (1974). Note: Shepard's *Criminal Justice Citations* cites to cases and selected law reviews citing these standards. The West Digests (*Abbott's New York Digest, Federal Practice* 2d, etc.) and current issues of the advance pamphlets to the *National Reporter System* (*Federal Reporter, New York Supplement*, etc.) carry references to the standards.

American Criminal Law Review (ABA).
V. 14 published in 1977.

American J. of Criminal Law (University of Texas).
V. 5 published in 1977.

American Law Institute. *A Model Code of Pre-Arraignment Procedure.* 1975.

______. *Uniform Laws Annotated* (West 1974; 1977 supp.).
v.10—Uniform Rules of Criminal Procedure, Model Penal Code.
v. 11—Attendance of Witnesses, etc., Crime Victims Reparations Act, Criminal Extradition Act, Criminal Statistics Act, Mandatory Disposition of Detainers Act, Military Justice Code, Motor Vehicle Certificate of Title and Anti-Theft Act, Post-Conviction Procedure Act, Rendition of Accused Persons Act, Rendition of Prisoners as Witnesses in Criminal Proceedings Act, Status of Convicted Persons.

Amsterdam et al. *Trial Manual for the Defense of Criminal Cases* IV (ALI-ABA 1976).

Anderson. *Wharton's Criminal Law and Procedure.* 3 v. (LCP 1957).
1977 pocket parts.

Bailey. *Complete Manual of Criminal Forms.* 2d ed. (LCP 1974).
1975 pocket part.

______. *Crimes of Violence* (LCP 1973).
1977 pocket parts. V. 1 homicide and assault; v. 2 rape and other sex crimes.

______. *Defending Business and White Collar Crimes* (LCP 1969).
1977 pocket part.

______. *Fundamentals of Criminal Advocacy* (LCP 1974).

______. *Handling Misdemeanor Cases* (LCP 1976).
1977 pocket part.

______. *Handling Narcotic and Drug Cases* (LCP 1972).

______. *Investigation and Preparation of Criminal Cases* (LCP 1970).
1975 pocket part.

______. *Successful Techniques for Criminal Trials* (LCP 1971).
1977 pocket part.

Bernheim. *Defense of Narcotic Cases.* Rev. ed. (M. Bender 1975).
Loose leaf.

Bernstein. *Criminal Defense Techniques.* 5 v. (M. Bender 1970; 1976 supp.).
Supplement by Cook.

Bond. *Plea Bargaining and Guilty Pleas* (Clark Boardman 1975).
Loose leaf.

Bureau of National Affairs. *Criminal Law Reporter.*
Loose leaf. Published weekly. V. 21 published in 1977.

Carrington. *Justice on Appeal* (West 1976).

Cook. *Constitutional Rights of the Accused* (LCP).
1977 pocket parts.
Pretrial Rights 1972 *Trial Rights* 1974 *Post-Trial Rights* 1977

Criminal Justice Periodical Index (University Microfilm 1975–to date).
Issued three times a year. Indexes approximately 100 titles.

Criminal Law Bulletin (Warren, Gorham and Lamont).
V. 10 published in 1977.

Criminal Law Digest (Warren Gorham and Lamont; 1977 supp.).

Davis. *The Rights of Juveniles* (Clark Boardman 1974).

Fox. *Juvenile Courts in a Nutshell.* 2d ed. (West 1977).

George. *Criminal Procedure Sourcebook.* 2 v. (PLI 1976).

Ginger. *Jury Selection in Criminal Trials: New Techniques and Concepts.* (Law Press 1975).
Loose leaf 1977 update.

Hermann and Haft. *Prisoners' Rights Sourcebook* (Clark Boardman 1973).

Israel and Lafave. *Criminal Procedure in a Nutshell.* 2d ed. (West 1975).

The Journal of Criminal Law and Criminology (Williams and Wilkins).
V. 68 published in 1977.

Juvenile Justice Standards (Institute of Judicial Administration–ABA (1977).

Volumes on: (1) Dispositions; (2) Noncriminal Misbehavior; (3) Abuse and Neglect; (4) Youth Service Agencies; (5) Appeals and Collateral Review; (6) Counsel for Private Parties; (7) Prosecution Functions; (8) Interim Status; (9) Rights of Minors; (10) Court Organization and Administration; (11) Pretrial Court Proceedings; (12) Planning for Juvenile Justice; (13) Transfer Between Courts; (14) Architecture of Facilities; (15) Correctional Administration; (16) Dispositional Procedures; (17) Delinquency and Sanctions; (18) Juvenile Records and Information Systems; (19) The Juvenile Probation Function: Intake and Predispositional Investigative Services; (20) Adjudication; (21) Rights of Minors; (22) Schools and Education; and (23) Police Handling of Juvenile Problems. See, in general, symposium on Juvenile Justice, 57 *Boston Univ. L. Rev.* 617–795 (1977).

Kerper and Kerper. *Legal Rights of the Convicted* (West 1974).

Krantz. *The Law of Corrections and Prisoners' Rights in a Nutshell* (West 1976).

Also a casebook by the author (1973).

LaFave and Scott. *Handbook on Criminal Law* (West 1972).

Loewy. *Criminal Law in a Nutshell* (West 1975).

Merksy et al. *Author's Guide to Journals in Law, Criminal Justice and Criminology* (Haworth 1977).

Morosco. *The Prosecution and Defense of Sex Crimes* (M. Bender 1976).

Loose leaf 1977 supplement.

National Lawyer's Guild. *Representation of Witnesses Before Grand Juries* (Clark Boardman 1976).

National Prison Project. *Prisoners' Self-Help Litigation Manual* by J.L. Potts, et al. (ACLU 1976).

Nedrud. *The Criminal Law* (LE Publishers).

Loose leaf. Published monthly.

Orfield. *Criminal Procedure under the Federal Rules.* 6 v. (LCP 1966; 1977 supp.).

Packer. *Limits of Criminal Sanction* (Stanford University Press 1968).

Poulos. *The Anatomy of Criminal Justice* (Foundation 1976).

Prison Decisions—A Case Digest (University of Toledo).

Monthly; cumulated with additions in Correctional Law Digest.

Prisoners' Legal Rights; A Bibliography of Cases and Articles. 2d. ed. (ABA and Prison Law Reporter 1974).

Ringel. *Searches and Seizures, Arrests and Confessions* (Clark Boardman 1972; 1977 supp.).

Rubin, S. *The Law of Criminal Correction.* 2d ed. (West 1973).
______. *The Law of Juvenile Justice* (Oceana 1976).
Rudovksy. *The Rights of Prisoners* (Avon 1977).
Other books in the "American Civil Liberties Union Handbooks on the Rights of Americans" are the *Rights of Candidates and Voters* (Neuborne and Eisenberg); *The Rights of Mental Patients* (Ennis and Siegel); *The Rights of Mentally Retarded Persons* (Friedman); *The Rights of Aliens* (Carliner); *The Rights of the Poor* (Law); *The Rights of Servicemen* (Rivkin); *The Rights of Students* (Levine et al); *The Rights of Suspects* (Rosengart); *The Rights of Teachers* (Rubin); *The Rights of Women* (Ross); *The Rights of Reporters* (Gora); *The Rights of Hospital Patients* (Annas); *The Rights of Gay People* Carrington, B. et al). See also Dorsen, *The Rights of Americans* (Random House 1971).
Sink. *Political Criminal Trials: How to Defend Them* (Clark Boardman 1974).
Sobel. *Eye-Witness Identification; Legal and Practical Problems* (Clark Boardman 1972).
Sokol. *Federal Habeas Corpus.* 2nd ed. (Michie 1960).
Tompkins. *Sentencing the Offender—A Bibliography* (University of California 1971).
Torcia. *Wharton's Criminal Evidence.* 13th ed. 4 v. (LCP).
1975 pocket parts.
______. *Wharton's Criminal Procedure.* 12th ed. 4 v. (LCP 1975). 1977 pocket parts.
Varon. *Searches, Seizures and Immunities.* 2d ed. 2 v. (Bobbs-Merrill 1974).

For a bibliography, in addition to those listed, see Association of American Law Schools, *Law Books Recommended for Libraries*, No. 15: Criminal Law and Procedure (Rothman 1968).

New York Law

Bender's Forms for Consolidated Law of New York.
V. 5 (pt. 1): Penal Law; V. 5 (pt. 2, 3): Criminal Procedure Law.
Dowsey. *Charges to the Jury and Requests to Charge in a Criminal Case in New York* (Acme 1968; 1977 supp.).
Loose leaf.
Marks and Paperno. *Criminal Law in New York under the Revised Penal Code* (Acme 1977 cum. supp.).
Loose Leaf.

New York. *Consolidated Laws of New York Annotated.*
McKinneys (West) Criminal Procedure Law Book 11a (4 v.); Penal Law Book 39 (2 v.).
Practice commentaries by practitioners, legislative history, law reviews, and so forth.
New York Consolidated Law Service (LCP) Criminal Procedure Law Book 7; Penal Law Books 23, 23A.
Commission staff reports; forms, research references to ALR, and so forth; law review, and so forth.
New York. *Criminal Practice* (M. Bender).
Loose leaf 1976 supplement. 11 v.
Pitler. *New York Criminal Procedure* (Clark Boardman 1976; 1977 cum. supp.).
Rothblatt. *Criminal Law of New York* (LCP 1971).

Checklist: 22–24B *C.J.S.* Criminal Law
21 *Am. Jur. 2d* Criminal Law
West Digest key number topic: Criminal Law

DAMAGES

Dobbs. *Handbook on the Law of Remedies: Damages, Equity, Restitution* (West 1973).
McCormick. *Handbook on the Law of Damages* (West 1935).
Stein. *Damages and Recovery* (LCP 1972).

New York Law

Encyclopedia of New York Law (West 1957–).
Fuchsberg. *Damages.* v 9–11.
1977 pocket parts.

Checklist: 25 *C.J.S.* Damages
22 *Am. Jur. 2d* Damages
13, 14 *N.Y. Jur.* Damages
West Digest key number topic: Damages

ENVIRONMENT LAW

Course description (environmental control seminar): An introduction to the legal problems of protecting and enhancing the quality of our natural environment. The roles carried out by administrative agencies and private litigants are considered. Particular attention is given to the interplay of law and economics in this area. (environmental quality controls): An interdisciplinary study of common law and statutory principles in relation to regional ecology; water supply and flood control; air and water pollution abatement and control; solid wastes disposal and control; problems of pesticides and noise; open space and small watershed programs; relation of land use standards to control of pollutants; legal sanctions for abatement and control measures; effluent charges and other nonregulatory sanctions; allocation of benefits and costs of control and abatement, for example, sewer-financing systems; problems of administrative organization and intergovernmental relations, federal, state, and local; current legislative programs.

Anderson. *NEPA in the Courts: A Legal Analysis of the National Environmental Policy Act* (Johns Hopkins University 1973).

Annual Survey of American Law *(New York University School of Law).*

Currently carries a survey article on this subject.

Bureau of National Affairs. *Energy Users Report.*

Loose leaf. 1977 update.

______. *Environment Reporter.*

Loose leaf. 1977 update. 13 loose leaf volumes; 7 volumes of cases.

Clark, ed. *Waters and Water Rights.* 7 v. (Allen Smith 1967–1976).

Columbia J. of Environmental Law.

V. 3 published in 1977.

Commerce Clearing House, *Pollution Control Guide.* 6 v.

Loose leaf. 1977 update, Cases in transfer binders.

______. *Urban Affairs Reports.* 3 v.

1977 update.

Dolgin and Guilbert. *Federal Environmental Law* (West 1974).

Earth Law J. (Sijhoff).

V. 2 published in 1976.

Ecology Law. Q. (University of California, Berkeley).

V. 6 published in 1977.

Environment Law Rev. (Clark Boardman).

V. 8 published in 1977. Reprints of law review articles.

Environmental Affairs (Boston College).

V. 5 published in 1976.

Environment Index 77 (EIC).

Environmental Law (Lewis & Clark, Northwestern School of Law, Portland, Oregon).

V. 7 published in 1977.

Environmental Law: Practice and Procedure Handbook (A.B.A. 1976).

Environmental Law Reporter (Environmental Law Institute). 2 v. 1977 update. Loose leaf.

Environmental Policy and Law (Elsevier).
V. 3 published in 1977.

Grad. *Treatise of Environmental Law.* 3 v. (M. Bender 1975). Loose leaf. 1977 supplement.

Hanks. et al. *Cases and Materials on Environmental Law and Policy* (West 1974).

Krier. *Environmental Law and Policy, Readings,* etc. (Bobbs-Merrill 1971).

Landau and Rheingold. *The Environmental Law Handbook* (Ballantine 1971).

Meshenber . *Environmental Planning: A Guide to Information Sources* (Gale 1976).

Natural Resources Lawyer (A.B.A.).
V. 17 published in 1977.

Polunin, ed. *The Environmental Future* (Macmillan 1972).

Rodgers. *Handbook on Environmental Law* (West 1977).

Sloane. A Summary of Sources of Research in Environmental Law. *N.Y.L.J.*., October 25, 1977, and December 20, 1977.
Discusses federal law, legislative history, case law, encyclopedias, treatises, law reviews, state and local environmental law and literature.

U.S. Government Manual (GPO 1977–1978).
Consult this manual for information on Environmental Protection Agency and other federal agencies concerned with the environment. The EPA publishes a great deal of material (Legal Compilation on Water Law for instance, including legislative history).

Yannacone, et al. *Environmental Rights and Remedies.* 2 v. (LCP 1972).

Checklist: 61 *Am. Jur. 2d* Pollution Control
45A *N.Y. Jur.* Pollution Control and Conservation Laws

ESTATE PLANNING (see TAXATION AND ESTATE PLANNING)

EVIDENCE (see also CIVIL PROCEDURE, TRIAL PRACTICE)

Course description: The rules of evidence in judicial tribunals. Judicial control and administration: functions of judge and jury, judicial notice, burden of proof, presumptions, problems of relevancy, remoteness, and undue prejudice. Witnesses: principles of examination and cross-examination, competency, and privilege. Exclusionary rules: the hearsay rule and its exceptions, expert and opinion evidence, rules relating to writings.

Am. Jur. Proof of Facts (LCP).
1977 pocket parts. 1st series—30 v.; 2d series—8 v. Includes medical glossary. Topics range from automobiles to zoning. Includes testimony at trial.

Binder. D. *The Hearsay Handbook* (McGraw-Hill N.Y. 1975).
Cross references to *Am. Jur.*, *C.J.S.*, and Wigmore.

Cederbaums and Arnold, eds. *Scientific and Expert Evidence in Criminal Advocacy* (PLI 1975).

Federal Rules of Evidence News (Callaghan).
V. 2 in 1977. Published ten times a year. Newsletter.

Houts. *Lawyers' Guide to Medical Proof.* 2 v. (M. Bender 1977).
Loose leaf. 1977 update.

Hughes and Cantor. *Photographs in Civil Litigation* (Bobbs-Merrill 1973).

Jones. *Jones on Evidence, Civil and Criminal.* 6th ed. By Gard. 4 v. (LCP 1972). 1975 pocket parts.

McCormick. *Handbook of the Law of Evidence.* 2d ed. (West 1972).

Redden and Salzburg. *Federal Rules of Evidence Manual.* 2d ed. (Michie 1977).

Rothstein. *Evidence in a Nutshell* (West 1970).

______. *Understanding the New Federal Rules of Evidence* (Law Journal Press 1973).

Scott. *Photographic Evidence, Preparation and Presentation.* 2d. ed. 3 v. (West 1969). 1974 pocket parts.

Torcia. *Wharton's Criminal Evidence.* 13th ed. 4 v. (CVP 1972).

Underhill. *Criminal Evidence.* 6th ed. 3 v. (Bobbs-Merrill (1973).
1976 pocket parts.

United States Code Annotated (West).
1977 pocket parts. Rules, annotations, legislative history.

United States Code Service (LCP).
1977 pocket parts. Rules, annotations, legislative history. (including Congressional Record), advisory committee notes, law review references, and references to LCP publications.

Weinstein and Berger's *Weinstein's Evidence.* (M. Bender 1975)
Loose leaf. 1976 update. Federal Rules of Evidence. 11 v.

Wigmore. *A Treatise on the Anglo-American System of Evidence.*
3d ed. 10 v. (Little, Brown). 1977 pocket parts.

New York Law

Bender's New York Evidence—CPLR. 6 v. (M. Bender).
Loose leaf. 1977 supplement.

Fisch. *New York Evidence—Civil and Criminal.* 2d ed. (Lond Publications 1977).

Kramer. *Evidence in Negligence Cases* (PLI 1973).

Mottla. *New York Evidence—Proof of Cases* (LCP).
1977 pocket parts. Subject breakdown—criminal and civil—refers to LCP publications.

For a bibliography, see Association of American Law Schools, *Law Books Recommended for Libraries*, No. 17: Evidence (Rothman 1968; 1974 supp.).

Checklist: 31-32A *C.J.S.* Evidence
29, 30 *Am. Jur. 2d* Evidence
21, 22 *N.Y. Jur.* Evidence
26 *N.Y. Jur.* Hearsay Evidence

FAMILY LAW

Course description (I): A study of decisional and statutory law governing divorce, separation, annulment, and marriage and the incidents thereto, including custody, alimony, and separation agreements. (II): Statutes and decisions relating to the care and protection of children, with emphasis on New York law. Selected materials and problems in the areas of adoption, custody, and visitation; delinquency, dependency, and neglect; illegitimacy, placement, and foster care; tort and contract liabilities of and to minors. Legislation regarding child support, child abuse, and parental responsibility for vandalism is also reviewed.

American Law Institute. *Uniform Law Annotated* (West).
1977 pocket part. V. 9—Matrimonial, Family and Health Laws: abortion, adoption, alcoholism, child custody jurisdiction, civil liability for support, controlled substances, divorce recognition, duties to disabled persons, juvenile court, marriage and divorce act, minor student capacity to borrow, narcotic drug act, act on paternity, reciprocal enforcement of support.

Bureau of National Affairs. *Family Law Reporter.* 2 v. (1974–).
Loose leaf. Weekly. V. 3 published in 1977.

Clark. *Domestic Relations.* 2d ed. (West 1974).

Conciliation Courts Review (Assn. of Family Conciliation Courts).
V. 15 published in 1977.

DeFuniak and Vaughn. *Principles of Community Property.* 2d ed. (University of Arizona Press 1971).

Family Law Q. (ABA).

V. 11 published in 1977.

Foster and Freed. *Law and the Family* (LCP 1972).

1976 pocket part.

J. of Family Law (University of Louisville School of Law).

V. 16 published in 1977.

Lindey. *Separation Agreements and Ante-Nuptial Contracts.* 2d ed. 2 v. (M. Bender 1961).

1977 supplement. Loose leaf.

Ploscowe, Foster, Freed. *Family Law, Cases and Materials* (Little, Brown 1972; 1977 supp.).

Reporter on Human Reproduction and the Law (Legal-Medical Studies.)

Loose leaf. 1977 update.

New York Law

Boardman's New York Family Law—with Forms. 1 v. (Clark Boardman).

Loose leaf. 1977 supplement.

Family Law, Bender Pamphlet Edition (M. Bender).

Annual. Domestic Relations Law, Family Court Act and Rules, Social Services Law and selected laws.

Rothenberg. *Matrimonial Allowances in New York.* 1 v. (Central Book Co.).

1977 supplement. Loose leaf.

Schatkin. *Disputed Paternity Proceedings.* 4th ed. rev. 2v. (M. Bender 1975).

Warren's Heaton on Surrogates' Courts—SCPA-EPTL by Markuson. 6th ed. (M. Bender).

1976 supplement. Loose leaf.

West's McKinney's Forms—Matrimonial and Family Law. 3 v.

1977 pocket parts. Covers Domestic Relations Law., GOL, Family Court. See also Bender's *Forms for the Consolidated Law of New York.*

Zett, et al. *New York Civil Practice—Family Court Proceedings.* 3 v. (M. Bender).

Loose leaf. 1977 update.

______. *Matrimonial Actions.* 3 v. (M. Bender).

Loose leaf. 1977 update.

For a bibliography, see Association of American Law Schools, *Law Books Recommended for Libraries,* No. 18 Family Law (Rothman 1968; 1974 supp.).

Checklist: 2 *C.J.S.* Adoption of Persons
27A, B *C.J.S.* Divorce
39 *C.J.S.* Guardian and Ward
41, 42 *C.J.S.* Husband and Wife
43 *C.J.S.* Infants
55 *C.J.S.* Marriage
23 *Am. Jur. 2d* Desertion and Support
24 *Am. Jur. 2d* Divorce and Separation
39 *Am. Jur. 2d* Guardian and Ward
41 *Am. Jur. 2d* Husband and Wife
42 *Am. Jur. 2d* Infants
52 *Am. Jur. 2d* Marriage
59 *Am. Jur. 2d* Parent and Child
73 *Am. Jur. 2d* Support of Persons
2 *N.Y. Jur.* Adoption
15, 16 *N.Y. Jur.* Domestic Relations
25 *N.Y. Jur.* Guardian and Ward
28 *N.Y. Jur.* Infants
57 *N.Y. Jur.* Support of Persons
West Digest key number topics: Adoption, Divorce, Guardian and Ward, Husband and Wife, Infants, Marriage

FOOD, DRUGS, AND COSMETICS (see also TORTS for products liability material)

Course description: A course in government regulation of three of our largest business enterprises, designed to provide an understanding of statutory materials and administrative actions that control the marketing of these important consumer products. Deals with the development of federal regulatory controls through the years, with insights into congressional response to such problems as the use of chemical additives in food, assurance of safety and reliability of drugs and therapeutic devices, and new directives in cosmetic control. Offers a study of administrative law in an operational setting by examining a variety of agency actions taken to implement an important federal statute. A number of specialists are invited to discuss industry reactions to the regulatory agency's actions.

Commerce Clearing House. *Food, Drug, Cosmetic Law Reporter.* 5 v.

Loose leaf. 1977 update.

Food Drug and Cosmetic Law J.

V. 32 published in 1977.

U.S. Department of Health, Education and Welfare. *The Review Panel on New Drug Legislation.* Final Report (GPO 1977).
A critique of the operation of the department's handling of foods and drugs with suggestions for improvement.

For a bibliography, see Association of American Law Schools, *Law Books Recommended for Libraries*, No. 19: Food, Drug, Cosmetics (Rothman 1968; 1974 supp.).

Checklist: 2 *C.J.S. Adulteration*
28 & Supp. *C.J.S.* Drugs and Narcotics
36 A. *C.J.S.* Food
25 *Am. Jur. 2d* Drugs, Narcotics and Poisons
17 *N.Y. Jur.* Drugs and Cosmetics
23 *N.Y. Jur.* Food
West Digest key number topics: Drugs and Narcotics, Food

FOREIGN LAW (see also CIVIL LAW, COMPARATIVE LAW, ROMAN LAW)

Consult books listed in the Introduction, particularly *Cohen*, pp. 349-59, and *How to*, ch. XV.

American Series of Foreign Penal Codes (Rothman).
V. 21 published in 1977.

Blaustein. *Constitutions of Dependencies and Special Sovereignties* 4 v. (Oceana 1975-76).
Loose leaf.

Blaustein and Flanz. *Constitutions of the Countries of the World.* 14 v. (Oceana 1971-75).
Loose leaf.

Index to Foreign Legal Periodicals. (AALL).
Published since 1960.

International and Comparative L.Q. (Inst. of International and Comparative Law).
V. 25 published in 1976.

International Encyclopedia of Comparative Law. 4 v. 1973 to date. (Mohr).

Martindale-Hubbell Law Directory (1978).
V. 7 digests fifty-two countries (see Part I: DIRECTORIES).

Szladits. *A Bibliography on Foreign and Comparative Law: Books and Articles in English* (Oceana 1955).
Supplements to 1974; also supplemented in *Am. J. Comp. Law.*

For specific codes, reports, and official gazettes (New York Public Library has a collection on microfilm) write or phone law libraries (Los Angeles County, Harvard, Texas, to name three), consulates, Library of Congress, and possibly, a law firm doing business with that particular country.

It is extremely difficult to do research in foreign law because there is no effective cooperative purchasing among those collecting foreign law. Cost is simply prohibitive ($100 is not outlandish for one volume), and until those responsible for foreign law collections assign particular collection responsibilities, including sending specialists abroad, it will be a hit-or-miss affair trying to locate significant foreign codes and commentaries.

For bibliographies, see Association of American Law Schools, *Law Books Recommended for Libraries*, No. 39: African Law; No. 40: Chinese Law; No. 41: Islamic Law; No. 42: Latin American Law; No. 43: Roman Law; No. 44: Russian Law; and No. 45: Foreign Law (Rothman 1968; 1974 supp. for nos. 39, 41, 43–45).

GOVERNMENT CONTRACTS

Course description (government contracts); The primary emphasis of this course is on contracts with the United States. Subjects covered include methods of obtaining government contracts, fixed price contracts, cost reimbursement contracts, incentive contracts, construction contracts, the role of the contracting officer, the types of government contract clauses, the concepts of allowable and unallowable costs, financing, payment, default, disputes and appeals, renegotiation, sovereign immunity, and judicial review. (the law of public contracts): In our system, the federal government pursues national goals and seeks to satisfy needs that have been identified as requiring federal action—such as those concerning environmental protection, mass transportation, urban development, and indeed the national economy—by public contracts. One-fourth of all federal spending is done this way. Covered in this course are the basic legal considerations underlying the public contracts of the federal government, the legal rules affecting the formation of such contracts, the social and economic uses of federal contracts, the major legal problems that arise during their performance, and claims and litigation resulting from them.

Bureau of National Affairs. *Federal Contracts Report.* Weekly.

Commerce Clearing House. *Contract Appeals Decisions.* 1 v. Loose leaf. 1977 update.

_____. *Government Contracts Reporter.* 8 v.
Loose leaf. 1977 update.

McBride. *Government Contracts: Law, Administration and Procedures.* 11 v. (M. Bender 1967).
Loose leaf.

Nash. *Government Contract Changes* (Federal Publications 1975).

Public Contract Law. J. (A.B.A.).
V. 9 published in 1977.

Whelan and Pasley. *Cases and Materials on Federal Government Contracts* (Foundation 1975).

Checklist: 72 *C.J.S. Supp.* Public Contracts
64, 65 *Am. Jur. 2d* Public Works and Contracts
West Digest key number topic: Public Contracts

IMMIGRATION AND NATIONALITY

Course description: A thorough study of the immigration, nationality, and naturalization laws of the United States. Among the topics discussed are: the immigrant selection system; issuance of nonimmigrant and immigrant visas; grounds of excludability; grounds for deportation of aliens and for relief from deportation; change of status within the United States; administrative procedures, administrative appeals, judicial review; nationality at birth and by naturalization; revocation of naturalization; and expatriation.

Carliner. *The Rights of Aliens* (Avon 1977).

Gordon and Rosenfield. *Immigration Law and Procedure.* 3 v. (M. Bender 1959).
Loose leaf. 1977 update.

Harper. *Immigration Laws of the United States* (Bobbs-Merrill 1975).

Immigration and Nationality Law Rev. (Hein).
V. 1 published in 1977.

National Lawyers Guild. *Immigration Defense Manual* (1977).
Loose leaf. Appendix lists primary and secondary sources in field.

Wasserman. *Immigration Law and Practice.* 2d ed. (ALI-ABA (1973).

Checklist: 3, 3A *C.J.S.* Aliens
3 *Am. Jur. 2d* Aliens and Citizens
West Digest key number topic: Aliens

INSURANCE

Course description: The fundamental legal principles of fire, life, and marine insurance such as insurable interest, concealment, representation, warranty, illegality, waiver and estoppel, subrogation, contribution, and rights of assignees and beneficiaries.

Appleman. *Insurance Law and Practice.* 26 v. (West 1941–1966).
Pocket parts.

Athearn. *Risk and Insurance* (West 1977).

Becker. *Index/Citator to Insurance Law* (1969).

Benefits Review Board Service (M. Bender 1977).
Loose leaf.

Commerce Clearing House. *Insurance Law Reporter.*
Loose leaf.

______. *Unemployment Insurance Reporter.*
Loose leaf.

Couch. *Cyclopedia of Insurance Law.* 2d ed. 24 v. (LCP 1959–1970).
Pocket parts.

Federation of Insurance Counsel Q.
V. 27 published in 1977.

Forum (A.B.A.).
V. 13 published in 1977.

Harnett. *Responsibilities of Insurance Agents and Brokers* (M. Bender 1974).
Loose leaf.

Insurance Counsel J.
V. 44 published in 1977.

Insurance Law J. (CCH).
No. 658 published in November 1977.

Keeton. *Basic Text on Insurance Law* (West 1971).

Long. *The Law of Liability Insurance.* 3 v. (M. Bender 1975).
Loose leaf.

Magarick. *Casualty Investigation Checklists.* 2d ed. (Clark Boardman 1977).

______. *Excess Liability, Duties and Responsibilities of the Insurer* (Clark Boardman 1976).

______. *Successful Handling of Casualty Claims* (Clark Boardman 1974).

Meyer. *Life and Health Insurance Law* (LCP 1972).
Pocket part.

Practical Lawyer's Insurance Manual No. 1 (ALI-ABA 1975).

Prentice-Hall. *Insurance Guide.*
 Loose leaf.
Risjord and Austin. *Automobile Liability Insurance Cases.* 2d ed. 9 v. (E. L. Mendenhall 1965–).
Schermer. *Automobile Liability Insurance* (Clark Boardman 1974).
 Loose leaf. 1977 update.
Woodroof et al. *Automobile Insurance and No-Fault Law* (LCP 1974).
Young. *Cases and Materials on the Law of Insurance* (Foundation 1971).

For a bibliography, see Association of American Law Schools, *Law Books Recommended for Libraries*, No. 20 Insurance (Rothman 1968; supp. 1974).

Checklist: 44–46 *C.J.S.* Insurance
43–44 *Am. Jur. 2d* Insurance
29–31 *N.Y. Jur.* Insurance
West Digest key number topic: Insurance

INTERNATIONAL LAW (see also CIVIL LAW, COMPARATIVE LAW)

Course description: An introduction to the role law and legal considerations plays in the development and resolution of international disputes.The course is taught by the problem method. Topics include the role of national courts in determining issues of international law, the function of the International Court of Justice, expropriation, bilateral and multilateral treaty relations, national uses of force, and United Nations peacekeeping.

International law is too vast a topic for this short monograph. To scratch the surface, consult *Cohen*, pp. 306–31; *How to*, pp. 412–45; *Jacobstein*, p. 378. What might be helpful is the following list of selected periodicals in the international field (see the *Index to Legal Periodicals*, *International Law Perspective*, and *Index to Foreign Legal Periodicals* to locate articles on specific topics):

ASILS International Law J. (American Society International Law). V. 1 in 1977.
American J. of International Law (American Society International Law). V. 71 in 1977.
Brooklyn J. of International Law. V. 3 in 1977.

California Western International Law J. V. 7 in 1977.
Case Western Reserve J. of International Law. V. 9 in 1977.
Columbia J. of Transnational Law. V. 16 in 1977.
Cornell International Law J. V. 10 in 1977.
Denver J. of International Law and Policy. V. 6 in 1976.
Foreign Affairs (Council on Foreign Relations). V. 56 in 1977.
Foreign Policy. V. 28 in 1977.
Georgia J. of International and Comparative Law. V. 7 in 1977.
Harvard International Law J. V. 18 in 1977.
Hastings International and Comparative Law Rev. V. 1 in 1977.
International Bar J. (International Bar Association). 1977 issues.
International Lawyer (A.B.A.). V. 11 in 1977.
International Legal Materials (American Society International Law). V. 16 in 1977.
International Organization (Stanford University). V. 31 in 1977.
International Relations (David Davies. . .Institute).
Journal of International Affairs (Columbia University). V. 29 in 1975.
Journal of Law and Economics (George Washington Law Center). V. 12 in 1977.

Research Sources on international law; international law bibliographies, v. 11:202; bulletins and newletters, v. 11:379; international law digests, v. 11:583; international and foreign law loose leaf services, v. 12:131.

Law and Policy in International Business (Georgetown University Law Center). V. 9 in 1977.
New York University J. of International Law and Politics. V. 9 in 1976.
North Carolina J. of International Law and Commercial Regulation. V. 2 in 1977.
Public International Law, A Current Bibliography of Articles (Max Planck Institute for Comparative Public Law and International Law). V. 3 in 1977.
Stanford J. of International Studies. V. 11 in 1976.
Suffolk Transnational Law J. V. 1 in 1977.
Syracuse J. of International Law and Commerce. V. 4 in 1976.
Texas International Law J. V. 13 in 1977.
U.S. Department of State. *Bulletin* (GPO). V. 76 in 1977.
United Nations. *Juridical Yearbook.* V. 13 in 1977.
Vanderbilt J. of Transnational Law. V. 4 in 1976.
Virginia J. of International Law. V. 17 in 1976.

See also *A Uniform System of Citation*, 12th ed., for citations and abbreviations to material in this field. For a bibliography in this field, see also Association of American Law Schools, *Law Books Recommended for Libraries*, No. 46: *International Law* (Rothman 1968; supp. 1974); and Delupis, *Bibliography of International Law* (Bowker 1975).

Checklist: 48 *C.J.S.* International Law
45 *Am. Jur. 2d* International Law
West Digest key number topic: International Law

INTERVIEWING AND COUNSELING (see also CLINICAL PROGRAMS)

Binder and Price. *Legal Interviewing and Counseling, A Client-Centered Approach* (West 1977).
Edwards and White. *Problems, Reading and Materials on the Lawyer as Negotiator* (West 1977).
Freeman. *Counseling in the United States* (Oceana 1967).
Freeman and Freeman. *Counseling, A Bibliography* (1964).
Shaffer. *Legal Interviewing and Counseling in a Nutshell* (West 1976).
Watson. *The Lawyer in the Interviewing and Counseling Process* (Bobbs-Merrill 1976).

JUDICIAL ADMINISTRATION (see also COURTS)

Course description: A critical study of the functioning of the machinery of justice in the United States, covering such matters as court structure; the selection tenure and the removal of judges; the use of juries; the delivery of legal services; discipline of the bench and bar; and other matters affecting the quality of justice. Contrasts between English and American justice are explored.

Advisory Council for Appellate Justice. *Appellate Justice*: 1975 (National Center for State Courts and Federal Judicial Center 1975).
Aldisert. *The Judicial Process: Readings, Materials and Cases* (West 1976).
Annual Survey of American Law (N.Y.U. School of Law).
Annual. Each volume carries an article on this topic.
Carrington, et al. *Justice on Appeal* (West 1976).
Klein. *The Administration of Justice in the Courts.* 2 v. (Oceana 1976).
Bibliography.
Klein. *Federal and State Court Systems—A Guide* (Ballinger (1976).

Covers court structures of United States, Alaska, California, Colorado, District of Columbia, Hawaii, Illinois, Mass., New Jersey, New York, Puerto Rico. Includes a bibliography for each section of book. Chapters on legal research by E.J. Bander and on comparative structures by J. P. Richert.

Kramer. *Outline of Basic Appellate Court Structure in the U.S.* (West 1975).

Basic information on courts, briefs, oral argument, and so forth.

Leflar. *Appellate Judicial Opinions* (West 1974).

Leflar. *Internal Operating Procedures of Appellate Courts* (ABA 1977).

National Survey of Court Organization (LEAA 1971; 1975 supp.).

Listing of all state court structures and their personnel categories—includes addresses of court administrators.

Martindale-Hubbell (see Part I: DIRECTORIES).

Witkin. *Manual on Appellate Court Opinions* (West 1977).

Bibliography.

For a complementary bibliography to the Klein item, see Association of American Law Schools, *Law Books Recommended for Libraries*, No. 22: Judicial Administration (Rothman 1968; 1974 supp.). (Note: Rothman is publishing in microfiche the items cited in these bibliographies. Judicial Administration is available.)

JURISPRUDENCE

Course description (introduction to legal philosophy): A study of the concept of law viewed through the work of the leading legal philosophers of the last hundred years. The course involves discussion of the relationships between law and coercion and law and morality and an attempt to elucidate the nature of decision-making under rules. (recent analytical jurisprudence): Studies a variety of issues in legal philosophy grouped about the analysis of the concept of law and the problem of describing and justifying adjudication. Hart. *The Concept of Law* (Clarendon 1961), and Dworkin, *Taking Rights Seriously* (Harvard University Press 1977), are the principal readings.

American J. of Jurisprudence (Notre Dame University).

V. 21 in 1976 (v. 1–18 *Natural Law Forum*—Hein).

Bodenheimer. *Jurisprudence: The Philosophy and the Method of the Law.*

Rev. ed. (Harvard University Press 1974).

Davitt. *Elements of Law* (Little, Brown 1959).
Dworkin, ed. *The Philosophy of Law* (Oxford 1977).
Includes Hart, Devlin, Rawls.
Ethics (University of Chicago).
V. 88 in 1977.
Feinberg and Gross. *Philosophy of Law* (Dickenson 1975).
Includes Dworkin, Pound, Austin, Rawls, Hart—also cases.
Friedrich and Chapman. *Justice* (Atherton 1963).
NOMOS VI—Yearbook of Amer. Soc. for Political and Legal Philosophy. Current volumes published by N.Y.U. Press (this issue includes Rawls, Feinberg).
Fuller. *The Morality of Law* (Yale University Press 1964).
Golding. *Philosophy of Law* (P-H 1975).
Hall. *Foundations of Jurisprudence* (Bobbs-Merrill 1973).
Hart. *The Concept of Law* (Oxford University 1961).
Henson. ed. *Landmarks of Law* (Beacon 1960).
Oldies by Holmes, Fuller, Pound, Warren and Brandeis, Leach, Million, Seavey.
Hughes. ed. *Law, Reason and Justice* (N.Y.U. Press 1969).
Dworkin et al.
Kelsen. *General Theory of Law and State* (Harvard University Press 1945).
Llewellyn. *Jurisprudence: Realism in Theory and Practice* (University of Chicago Press 1962).
Morris, C. *The Great Legal Philosophers, Selected Readings in Jurisprudence* (University of Pennsylvania Press 1969).
Aristotle to Montesquieu to Hegel to Cardozo.
Nozick. *Anarchy, State, and Utopia* (Basic Books 1974).
See Symposium, 19 *Ariz. L. Rev.* 1-283 (1977).
Patterson. *Jurisprudence: Men and Ideas of the Law* (Foundation 1953).
Pound. *Jurisprudence.* 5 v. (West 1959).
Rawls. *A Theory of Justice* (Harvard University Press 1971).
Richard. *Moral Criticism of Law* (Dickenson 1977).
Sokol. *Justice after Darwin* (Michie 1975).
Twining. *Karl Llewellyn and the Realist Movement* (Rothmann 1973).
White. *The Legal Imagination: Studies in the Nature of Legal Thought and Expression* (Little, Brown 1973).

See also Association of American Law Schools, *Law Book Recommended for Libraries*, No. 23: Jurisprudence (Rothman 1968; 1974 supp.).

JUVENILES (see also CRIMINAL LAW, FAMILY LAW)

Course description: Examines the philosophical and historical underpinnings of the development of separate system of justice for juveniles. Analyzes the juvenile court process, including the scope of due process rights juveniles enjoy and the statutory bases for jurisdiction. Additionally, considers the legal status of children in the United States, focusing on such topics as education, medical treatment, employment, curfew laws, emancipation, right to contract.

Davis. *Rights of Juveniles: The Juvenile Justice System* (Clark Boardman 1974).

Faust and Brantingham. *Juvenile Justice Philosophy—Readings, Cases, Comments* (West 1974).

Foster. *A "Bill of Rights" for Children* (Thomas 1974).

Fox. *The Law of Juvenile Courts in a Nutshell.* 2d ed. (West 1977). Also a case book by this author (West 1972).

Goldstein, et al. *Beyond the Best Interests of the Child* (Free Press 1973.

Journal of Juvenile Law (La Verne College of Law Center, Calif.). V. 1 published in 1977.

Juvenile Court Digest (University of Nevada). V. 28 in 1977.

Juvenile Justice (University of Nevada). V. 28 published in 1977.

Juvenile Justice Standards (see CRIMINAL LAW).

Levine, et al. *The Rights of Students* (Avon 1973).

Miller, F.W., et al. *The Juvenile Justice Process* (Foundation (1971).

Piersma, et al. *Law and Tactics in Juvenile Cases.* 3d ed. (ALI-ABA 1977).
Bibliography follows each section.

Strouse. *Up Against the Law, The Legal Rights of People Under 21* (New American Library 1970).

Sussman. *The Rights of Young People* (Avon 1977).

LABOR LAW (see also ARBITRATION)

Course description (labor law): The common law and federal statutes applicable to concerted labor activity and collective bargaining. A brief examination of the common law applicable to strikes, picketing, and boycotts; extended examination of the National Labor

Relations Act as amended; a survey of the developing law of enforcement of the collective labor agreement, (labor relations in public employment): Deals with statutory and executive labor relations systems for federal, state, and local government employees. Subjects covered include unit determination, choice of representatives, wage comparability, collective bargaining, impasse resolution, use of economic weapons, and relationship of civil service laws. Prior completion of the basic labor law course is desirable, though not essential. (Other courses are: labor-management relations seminar, National Labor Relations Board practice and procedure, practice and procedure of labor arbitration, the Railway Labor Act, strikes and injunctions, the union and its members: rights and responsibilities.)

A.B.A. Section of Labor Relations Law.
  1977 *Committee Reports*—2 v.

Bartosic and Hartley. *Labor Relations Law in the Private Sector.* (ALI-ABA 1977).

Bureau of National Affairs. *Affirmative Action Compliance Manual for Federal Contractors.* 2 v.
  Loose leaf.

_____. *Collective Bargaining.* 2 v.
  Loose leaf.

_____. *Daily Labor Report.*
  Loose leaf. Published five times a week. Very expensive.

_____. *Developing Labor Law.*
  Morris volume. 1971; 1971-1975 cum. supp.; 1976 supp.

_____. *EEOC Compliance Manual.* 1 v.
  Loose leaf.

_____. *Fair Employment Practice Cases.*
  V. 14 published in 1977.

_____. *Government Employee Relations Reporter.* 2 v.
  Loose leaf. No. 714 issued in June 1977.

_____. *Labor Arbitration Reports.*
  V. 67 published in 1977.

_____. Labor Relations and Social Problems—A course book. 1971-1973.
  1.—*Unionization and Collective Bargaining*; 2.—*Social Legislation*; 3.—*Discrimination in Employment*; 4.—*Collective Bargaining in Public Employment*; 5.—*Cases and Materials on Negotiation*; 6.—*Myths and Assumptions in Labor Law*; 7.—*Processes for Conflict Resolution: Self-Help, Voting, Negotiation, and Arbitration*; 8.—*Arbitration as a Method of Resolving Disputes*; 9.—*Individuals and Unions*; 10—*Allocation of Power and Individual Rights*; Reference Supplement.

______. *Labor Relations Reference Manual.*
V. 94 published in 1977 (federal and state court decisions).

______. *Labor Relations Reporter.*
Loose leaf. 1977 update. News and Background (v. 1), Decisions of Boards and Courts (v. 2), Labor Arbitration and Dispute Settlement (v. 3), State Laws (v. 4, 4A), Wages and Hours (v. 5, 6, 6A), Fair Employment Practices (v. 7, 8, 8A); Master Index (1 v.), Expediter (2 v.).

______. *Labor Relations Yearbook.*
1976 bound volume.

______. *Occupational Safety and Health Reporter.* 5 v.
Loose leaf.

______. *Policy and Practice Series.*
Loose leaf. Compensation (2 v.), Labor Relations (2 v.), Personnel Management (1 v.), Wages and Hours (2 v.), Fair Employment Practice (2 v.).

______. *Wage and Hour Cases.*
V. 22 in 1977.

Commerce Clearing House. *Employment Practices Decisions.*
V. 13 published in 1977.

______. *Labor Arbitration Awards.*
V. 77-1 published in 1977.

______. *Labor Cases.*
V. 80 published in 1977—state and federal court decisions.

______. *Labor Law Reporter.*
Loose leaf. Case Table (1 v.), Labor Relations (5 v.), Wages and Hours (2 v.), State Laws (3 v.), Union Contract Arbitration (1 v.), Employment Practices (3 v.), Public Employee Bargaining (2 v.), Labor Arbitration Awards (1 v.).

______. *N.L.R.B. Decisions.*
1976-1977 volume published.

______. *Public Bargaining Cases.*
V. 2 published in 1977.

Employee Relations Law J. (Executive Enterprises, N.Y.C.).
V. 3 in 1977.

Federal Regulation of Employment Services. 9 v. (LCP 1976).
Pocket parts.

Industrial and Labor Relations Forum (Cornell).
V. 12 published in 1976.

Industrial and Labor Relations Rev. (Cornell).
V. 31 in 1977.

Industrial Relations (University of California, Berkeley).
V. 16 published in 1977.

Industrial Relations Law Digest (University of Michigan).
V. 19 published in 1977.

Industrial Relations Law J. (University of California School of Law).
V. 2 published in 1977.

Jenkins. *Labor Law* (Anderson 1968).
Loose leaf. 1974 supplement.

J. of Collective Negotiating in the Public Sector (Baywood Pub. (Co.).
V. 6 published in 1977.

Kheel. *Labor Law.* 8 v. (M. Bender).
Loose leaf. 1977 update. V. 18–18H of their Business Organization set.

Labor Law. J. (CCH).
V. 28 published in 1977.

Larson. *Employment Discrimination: Sex.* 3 v. (M. Bender).
Published loose leaf. 1977 update.

______. *Workmen's Compensation* (M. Bender).
Loose leaf. V. 1, 1A, 2, 2A.

Law Reprints. *Labor Series.*
Briefs and records of current labor cases; v. 10 published during 1976–1977 term of U.S. Supreme Court.

McGuinness. *How to Take a Case Before the NLRB.* 4th ed. (BNA 1976).

New York University. *Conference on Labor* (M. Bender).
V. 29 published in 1976.

Player. *Federal Law of Employment Discrimination in a Nutshell* (West 1976).

Prentice-Hall. *Labor Relations Guide.* 3 v.
Loose leaf.

Roberts' *Dictionary of Industrial Relations* (BNA 1971).

Schwartz, B. *Statutory History of the United States. Labor Organization* (Chelsea 1970).

Shepard's *Federal Labor Law Citations. . . .*(1975 to date).

Southwestern Legal Foundation. *Labor Law Developments* (M. Bender). 1977 v.

Sullivan. *Public Employee Labor Law* (Anderson 1970).
Loose leaf.

U.S. *Legislative History of*
Labor-Management Relations Act 1947 (GPO).
Labor-Management Reporting and Disclosure Act of 1959 (GPO).
National Labor Relations Act 1935 (GPO).

_____. *National Labor Relations Board Reports.*
V. 225 in 1976.

_____. *OSAHRC Reports.*
V. 20 bound, v. 21 (1977) on microfiche.

Werne. *The Law and Practice of Public Employment Labor Relations.* 3 v. (Michie 1974).

Wilson. *Labor Law Handbook* (Bobbs-Merrill) 1963.
1976 pocket part.

New York

New York. Department of Labor. *Labor News Memorandum.*
V. 32 in 1977.

New York. Public Employment Relations Board. *Official Decisions.*
V. 10 in 1977.

New York. Public Employment Relations Board. *PE News.*
V. 10 in 1977.

See also Association of American Law Schools, *Law Books Recommended for Libraries*, No. 24: Labor Law (Rothman 1968; 1974 supp.).

Checklist: 51–51B *C.J.S.* Labor Relations
48 *Am. Jur. 2d.* Labor and Labor Relations
33 *N.Y. Jur.* Labor and Labor Relations
West Digest key number topic: Labor Relations

LAW AND LITERATURE (including Humor and Quotations)

Course description: One cannot be an effective advocate or legal draftsman without being skilled in the use of language. The purpose of the course is to improve students' verbal and writing skills through a study of legal writing, legal argument, judicial opinions as literature, literature about the law, the law's effects on literature, and the effects of literature on the law.

Adler and Van Doren. *Great Treasury of Western Thought. . .* (Bowker 1977).
Ch. 12: Law and Justice.

Blom-Cooper. *The Literature of the Law* (Macmillan 1967).
Anthology.

Davenport. *Voices in Court. . .* (Macmillan 1958).
Anthology—see also the author's Readings in Legal Literature, 41 *A.B.A.J.* 939 (1955); 43 *A.B.A.J.* 813, 1018 (1957).

Dunne. *Mr. Dooley on the Choice of Law.* Comp. by E.J. Bander (Michie 1963).

Gerhart. *Quote It! Memorable Legal Quotations. . .* (Clark Boardman 1969).

Herbert. *Misleading Cases on the Common Law* (Methuen 1927).

Kretschtman. *Legal Novels: An Annotated Bibliography* (University of Texas Law School 1976).

Law in Action. *An Anthology of the Law in Literature.* Ed. by Amicus Curiae, (Edmund Fuller) (Crown 1947).

London. *The World of Law; A Treasury. . .* 2 v. (Simon & Schuster 1960).

Marke. *Dean's List of Recommended Reading for Pre-Law and Law Students, Selected by Deans and Faculties at American Law Schools* (Oceana 1958).
New edition in preparation.

McNamara. *2000 Famous Legal Quotations* (LCP 1967).

Megarry. *Miscellany-at-Law* (Stevens 1955).

______. *Miscellany-at-Law 2d* (Stevens 1974).

Prosser. *Judicial Humorist* (Little, Brown 1952).

Weisberg. Wigmore "Legal Novels" Revisited: New Resources for the Expansive Lawyer, 71 *Nw. Univ. Law Rev.* 17 (1976).

LAW FOR THE LAYMAN

Course description: This course is intended for laypeople—the professional, the office worker, and the homemaker. The class discusses marriage as a contract, marital obligations, the rights of husband and wife, parent and child, both in and out of marriage; forms of business enterprises—corporation, partnership or doing it alone, profits, responsibilities, and taxes, other forms of business; rights and duties with regard to neighbors, property, reputation, and person, how to protect one's interests and relationships; the importance of a good will—who may draw one, what is involved, a widow's rights and exemptions, how to provide for children; examination of contracts; landlord-tenant relationships, rights and duties; consumer rights; negotiable instruments; constitutional law—current developments; how to use small claims court.

American Civil Liberties Union.
For their Rights of Americans series, see CRIMINAL LAW, Rudovsky.

Brieland and Lemmon. *Social Work and the Law* (West 1977). Pp. 1–29 general; pp. 30–52 legal research.

Fisher. *Introduction to the Legal System—Theory—Overview—Business.* 2d. ed. (West 1977).

For non-law-school course—anatomy of criminal and civil suits, legal reasoning, property, contracts, agency, partnership, corporations; glossary.

Fuller. *Anatomy of the Law* (Praeger 1968).

Cerebral and readable.

Grilliot. *Introduction to Law and the Legal System* (Houghton Mifflin 1975).

Hanna. *The Complete Layman's Guide to the Law* (P-H 1974).

Institute for Business Planning. *Lawyer's Desk Book.* 5th ed. (I.B.P. 1978).

Checklists and black letter rules (with a modicum of primary and secondary source materials) on agents, arbitration, commercial law, estate planning, patents, insurance, landlord and tenant, copyright, business organization, attorney-client, uniform commercial code, taxation, and so forth. Appendix has breakdown of state laws on incorporation, blue sky laws, attachments, tax rates, rules against perpetuities, interest tables, and so forth. See also Am. Jr. Desk Book, Am. Jur. Pleading and Practice, Martindale-Hubell Law Directory, and other books listed under this topic for similar breakdowns of state laws.

Landsman, et al. *What to do Until the Lawyer Comes: An Invitation to Law*.(Anchor Press 1977).

Miller. *What Some People Ought to Know about Personal Injury Law* (Vantage 1977).

Murphy. *Canadian Legal Research Guide* (University of Windsor 1976).

Post. *An Introduction to the Law* (P-H 1963).

Radin. *The Law and You* (New American Library 1947).

Readable and cerebral.

Reader's Digest. *You and the Law.* 2d rev. ed. (1973).

The nonlawyer's *Martindale-Hubbell* digest: charts of court systems, charts of state laws; glossary.

Rezny and Remmlein. *A Schoolman in the Law Library* (Interstate 1962).

Succinct with glossary.

Rosengart. *Busted—A Handbook for Lawyers and Their Clients. . .* (St. Martin's Press 1972).

Striker and Shapiro. *New York City Tenant Handbook* (Holt (1978).

Swartz. *Making the Law Work for you—A Prisoner's Guide* (New York Community Fund 1976).

Practical guide for prisoners—how to use law library; glossary.

The Time-Life Family Legal Guide (1971).

Zelermyer. *The Legal System in Operation: A Case Study from the Procedural Beginning to the Judicial Conclusions* (West (1977).

Biography of *Lowe v. Quinn*—includes summons, complaint, memorandum of law, motions, briefs, opinions, and so forth.

LEGAL EDUCATION (see also ADMISSION TO THE BAR)

Course description (seminar): The objectives, methods, and developments of legal education and the function and obligations of the law teacher in the present-day society. Analysis and appraisal of law teaching techniques, compared with those of other professions and with those of other legal systems. Curriculum planning and interrelationship of law school courses and law practice. Law school administration, including interdepartmental university relationships, cooperation with professional groups and the community, and other extracurricular responsibilities of the legal educator.

A.B.A. *Schools and Bar Admission Requirements in the U.S.: Review of Legal Education.* Fall 1976 ed.

ABA approved schools, bar exam directory, and so forth. Note: *Directory of Law Teachers* 1976 has list of AALL-approved, ABA-approved, nonapproved, Canada.

Association of American Law Schools.

Publish proceedings, directory, *J. of Legal Education*, and so forth.

Catalog of Continuing Legal Education Programs in the United States (ALI-ABA).

V. 21 in 1975-1976.

Djonovich, comp. *Legal Education Bibliography* (Oceana 1970).

Updated in *Annual Survey of American Law* 1970-71, 1971-72, 1972-73, 1973-74. 1975-77 in forthcoming issue of *New York University Law Review.*

Gillers, ed. *Looking at Law School* (Taplinger 1977).

Gordon. *Directory of Graduate Law Programs Offered throughout the World.* 11th ed. (1977).

______. *Directory of Summer Law Programs Offered throughout the World.* 6th ed. (1977).

J. of Legal Education (AALS).
V. 28 published in 1977.
Kinyon. *Introduction to Law Study and Law Examination in a Nutshell* (West 1971).
Law Library J. (AALL).
V. 69 published in 1976.
Learning and the Law (ABA).
V. 3 published in 1977.
Llewellyn. *The Bramble Bush* (Oceana 1951).
Mayer, M. *The Lawyers* (Harper 1967).
Osborne. *Paper Chase* (Houghton-Mifflin 1971).
Novel about Harvard Law School.
Packer. *New Directions in Legal Education* (McGraw-Hill 1972).
Pre Law Handbook (AALS 1977).
1977–78 ed. All you need to know about getting into law school according to those who are in. Reading lists.
Seligman. *The High Citadel: The Influence of Harvard Law School* (Houghton-Mifflin 1978).
Shaffer and Redmount. *Lawyers, Law Students and People* (Shepard's 1977).
Learning the law, studies of law students, classroom experience, and so forth. Good bibliography on law teaching.
Siegel. *How to Succeed in Law School* (Barron 1975).
Strickland. *How to Get into Law School* (Hawthorn 1971).
Student Lawyer (ABA).
V. 6 published in 1977; see 6 *Student Lawyer* 21–32 (September 1977) for "How to Survive in Law School."
Turow. *One L* (Putnam 1977).
Fact and fiction about first year at Harvard Law School.

New York

Code, Rules and Regulations.
Title 22 Judiciary (A); Rule 520—Rules for admission of attorneys and counselors at law.

Checklist: 14 *C.J.S.* Colleges and Universities
15A *Am. Jur. 2d* Colleges and Universities
52, 53 *N.Y. Jur.* Schools, Colleges, and Universities
West Digest key number topic: Colleges and Universities

LEGAL HISTORY

Course descriptions (American legal history): Beginning with the Colonial period and emphasizing the nineteenth century; covering the formative era of American law in early Massachusetts Bay Colony;

status and manipulation of the legal process during the struggle for independence; land tenure on the western frontier; the law of the clan and of the blood feud among the Cherokees; jurisdiction in the Indian country; the American law of slavery; customary law as employed in the mining camps. (English legal history): An introduction to the history of the law of England. Emphasis on the origins of the common law in Anglo-Saxon times, the question of Norman contributions, the early modes of proof, the rise of land actions, and the status of villeins; the evolution of the King's Courts, the struggle within the judicial system, the jurists who shaped our legal heritage, the development of torts and contracts.

American J. of Legal History.
V. 21 in 1977.

Essays in Nineteenth-Century American Legal History. Ed. by Holt (Greenwood Press 1976).

Flaherty, comp. *Essays in the History of Early American Law* (University of North Carolina 1965).

Friedman. *A History of American Law* (Simon and Schuster 1973).

Haar, ed. *Golden Age of American Law* (Braziller 1965).

History of the Supreme Court of the United States. 3 v. (Macmillan 1971-) (see also UNITED STATES SUPREME COURT).

Holdsworth. *History of English Law.* 16 v. (Sweet and Maxwell 1937).

Horwitz. *The Transformation of American Law* (Harvard University Press 1977).

Howe. *Readings in American Legal History* (Harvard University Press 1949).

Hurst. *Growth of American Law: The Law Makers* (Little, Brown 1950).

Kempin. *Historical Introduction to Anglo-American Law in A Nutshell.* 2d ed. (West 1973).

Marke. *Vignettes of Legal History* (Rothman 1965).

______. *Vignettes of Legal History Second* (Rothman 1977).

Morris. *Studies in the History of American Law* (Columbia University Press 1930).

Plucknett. *A Concise History of the Common Law.* 5th ed. (Butterworth 1956).

Pollock. *History of the English Law.* 2d ed. 2 v. (Cambridge University 1968).

Radin. *Handbook of Anglo-American Legal History* (West 1936).

Schwartz. *The American Heritage History of the Law in America* (American Heritage 1974).

Also published in nonillustrated ed. (McGraw-Hill 1974).

Warren. *The Supreme Court in United States History.* Rev. ed. 2 v. (Little, Brown 1937).

Wigmore. *A Panorama of World's Legal Systems.* 3 v. (West 1928).

For a bibliography see, Association of American Law Schools, *Law Books Recommended for Libraries,* No. 25: Legal History (Rothman 1968; 1974 supp.).

LEGAL PROCESS

Course description: Advanced legal analysis that explores intensively and in a practical context the nature and interrelationships of the main institutions that compose our legal system. The respective roles of the legislature, judiciary, administrative agency, and lawyer-planner are considered in a series of imaginative problems. Among the subjects covered are the formulation and interpretation of legislation, the limits of the courts' function in making and applying law, *stare decisis,* and the drafting of private arrangements.

LEGAL PROFESSION AND PROFESSIONAL RESPONSIBILITY

Course description: A study of the legal profession and of many of the ethical decisionmaking problems that the American lawyer is likely to encounter in all phases of practice. The American Bar Association's Rules of Professional Responsibility and the (state) Rules of Professional Conduct are considered. Principal emphasis is given to the origins and organization of the profession, building a law practice, the differing roles of lawyer as counselor, negotiator, advocate, judge and teacher, obligations to provide effective legal assistance to the entire community, and the wider professional responsibilities of the lawyer.

Altman and Weil. *How to Manage your Law Office—Private Practice—Law Departments—Government* (M. Bender).

Loose leaf. 1976 update.

American Bar Association J.

V. 63 published in 1977. The A.B.A. puts out a wide variety of material on the profession. There are also state and city and county bar associations (see 7 *Martindale-Hubbell Law Directory*

1978 for a listing); as well as organizations such as National Lawyers Guild, American Civil Liberties Union that reflect the role of the law in our society.

______. *Code of Professional Responsibility.*

Also published in *Martindale-Hubbell* and by state bar associations.

______. *Opinions of the Committee on Professional Ethics* (1967).

Kept up to date in loose leaf volume: *Recent Ethics Opinions*—formal and informal opinions. Opinions also appear in *A.B.A.J.* In New York, opinions can be found in *New York State Bar J.* and proceedings of local associations.

American Bar Foundation. *Lawyer Statistical Report.*

1971 statistical report.

______. ______. *Women Lawyer Supp.* (Grossblat and Sykes). See also *United States Statistical Abstract.*

______. *Legal Profession in the United States.* 2d ed. (1970).

American Statistical Directory (CIS 1974–1977).

Current update index with entries for "Judges," "Lawyers," and so forth.

Association of the Bar of the City of New York. *Professional Responsibility of the Lawyer—The Murky Divide Between Right and Wrong* (Oceana 1976).

Auerbach. *Unequal Justice: Lawyers and Social Change in Modern America* (Oxford University Press 1976).

Bibliography on pp. 370–80.

Barrister (ABA).

V. 4 published in 1977.

Black. *Radical Lawyers. . .*(Avon 1971).

Bloom. *The Trouble with Lawyers* (Simon and Schuster 1968).

Countryman and Finman. *The Lawyer in Modern Society.* 2d ed. (Little, Brown 1976).

Drinker. *Legal Ethics* (Colorado University Press 1953).

Fischer and Lachmann. *Unauthorized Practice Handbook* (ABA 1972).

Foonberg. *How to Start and Build a Law Practice* (ABA 1976).

Gillers. *"I'd Rather Do It Myself"; How to Set Up Your Own Law Firm* (Law Journal Press 1977).

Goulden. *The Super-Lawyers; the Small and Powerful World of the Great Washington Law Firms* (Weybright and Talley 1972).

Green. *The Other Government; The Unseen Power of Washington Lawyers* (Grossman 1975).

Hoffman. *Lions in the Street: The Inside Story of the Great Wall Street Law Firms* (Saturday Review 1973).

Hudson. *Outside Counsel: Inside Director; Lawyers on the Boards of American Industry* (Law Journal Press 1973).

James. *People's Lawyers* (Holt, Rinehart 1973).

Johnstone and Hopson. *Lawyers and Their Work. . .*(Bobbs-Merrill 1967).

Kaufman. *Problems in Professional Responsibility* (Little, Brown 1976).

Conflicting interests, confidences, corporate lawyer, government lawyer, legal services, admission to bar, discipline, bibliography.

Law Notes for the General Practitioner (ABA).

V. 13 published in 1977.

Legal Economics (ABA).

V. 3 published in 1977.

Mallen and Levit. *Legal Malpractice* (West 1977).

Forms, bibliography, table by jurisdiction, and so forth.

Maru and Clough. *Digest of Bar Association Ethics Opinions* (ABA 1970; 1975 supp.).

Mayer. *Lawyers* (Harper 1967).

Morgan and Rotunda. *Problems and Materials on Professional Responsibility* (Foundation 1976).

Bibliography following each section: ethical problems, loyalty to client, legal services, obtaining clients, discipline, conduct of judges, criminal law practice, government service, public interest law.

Nader and Green, ed. *Verdicts on Lawyers* (Crowell 1976).

NCBL Notes (National Conference of Black Lawyers).

V. 3 in 1977.

Practical Lawyer (ABA).

V. 23 published in 1977.

Redlich. *Professional Responsibility—A Problem Approach* (Little, Brown 1976).

Singer. *How to Go Directly Into Solo Practice Without Missing a Meal* (LCP 1976).

Smigel. *Wall St. Lawyer. . .*(Free Press 1964; 1969).

Stern. *An Attorney's Guide to Malpractice Liability* (Michie 1977).

Utley. *Where Do I Go From Here: A Career Planning Manual for Lawyers* (ABA 1973).

New York State

New York State Bar Association, *Handbook on Professional Ethics and Responsibility*, Buckley, ed. (1974).

Bibliography.

Fishman and Kaufmann, ed. *Practicing Law in New York City* (Council of New York Law Associates 1975).

For a bibliography, see Association of American Law Schools, *Law Books Recommended for Libraries*, No. 26: Legal Profession (Rothman 1968; 1974 supp.).

Checklist: 7 *C.J.S.* Attorney and Client
7 *Am. Jur. 2d* Attorneys at Law
3 *N.Y. Jur.* Attorney and Client

LEGAL SERVICES

American Bar Association. *Compilation of Reference Materials on Prepaid Legal Services* (1973).

Clearinghouse Review (National Clearinghouse for Legal Services).
V. 11 in 1977 covers paralegals, poverty law, class actions, criminal law, case developments by subject, and so forth.

New Directions in Legal Services.
V. 2 published in 1977.

Pfennigstorf and Kimball. *Legal Service Plans, Approaches to Regulation* (ABA 1977).
Types of plans, model act, bibliography, state legislation, and so forth.

LEGAL WRITING

Course description (introductory seminar and moot court): Legal research, legal writing and Moot Court law notes, appellate briefs, and oral argument. Discussion of topics and problems within the scope of first year work to give the student additional opportunity for participation in legal argument and to increase his or her understanding of legal processes.

Note: the following material is selected (with additions) from the N.Y.U. *Moot Court Handbook* (1978), which this author assisted in preparing.

Association of the Bar of the City of New York, Committee on Federal Courts.
Appeals to the Second Circuit. . .(1975).

Biskind. *Simplify Legal Writing* (Arco 1975).

Board of Student Advisors. *Introduction to Advocacy.* 2d ed. (Foundation 1976).
Harvard's Moot Court Handbook.

Bodin. *Civil Litigation and Trial Techniques* (PLI 1976).
Cohen. *How to Find the Law.* 7th ed. (West 1976).
487 *et seq.* contains memorandum, sample brief, and so forth.
Djonovich. *Legal Education Bibliography* (Oceana 1970).
Books and articles on legal writing, p. 214. For supplement information see LEGAL EDUCATION.
Figg. et al. *Civil Trial Manual* (ALI-ABA 1974).
Art of advocacy, p. 353; trial brief, pp. 384, 389.
Greenbaum. Lawyers Talk Too Much, 19 *F.R.D.* 217 (1957).
Henke. *California Law Guide.* 2d ed. (Parker and Son 1976).
Court briefs, pp. 419 *et seq.*; memoranda, pp. 400–45, opinion letters, pp. 445–47.
Leflar, ed. *Appellate Judicial Opinions* (West 1974).
Chapter 7: writing of opinions.
Mehler. *Effective legal communication* (Philgor 1975).
Forms for summons, briefs, memorandum of law, and the like.
Melinkoff. *The Language of the Law* (Little, Brown 1963).
Newman. *Strictly Speaking* (Bobbs-Merrill 1974).
See 22 *U.C.L.A. L. Rev.* 999 (1975) as Newman book applies to law.
Re. *Brief Writing and Oral Argument.* 4th ed. (Oceana 1973).
Rombauer. *Legal Problem Solving: Analysis, Research and Writing.* 3d ed. (West 1978).
Statsky. *Legal Research—Writing and Analysis* (West 1974).
Statsky and Wernet. *Case Analysis and Fundamentals of Legal Writing* (West 1977).
Office memo in typed form, pp. 458–70.
vom Baur. *The Practical Lawyer's Manual Memorandum of Law.* 2d ed. (ALI-ABA 1973).
White. *The Legal Imagination. . .*(Little, Brown 1973).
Witkin. *Manual on Appellate Court Opinions* (West 1977).

LEGISLATION (see also Part I: LEGISLATIVE HISTORY)

Course description: A study of the legislative process in the context of statutory construction and drafting. Special attention given to constitutional limitations on the subject matter and form of statutes as well as to the judicial interpretation of statutes. Emphasis placed on the rules and guides to the drafting of statutes, with illustrative drafting problems.

Barber. *The Constitution and the Delegation of Congressional Power* (University of Chicago 1975).

Congressional Quarterly. *Guide to Congress.* 2d ed. (1976).
Extensive bibliographies; how a bill becomes a law, p. 345.

Davies. *Legislative Law and Process in a Nutshell* (West 1975).

Dickerson. *The Fundamentals of Legal Drafting* (Little, Brown 1965).

———. *The Interpretation and Application of Statutes* (Little, Brown 1975).

Froman. *The Congressional Process: Strategies, Rules and Procedures* (Little, Brown 1967).

Gowers. *The Complete Plain Words.* Rev. ed. by Fraser (HMSO 1973).

Hamilton. *The Power to Probe: A Study of Congressional Investigations* (Random House 1976).

Harvard J. of Legislation.
V. 14 published in 1977.

How to find Statutes and U.S. Code Citations. 3d rev. ed. (GPO 1977). See Appendix.

J. of Legislation (Notre Dame Law School).
V. 4 published in 1977.

Lammers. *Legislative Process and Drafting in U.S. Law Schools* (ABA 1977).
Ch. 5—teaching materials and methods discusses legal research texts and how to teach legal research; bibliography for courses on the legislative process, pp. 77–86.

Nutting, et al. *Legislation.* 5th ed. (West 1977).

Pettit. *The Legislative Process in the U.S. Senate* (Rand McNally 1969).

Read, et al. *Materials on Legislation.* 3d ed. (Foundation 1973).
Bibliography, p. xlii *et seq.*

Redman. *The Dance of Legislation* (Simon and Schuster 1973).

Seton Hall Legislative J.
V. 2 in 1976.

Statsky. *Legislative Analysis: How to Use Statutes and Regulations* (West 1975).

Sutherland. *Statutes and Statutory Construction.* 4th ed. by C.D. Sands. 6 v. (Callaghan).
1977 pocket parts. Extensive bibliographies.

United States Government Printing Office. *Style Manual.* Rev. ed. (GPO 1967).

University of Michigan J. of Law Reform.
V. 10 in 1977.

Zinn. *How Our Laws are Made.* Rev. ed. (GPO 1974).

See also *Cohen*, pp. 160–200; *How to*, pp. 184–218, 331–32; *Jacobstein*, pp. 136, 164, 188.

Checklist: 82 *C.J.S.* Statutes
73 *Am. Jur. 2d* Statutes
56 *N.Y. Jur.* Statutes
West Digest key number topic: Statutes

LOCAL GOVERNMENT (see also URBAN LAW)

Advisory Commission on Intergovernmental Affairs (Washington, D.C. 20575).
Write for list of publications.

Antieau. *Local Government Law.* 7 v. (M. Bender 1955).
Loose leaf. 1976 update.

Council of State Governments (P.O. Box 11910, Lexington, Ky. 40511).

McCarthy. *Local Government Law in a Nutshell* (West 1975).

McQuillin. *Law of Municipal Corporations.* 3d ed. 23 v. (Callaghan).
1976 pocket parts.

Matthews. *Municipal Ordinances, Text and Forms.* 2d ed. (Callaghan).

National Institute of Municipal Law Officers (839 17 St. N.W. Washington, D.C. 20006).
Publishers of *NIMLO Municipal Law Rev., Municipal Attorney, Municipal Law Court Decisions, Municipal Ordinance Rev.*, and so forth.

National League of Cities and U.S. Conference of Mayors (1620 Eye St. N.W. Washington, D.C. 20006).
Write for list of publications such as *Urban Affairs Abstracts.*

Rhyne. *Municipal Law* (National Institute of Municipal Law Officers 1957).

Shepard's Citations. *Ordinance Law Annotations.* 6 v.
1977 pocket parts. Arranged by subject with citations to cases, annotations, law review articles.

Urban Lawyer (ABA).
V. 9 published in 1977.

Yokley. *Municipal Corporations.* 4 v. (Michie 1956).

For a bibliography on this topic, see Association of American Law Schools. *Law Books Recommended for Libraries*, No. 27: Local Government (Rothman 1968; supp. 1974).

Checklist: 62-64 *C.J.S.* Municipal Corporations
20 *Am. Jur. 2d* Counties
40 *Am. Jur. 2d* Housing Laws and Urban Redevelopment
56, 57 *Am. Jur. 2d* Municipal Corporations, etc.
13 *N.Y. Jur.* Counties
27 *N.Y. Jur.* Housing Laws and Urban Renewal
39, 40 *N.Y. Jur.* Municipal Corporations
West Digest key number topics: Municipal Corporations, States

MEDICO-LEGAL

Course description (law and medicine): Survey course designed to introduce students to the various aspects of the field of legal medicine from the point of view of the attorney. Subject matter covers the medical-scientific approach and mode of analysis of legal issues of injury definition, causation assessment, disability evaluation and measurement of medical damages, as well as legal problems of health care delivery, planning and financing, patients' rights, medical malpractice, population control, genetics, human experimentation and other issues involving medical ethics. (law and psychiatry): Exploration of the significant areas of interaction between the legal and psychiatric disciplines. Matters to be covered include the insanity defense, disposition of the mentally ill offender, treatment of sex offenders and dangerous offenders, civil commitment, right to treatment, alternatives to incarceration, divorce and child custody.

Alexander. *Jury Instruction on Medical Issues* (Allen Smith 1966).

Allen. et al. *Readings in Law and Psychiatry.* Rev. ed. (Johns Hopkins Press 1975).

Am. Jur. Proof of Facts. *Medical Glossary* (LCP).

Annas. *The Rights of Hospital Patients* (Avon 1975).

Aspen Systems Corp. Health Law Center. *Problems in Hospital Law.* 2d ed. (1974).

Bender's Courtroom Medicine Series. 18 v. (M. Bender). Loose leaf. 1976 update.

Blinder. *Psychiatry in the Everyday Practice of Law* (LCP 1973). 1977 pocket part.

Brooks. *Law, Psychiatry and the Mental Health System* (Little, Brown 1974).

Bulletin of the American Academy of Psychiatry and the Law. V. 5 published in 1977.

Charfoos. *The Medical Malpractice Case: A Complete Handbook* (P-H 1973).

Chartel. *The Law of Medical Practice* (C.C. Thomas 1959).
Commerce Clearing House. *Medicare and Medicaid.* 3 v.
Loose leaf. 1977 update.
Curran and Shapiro. *Law, Medicine and Forensic Science.* 2d ed. (Little, Brown 1970).
1974 update—cases and materials.
DeMarco. *Pharmacy and the Law* (Aspen Systems 1975).
Ennis. *The Rights of Mental Patients* (Avon 1973).
Gosfield. *PSRO's: The Law and Health Consumer* (Ballinger 1975).
Gray. *Attorneys' Textbook of Medicine.* 3d ed. 12 v. (Bender 1934).
Loose leaf. 1977 update.
Harney. *Medical Malpractice* (Allen Smith 1973).
Hershey. *Human Experimentation and the Law* (Aspen 1976).
Holder. *Medical Malpractice Law* (Wiley 1975).
Houts. *Lawyers' Guide to Medical Proof.* 2 v. (M. Bender 1966).
Loose leaf. 1977 update.
Humber. *Biomedical Ethics and the Law* (Plenum Press 1976).
Katz. *Experimentation with Human Beings* (Russell Sage 1972).
Katz, et al. *Psychoanalysis, Psychiatry and Law* (Free Press 1967).
Kindred. *The Mentally Retarded Citizen and the Law* (Free Press 1976).
King. *The Law of Medical Malpractice in a Nutshell* (West 1977).
Lawyers' Medical Cyclopedia of Personal Injuries. 8 v. (Allen Smith 1958).
1976 pocket parts.
Lawyer's Medical J., 2d series (LCP).
V. 6 in 1977.
Legal Aspects of Medical Practice/J. of Legal Medicine.
V. 5 in 1977.
Legal Medical Q.
V. 1 published in 1977.
Lex et Scientia.
V. 13 published in 1977.
Louisell and Williams. *Medical Malpractice.* 2 v. (M. Bender 1969).
Loose leaf. 1977 update.
Medical Trial Technique Q. (Callaghan).
Published in 1977.
The Mentally Retarded Citizen and the Law (Free Press 1976).
Milunsky. *Genetics and the Law* (Plenum 1976).
Reporter on Human Reproduction and the Law (Legal-Medical Studies).

Loose leaf 1977 update—abortion, conception, malpractice, and so forth.

Sadoff. *Forensic Psychiatry: A Practical Guide for Lawyers and Psychiatrists* (C.C. Thomas 1975).

Schmidt. *Attorney's Dictionary of Medicine.* 2 v. (M. Bender 1962).

Loose leaf.

Slovenko. *Psychiatry and Law* (Little, Brown 1973).

Stedman's *Medical Dictionary.* 23d ed. (Williams 1976).

Streiff. *Nursing and the Law* (Aspen 1975).

Watson. *Psychiatry for Lawyers* (International Universities 1968).

Wilson. *Death by Decision, The Medical, Moral and Legal Dilemmas of Euthanasia* (Westminster 1975).

Woody. *Legal Aspects of Mental Retardation; A Search for Reliability* (C.C. Thomas 1974).

For a bibliography, see Association of American Law Schools, *Law Books Recommended for Libraries,* No. 28: Medical Jurisprudence (Rothman 1968; supp. 1974).

Checklists: 61 *Am. Jur. 2d* Physicians and Surgeons
45 *N.Y. Jur.* Physicians and Surgeons

MILITARY LAW

Course description: Involves essentially a critical study of the scope and limits of military authority in the United States. Military law is examined not only as it is but also in the context of what should be the proper role of a military establishment in modern American society. Areas covered include the war and military powers of Congress and the president and their constitutional limitations; conscription, conscientious objection to military service; the authority of the military over its own personnel; the relationship between military discipline and military law; the court martial system and court martial jurisdiction; due process rights under military justice; command influence; First Amendment rights of military personnel; limitations on the validity of military orders and the imposition of punishment for disobedience; civilian court review of military determinations.

Air Force Law Rev. (USAF).

V. 18 published in 1976.

Air University Library Index to Military Periodicals.
V. 28 in 1977. Published quarterly—covers seventy-three military and air journals.

The Army Lawyer (JAG).
Published in 1977.

Bishop. *Justice Under Fire; A Study of Military Law* (Charterhouse 1974).

JAG J. (Navy).
V. 29 published in 1976.

Military Justice Reporter (West).
V. 3 in 1977; cases decided in Court of Military Appeals and selected decisions.

Military Law Reporter (Public Law Education Institute).
Loose leaf.

Military Law. Rev.
V. 77 published in 1977.

Moyer. *Justice and the Military* (Public Law Education Institute).
Loose leaf.

Rivkin. *The Rights of Servicemen* (Avon 1972).

United States. *Air Force JAG Law Rev.*
V. 18 published in 1976.

For a bibliography, see Association of American Law Schools, *Law Books Recommended for Libraries*, No. 29: Military Law (Rothman 1968; supp. 1974).

Checklist: 6 *C.J.S.* Armed Services
57 *C.J.S.* Militia
93 *C.J.S.* War and National Defense
53, 54 *Am. Jur. 2d.* Military and Civil Defense
78 *Am. Jur. 2d.* War
79 *Am. Jur. 2d.* Weapons and Firearms
37 *N.Y. Jur.* Military and Civil Defense
West Digest key number topics: Militia, Military Justice, War and National Emergency

NATURAL RESOURCES

Course description (oil and gas): The study of the nature and protection of various interests in the oil and gas mineral estate; legal principles concerning the rights and remedies of the oil and gas mineral owner, owner-lessor, and lessee; major clauses of the oil and gas lease; the problems incident to conveyancing of the various interests in the oil and gas mineral estate; and governmental regulation, polling, and unitization.

2 *American Law of Property* (Little, Brown) 1952–1976.
Bound supplement.
Brown. *Law of Oil and Gas Leases.* 2d ed. 2 v. (M. Bender 1967).
Loose leaf.
Hemingway. *The Law of Oil and Gas* (West 1971).
Institute on Oil and Gas Law and Taxation (M. Bender).
1977 volume.
Kuntz. *A Treatise on the Law of Oil and Gas. . . .*6 v. (Anderson 1962).
Miller. *Oil and Gas: Federal Income Taxation.* 13th ed. (CCH 1975).
Myers. *The Law of Pooling and Unitization.* 2d ed. 2 v. (M. Bender 1957).
Loose leaf.
Oil and Gas Tax Q. (M. Bender).
V. 26 published in 1977.
Prentice-Hall. *Federal Taxes: Oil and Gas.* 1 v.
Loose leaf.
Sigler. *Wildlife Law Enforcement.* 2d ed. (W.C. Brown 1972).
Southwestern Legal Foundation. *Oil and Gas Reporter.* 55 v. (M. Bender).
Monthly loose leaf service.
Summers. *The Law of Oil and Gas.* (West 1938).
Pocket parts.
Waters and Water Rights. 7 v. (Allen Smith 1967).
Pocket parts.
Williams and Meyers. *Oil and Gas Law.* 7 v. (M. Bender 1959).
Loose leaf.
______. *Oil and Gas Terms.* 3d ed. (M. Bender).
Loose leaf.

For a bibliography, see Association of American Law Schools, *Law Books Recommended for Libraries*, No. 31: Oil and Gas Law (Rothman 1968; 1974 supp.).

Checklists: 38 *C.J.S.* Gas
58 *C.J.S.* Mines and Minerals
93 *C.J.S.* Waters
38 *Am. Jur. 2d.* Gas and Oil
54 *Am. Jur. 2d* Mines and Minerals

78 *Am. Jur. 2d.* Waters
8 *N.Y. Jur.* Conservation
37 *N.Y. Jur.* Mines and Minerals
63 *N.Y. Jur.* Waters and Water Courses
West Digest key number topics: Gas, Mines and Minerals, Water and Water Courses

PARALEGALS

Course description (basic concepts in paralegal education): Designed to give the student a broad background in the basic concepts of the legal field. Material covered includes fundamentals of legal research, Civil Practice law, torts, matrimonial (family) law, criminal law, federal income, estate and gift taxation, federal regulatory agencies, debtor-creditor relations, business organizations, wills, estates and trusts, and real property law. The objective of this course is to acquaint the beginning student with the principles of Anglo-American jurisprudence, the vocabulary of the law, and the basic concepts of the legal system in general. (advanced concepts in business organizations): Trains the student to handle the practical problems of business organizations, particularly the regulation of business by various government agencies. Material covered includes basic accounting concepts, N.L.R.B., fair employment practices, deferred compensation and ERISA, incorporation procedures and forms, S.E.C., and federal income tax. The student will be trained to function in major areas of business-related law. (advanced concepts in wills, estates, and trusts): Designed to develop a legal technician in wills, estates, and trust administration. Material covered includes the law of inheritance of property—wills and intestacy; requirements of will preparation—information, form and substance; the law of trusts; requirements of trust preparation, forms: administration of trusts and estates—the surrogate court, techniques of probate, record keeping and bookkeeping; state and federal taxation, preparation of returns; techniques of closing estates, and termination of trusts. The student will be trained to assist a lawyer in rendering legal services to clients in the probate and trust area. (advanced concepts in litigation): Trains the student to be a technician in the area of litigation by exposure to practical problems and procedures encountered by litigating attorneys. Material covered includes courts and jurisdiction actions and special proceedings, matrimonial actions, landlord and tenant, pleadings and motions, trials and appeals. The student will be trained to assist attorneys in all areas of litigation.

Rock. *Preparation and Pursuance of Civil Litigation* (National Center for Paralegal Training, N.Y.C.).

Cases and forms relating to courts, substantive law, and so forth.

Shayne. *The Paralegal Profession—A Career Guide* (Oceana 1977).

Statsky. *Introduction to Paralegalism; Perspectives, Problems, and Skills* (West 1974).

West also publishes specific titles such as *Introduction to Corporate Law* (Institute for Paralegal Training 1978).

For bibliographic material, see *Index to Legal Periodicals*: Paraprofessionals.

PARTNERSHIP (see BUSINESS ORGANIZATIONS)

Checklist: 68 *C.J.S.* Partnership
59, 60 *Am. Jur. 2d* Partnership
43 *N.Y. Jur.* Partnership
West Digest key number topic: Partnership

PATENTS, TRADEMARKS, AND COPYRIGHT (see also ART LAW)

Course description (copyright I): Covers constitutional and statutory requirements for copyright protection of books, periodicals, maps, musical works, photographic works, motion pictures, television programs, commercial prints and labels, artistic designs, and so forth; how such protection may be secured under the statute (problems of copyright notice, manufacturing clause, deposit of copies and registration, etc.); who may secure copyright (alien authors, etc.) including problems of copyright renewal and current international copyright problems. (copyright II): Topics include fair use; infringement by news media including photocopying, computers, and video cassettes; performing rights and musical performing rights societies; problems of the recording industry; the right to vend, translate, and make new versions; and rights outside the Copyright Act. Consideration is given to litigation problems including jurisdiction, venue, pleadings, discovery, preliminary and permanent injunctions, restraining orders, proof of access and similarity, actual damages and profits, statutory damages, and attorneys' fees and trials. (advanced copyright seminar): Advanced seminar with participation by expert practitioners on current legal and business problems in industries affected by copyright law including music, book and periodical publishing, recording, motion pictures, and broadcasting. Separate consideration will be given to character licensing, techniques of searching and clearing rights and titles, and problems from the copyright office point of view. (industrial property seminar): Each seminar is devoted to one or more special problems of active interest in the field of industrial property, for example, trade secrets, patent and trade secret antitrust policy, patent and trade secret licensing; and interface problems with other forms of intellectual property. The specific subject matter to be covered in a seminar is designated by the instructor. (patent law I): Directed to the nature of patents as property and the substantive law governing questions of validity and infringement in actions to enforce patents. Covers transfers of patent property; interpretative rules of claim construction, the doctrine of equivalents and file wrapper estoppel, novelty, utility, and nonobviousness; presumptions of validity; late claiming; intervening rights; the statutory bars; the experimental use exception. (patent law II): Directed to patent procurement problems. Covers the substantive law connected with filing and obtaining patents; means for obtaining and keeping the earliest filing date, including continuing applications, *res judicata* in the patent office, foreign priority dates, and misjoinder and nonjoinder difficulties; requirements of prior art references; Rules 131 and 132 affidavits; technical rejections; double patenting; reissue applications; forms and substance of appellate review. (trademark registration and protection): Deals with the common law and statutory protection of trademarks and trade names. Includes a thorough discussion of the Lanham Trade-Mark Act of 1946; covers, inter alia, acquisition and loss of trademarks at common law; opposition, interference, cancellation, and concurrent use proceedings; registrability of trademarks, service marks, certification marks, collective marks; assignment, licensing, and "franchising" of trademarks; jurisdiction and remedies. (unfair trade practices I): Deals with misappropriation of intangible business values (news piracy, design piracy, betrayal of trade secrets, etc.), disparagement and trade libel, false and "bait" advertising, and related problems.

Also covers major aspects of "passing off" and trademark infringement, including acquisition, preservation, and loss of trademarks, "dilution" of trademark rights, and other contemporary problems. (Trademark registration problems and procedures are treated in a separate course.) (unfair trade practices II): Deals exclusively with Federal Trade Commission, including extensive coverage of FTC enforcement and regulatory authority with respect to unfair and deceptive trade practice. Also covers FTC practices and procedure, judicial review of FTC orders, and FTC enforcement of its power to prevent unfair methods of competition.

APLA J. (American Patent Law Association).
V. 5 published in 1977.

Annual Survey of American Law.
Survey articles on copyright, patents, and so forth.

Brylawski and Goldman. *Legislative History of the 1909 Copyright Act* (Rothman 1976).

Bulletin of the Copyright Soceity (Rothman).
V. 24 published in 1977.

Callman. *The Law of Unfair Competition, Trademarks and Monopolies.* 3d ed. 5 v. (Callaghan 1967).
Loose leaf.

Chee. How to Research Copyright Law, 70 *Law Lib. J.* 171 (1977).

Copyright Bulletin (UNESCO).
V. 11 published in 1977.

Copyright Law Symposium (Columbia University Press).
V. 23 published in 1977.

Costner. *Patent Licensing Transactions.* 2 v. (M. Bender 1968).
Loose leaf. V. 14 of Business Organizations.

Deller. *Deller's Walker on Patents.* 2d ed. 9 v. (Baker, Voorhis 1964).
1975 pocket parts.

Dunner, et al. *Patent Law Perspectives* (M. Bender).
Loose leaf. 1977 update.

Eckstrom. *Licensing in Foreign and Domestic Operations* 3d ed. (Clark Boardman).
Loose leaf. 1976 update.

Finnegan. *The Law and Business of Licensing.* 2 v. (Clark Boardman (1975).
Loose leaf.

IDEA (Franklin Pierce Law Center).
V. 18 published in 1976.

Kintner. *Intellectual Property Law Primer* (Macmillan 1975).

Ladas. *Patents, Trademarks and Related Rights: National and International Protection.* 3 v. (Harvard University Press 1975).

Lieberstein. Through the Patent Maze: A Guide for the General Lawyer, 32 *Record* (Association of the Bar of the City of New York) No. 5/6: 339 (1977).

Lindey. *Entertainment Publishing and the Arts: Agreements and the Law.* 2 v. (Clark Boardman 1963).
Loose leaf. 1977 update.

Martindale-Hubbell. Vol. 7, pt. 2: Digests of copyright, patents and trademarks.

Milgrim. *Trade Secrets* (M. Bender 1967).
Loose leaf. 1977 update.

Nimmer. *Copyright.* 2 v. (M. Bender 1963).
Loose leaf.

Nordhaus. *Patent License Agreements: Law and Forms* (Jural 1976).
Loose leaf.

Patent and Trademark Rev. (Trade Activities, N.Y.C.).
V. 75 published in 1977.

Patent Law Rev. (Clark Boardman).
V. 8 published in 1976.

Patent, Trademark and Copyright J. (BNA)
No. 358 published in December 1977.

Pollzien. *International Licensing Agreements.* 2d ed. (Bobbs-Merrill 1973).

Publishing, Entertaining, Advertising and Allied Fields (Callaghan).
V. 16 published in 1977.

Rosenberg. *Patent Law Fundamentals* (Clark Boardman 1975).

Seidel. *What the General Practitioner Should Know about Patent Law and Practice* 3d ed. (ALI-ABA 1976).

———. *What the General Practitioner Should Know about Trademarks and Copyrights.* 3d ed. (ALI-ABA 1976).

Shepard's *United States Patents and Trademarks Citations.*
1977 update includes copyright.

Sperber. *Intellectual Property Management: Law—Business—Strategy* (Clark Boardman).
Loose leaf. 1976 update. V. 3 of series: v. 1: Hamburg, *Patent Fraud*; v. 2: Sperber, *Patent Invalidity.*

Trademark Reporter (U.S. Trademark Association).
V. 67 published in 1977.

United States Patent Q. (BNA).
V. 195 published in 1977. Published weekly as *Patent, Trademark and Copyright Weekly Reports*—quarterly cumulation; annual and five year digests. Lists patents, trademarks, books, plays, music that have been subject of litigation.

Vandenburgh. *Trademark Law and Procedure.* 2d ed. (Bobbs-Merrill 1968).
1974 pocket part.

West's *Federal Practice Manual.* 2d ed. (West).
1977 pocket parts. V. 4: patents sec. 3911; copyright sec. 4011; trademarks sec. 4121.
World Patent Law and Practice (M. Bender 1969).
Loose leaf.

For a bibliography, see Association of American Law Schools, *Law Books Recommended for Libraries,* No. 21: Intellectual and Industrial Property (Rothman 1968; 1974 supp.).

Checklist: 18 *C.J.S.* Copyright and Literary Property
69 *C.J.S.* Patents
87 *C.J.S.* Trade-Marks, Trade-Names, and Unfair Competition
18 *Am. Jur. 2d* Copyright and Literary Property
60 *Am. Jur. 2d* Patents
74 *Am. Jur. 2d* Trademarks and Tradenames
36 *N.Y. Jur.* Literary Property and Copyright
43 *N.Y. Jur.* Patents
60 *N.Y. Jur.* Trademarks, Tradenames, and Unfair Competition
West Digest key number topics: Copyright, Literary Property, Patents, Trade-Marks, Trade-Names, and Unfair Competition

PRODUCTS LIABILITY (see also TORTS)

Course description: A study of the source, development, and limits of the law of product liability, with particular attention to theories rooted in negligence, fraud, warranty, and strict liability in tort as they are applied to the problems of a technological society. Includes problems of evidence and proof, and focuses on an in-depth study of a current major problem area such as automobile design.

Checklists: 72 *C.J.S.* Supp. Products Liability
63 *Am. Jur. 2d* Products Liability
47 *N.Y. Jur.* Products Liability
West Digest key number topic: Products Liability

PROPERTY

Course descriptions (property): The institution of property; property interests in land and in wealth other than land. Formation of interests in land; the "estate"concept; possessory and nonpossessory interests; concurrent interests; the landlord-tenant relation. The allocation and development of land resources by private arrangement and through community planning devices such as zoning and eminent domain. (mortgages): Legal and equitable mortgages, incidents of the mortgage relation; priorities; assignment; conveyancing of property subject to mortgage; assumption of mortgage debt; discharge, redemption, subrogation, contribution, marshaling; foreclosure. (land use regulation): A survey of legislative, administrative, judicial, and private controls utilized in the regulation of land use. Nuisance doctrines, zoning subdivision control, master plans and official maps, eminent domain, and new towns receive consideration. Emerging techniques and doctrines that constitute a societal response to current problems, such as growth control, exclusionary zoning, ecology, and environment are studied in an interdisciplinary context. (advanced real estate practice seminar): A study of the law and financing with respect to condominiums, cooperatives, planned unit development, and other types of mass housing and a review of the methods used in the negotiation and preparation of appropriate legal documents. (problems in conveyancing seminar): Problems involving real estate contracts; leases, searching titles, examining abstracts, surveys, title policies; closing titles, mortgages; financing; imposing and removing restrictions. Exercises in drafting contracts, deeds, mortgages and other instruments. (current problems in property law seminar): This seminar affords an opportunity for independent and collective research on and discussion of emergent problems of national concern as they relate to and affect property law. Such problems include (but are not limited to): landlord-tenant; sex and race discrimination in the ownership, use, and devolution of property; environmental controls; land use decisionmaking at the local, state, and national levels; zoning, subdivision control, and eminent domain.

American Law Institute. *Restatement of the Law of Property.* 5 v. (1936–1944).

______. *Property 2d. Landlord and Tenant.* 2 v. (1977).

______. *Restatement of the Law of Security* (1941).

______. *Restatement of the Law, Second: Trusts 2d.* 3 v. (1959).

Ackerman, ed. *Economic Foundations of Property Law* (Little, Brown 1975).

Anderson, R.M. *American Law of Zoning—Zoning, Planning, Subdivision Control.* 4 v. (LCP 1968).

Pocket parts.

Anderson. P.E. *Tax Planning of Real Estate.* 7th ed. (ALI-ABA 1977).

Arnold, et al. *Modern Real Estate and Mortage Forms: Ownership and Investment Forms.* 3 v. (Warren, Gorham and Lamont 1976).

Atlas. *Atlas' Tax Aspects of Real Estate Transactions.* 5th ed. (BNA 1971).

Basye. *Clearing Land Titles.* 2d ed. (West 1970).
1977 pocket part.

Berger. *Land Ownership and Use.* 2d ed. (Little, Brown 1975).

Bernhardt. *Real Property in a Nutshell* (West 1975).

Bicks. *Contracts for the Sale of Real Property* (PLI 1973).

Bogert. *Handbook on the Law of Trusts.* 5th ed. (West 1973).

______. *Law of Trusts and Trustees,* 2d ed. 15 v. (West).
Pocket parts.

Brown. *The Law of Personal Property.* 3d ed. by Raushenbush (Callaghan 1975).

Burby. *Handbook on the Law of Real Property.* 3d ed. (West 1965).

Bureau of National Affairs. *Housing and Development Reporter.*
Loose leaf. 1977 update.

Casner, ed. *American Law of Property.* 8 v. (Little, Brown 1953; supp. vol. 1952-76).

Clark. *Real Covenants and Other Interests which "Run with Land."* 2d ed. (Callaghan 1947).

Commerce Clearing House. *Urban Affairs Reporter.* 3 v.
Loose leaf. 1977 update.

Cribbet. *Principles of the Law of Property.* 2d ed. (Foundation 1975).

Davis. *Mobile Homes and Mobile Home Parks* (Shepard's 1975).

Ferrer and Stecher. *Law of Condominium with Forms, Statutes, Regulations.* 2 v. (Equity 1967).

Friedman. *Contracts and Conveyances of Real Property.* 3d ed. 2 v. (PLI 1975).

______. *Friedman on Leases.* 2 v. (PLI 1974).
1976 bound supplement.

Goldberg. *Sales of Real Property* (ALI-ABA 1971).

Gordon and Kurzman. *Modern Annotated Forms of Agreement* (P-H 1970).

Grimes. *A Treatise on the Law of Surveying and Boundaries.* 4th ed. (Bobbs-Merrill 1976).

Haar and Liebman. *Property and Law* (Little, Brown 1977).

Hecht. *Long Term Lease Planning and Drafting.* (Anderson 1974).

Hodes. *The Law of Mobile Homes.* 3d ed. (BNA 1974).

J. of Real Estate Taxation. (Warren, Gorham and Lamont).
V. 5 published in 1977.

Kratovil. *Real Estate Law.* 6th ed. (P-H 1974).

Land Use Law and Zoning Digest (American Society of Planning Officials).
V. 29 published in 1976.

Land Use Planning Abstracts '76–77 (EIC 1977).

Levine. *Real Estate Transactions—Tax Planning and Consequences.* 2d ed. (West 1976).

Lynn. *The Modern Rule Against Perpetuities* (Bobbs-Merrill 1966).

Moynihan. *Introduction to Real Property* (West 1962).

Nichols. *Eminent Doman.* 3d ed. 13 v. (M. Bender).
1977 update. V. 7 and 8 part of Rohan.

Osborne. *Handbook on the Law of Mortgages.* 2d ed. (West 1970).

Patton. *Land Titles.* 2d ed. 3 v. (West 1957).
1977 pocket parts.

Phipps. *Titles in a Nutshell* (West 1968).

Plager. *New Approaches in the Law of Property* (Foundation 1970).

Powell. *The Law of Real Property.* 10 v. (M. Bender).
Loose leaf. Also in one volume edition (1968).

Prentice-Hall. *Equal Opportunity in Housing.* 2 v.
Loose leaf. 1977 update.

Prentice-Hall. *Wills, Estates and Trusts.* 5 v.
Loose leaf.

Rathkopf. *The Law of Zoning and Planning.* 4th ed. 4 v. (Clark Boardman).
Loose leaf.

Real Estate Law. J. (Warren, Gorham and Lamont).
V. 6 published in 1977.

Real Estate Review (Warren, Gorham and Lamont).
V. 7 published in 1977.

Robinson. *Federal Income Taxation of Real Estate.* Rev. ed. (Warren, Gorham and Lamont 1974).
Loose leaf.

Rohan and Reskin. *Real Estate Transaction Series* (with forms) (M. Bender).
Loose leaf. v. 1, 1 pt. 2, 1A, 1B—Rohan and Reskin, *Condominium Law and Practice—Forms;* v. 2, 2A—Rohan and Reskin, *Cooperative Housing Law and Practice—Forms*; v. 3, 3A—Rohan and Reskin, *Condemnation Procedures and Techniques—Forms*; v. 4, 5—Rohan, *Real Estate Financing—Forms.*

Schwartz. *Future Interests and Estate Planning.* (Bobbs-Merrill 1965).
    1976 supplement.

Scott. *The Law of Trusts.* 3d ed. 6 v. (Little, Brown 1967).
    1975 pocket parts.

Simes. *Handbook on the Law of Future Interests.* 2d ed. (West 1966).

Simes and Smith, A.F. *The Law of Future Interests.* 2d ed. 4 v. (West 1956).

Smith, C.H., and Boyer. *Survey of the Law of Property.* 2d ed. (West 1971).

Thompson. *Commentaries on the Modern Law of Real Property.* (Bobbs-Merrill).
    1975 pocket parts.

Tiffany. *Law of Real Property.* 6 v. (Callaghan 1939).
    1977 pocket parts. Also in abridged edition (1970).

Title News (American Land Title Association).
    V. 56 in 1977.

Warren, et al. *Warren's Forms of Agreement.* 4 v. (M. Bender).
    Loose leaf. Update. Also in one volume edition.

Williams. *American Land Planning Law.* 5 v. (Callaghan 1974–1975).

Yokley. *Zoning Law and Practice.* 3d ed. (Michie 1965).
    1974 pocket parts.

New York Law

Bergerman and Roth. *New York Real Property Forms.* 2d ed. by Steinman. 2 v. (M. Bender).
    1977 update. Loose leaf.

Biskind and Barasch. *Law of Real Estate Brokers* (Clark Boardman 1969).
    1977 pocket part.

Harvey. *Law of Real Property and Title Closing* by Biskind. 3 v. (Clark Boardman 1966).
    Loose leaf. 1977 update.

Lee and LeForestier. *Review and Reduction of Real Property Assessments in N.Y.* 2d ed. (Clark Boardman 1977). Loose leaf.

Marks, et al. *Mortgages and Mortgage Foreclosure in N.Y.* Rev. ed. (Acme).
    Loose leaf. 1977 supplement.

New York Law of Landlord and Tenant. 3 v. (West).
    1977 pocket parts.

Rasch. *New York Landlord and Tenant Including Summary Proceedings.* 2d ed. 4 v. (LCP 1971).
1976 pocket parts.

______. *New York Law and Practice of Real Property.* 3 v. (LCP 1962).
1976 pocket parts.

Warren, et al. *Warren's Weed on the New York Law of Real Property.* 4th ed. 14 v. (M. Bender).
Loose leaf. 1977 update.

West's McKinney's Forms. Real Property Law, v. 11, 12, 13.
1977 pocket parts. Commentary following section of law.

Zoning and Planning Law Report (Clark Boardman).
Loose leaf. V. 1 published in 1977.

For a bibliography, see Association of American Law Schools, *Law Books Recommended for Libraries*, No. 32: Property (Rothman 1968; supp. 1974).

Checklists: 14 *C.J.S.* Chattel Mortgages
26, 26A *C.J.S.* Deeds
29A–30 *C.J.S.* Eminent Domain
52, 52A *C.J.S.* Landlord and Tenant
57 *C.J.S.* Mechanics' Liens
59 *C.J.S.* Mortgages
73 *C.J.S.* Property
101 *C.J.S.* Zoning
15A. *Am. Jur. 2d* Condominiums and Cooperative Apartments
23 *Am. Jur. 2d* Deeds
26, 27 *Am. Jur. 2d* Eminent Domain
28 *Am. Jur. 2d* Estates
49, 50 *Am. Jur. 2d* Landlord and Tenant
53 *Am. Jur. 2d* Mechanics' Liens
55 *Am. Jur. 2d* Mortgages
61 *Am. Jur. 2d* Perpetuitites and Restraints on Alienation
63 *Am. Jur. 2d* Property
82 *Am. Jur. 2d* Zoning and Planning
8 *N.Y. Jur.* Chattel Mortgages
11 *N.Y. Jur.* Cooperative Associations and Condominiums
15 *N.Y. Jur.* Deeds
19 *N.Y. Jur.* Eminent Domain
20 *N.Y. Jur.* Estates
33, 34 *N.Y. Jur.* Landlord and Tenant

35 *N.Y. Jur.* Life Estates, Remainders, and Reversions
38 *N.Y. Jur.* Mortgages and Deeds of Trust
47 *N.Y. Jur.* Property
67 *N.Y. Jur.* Zoning and Planning Board
West Digest key number topics: Chattel Mortgages, Deeds, Eminent Domain, Landlord and Tenant, Mechanics' Liens, Mortgages, Property, Zoning

PUBLISHERS

This list has been compiled from *Books in Print* (Bowker), *Ulrich's International Periodical Directory* (Bowker), *Law Books in Print* (Glanville), New York City directories, company letterheads, and advertisements in legal periodicals.

Acme Law Book Co.
Amityville, N.Y. 11701
516 799-8686

Advisory Commission on Intergovernmental Affairs
726 Jackson Place, N.W.
Washington, D.C. 20575
202 633-7051

Allen Smith
1435 North Meridian Street
Indianapolis, Ind. 46202
317 634-4098

American Academy of Psychiatry and the Law
47 East 88th Street
New York, N.Y. 10028
212 369-2468

American Arbitration Association
140 West 51st Street
New York, N.Y. 10020
212 977-2000

American Association of Law Librarians
53 West Jackson Boulevard #1201
Chicago, Ill. 60604
312 939-4764

American Bankers Association
1120 Connecticut Avenue, N.W.
Washington, D.C. 20036
702 467-4000

American Bar Association or American Bar Foundation (ABA or ABF)
1155 East 60th Street
Chicago, Ill. 60637
312 493-0533

American Business Law Association
c/o Wharton School
University of Pennsylvania
Philadelphia, Penn. 19174
215 243-7691

American Civil Liberties Union (ACLU)
22 East 40th Street
New York, N.Y. 10016
212 924-7800
or
1346 Connecticut Avenue, N.W. #1031
Washington, D.C. 20036
202 638-6263

American Enterprise Institute
for Public Policy Research
1150 17th Street, N.W.
Washington, D.C. 20036
202 296-5616

American Federation of
Information Processing
Societies (AFIPS)
210 Summit Avenue
Montvale, N.J. 07645
210 391-9810

American Judicature Society
1155 East 60th Street
Chicago, Ill. 60637
312 667-2727

American Land Title Association
1828 L Street, N.W.
Washington, D.C. 20036
202 296-3671

American Law Institute (ALI or
ALI-ABA)
4025 Chestnut Stret
Philadelphia, Penn. 19104
215 387-3000

American Maritime Cases
28 East 21st Street
Baltimore, Md. 21218
301 752-2939

American Patent Law
Association
20001 Jefferson David Highway
#203
Arlington, Va. 22202
703 521-1680

American Pilosophical Society
104 South Fifth Street
Philadelphia, Penn. 19106

American Society of
International Law
2223 Massachusetts Avenue,
N.W.
Washington, D.C. 20008
202 265-4313

American Society of Planning
Officials
1313 East 60th Street
Chicago, Ill. 60637
312 947-2560

American Trial Lawyers
Association (see also
Association of Trial Lawyers
of America)
20 Garden Street
Cambridge, Mass. 02138

Anchor Press (Doubleday)
501 Franklin Avenue
Garden City, N.Y. 11530
212 658-2222

W.H. Anderson Co.
646 Main Street
Cincinnati, Ohio 45201
513 421-4142

Appleton-Century-Crofts
292 Madison Avenue
New York, N.Y. 10017
212 532-1700

Arco Publishing Co.
219 Park Avenue S.
New York, N.Y. 10003
212 777-6300

Aspen Systems
20010 Century
Boulevard
Germantown, Md. 20767
301 428-0700

Association of American Law Schools (AALS)
1 Dupont Circle, N.W. #370
Washington, D.C. 20036
202 296-8851

Association of the Bar of the City of New York
42 West 44th Street
New York, N.Y. 10036
212 682-0606

Association of Trial Lawyers of America
1050 31st Street, N.W.
Washington, D.C. 20007
202 965-3500

Avon Books
959 English Avenue
New York, N.Y. 10019
212 262-5700

Baker-Voorhis
(see Lawyers Cooperative)

Ballantine Books
201 East 50th Street
New York, N.Y. 10022
212 751-2600

Ballinger Publishing Company
17 Dunster Street
Harvard Square
Cambridge, Mass. 02138
617 492-0670

Bancroft-Whitney Co. (LCP West)
301 Brannan Street
San Francisco, Calif. 94107
415 986-4410

Banking Law J.
(see Warren, Gorham and Lamont)

Banks-Baldwin Law Publishing Co.
1904 Ansel Road
Cleveland, Ohio 44106
216 721-7373

Barron's Educational Series
113 Crossways Park Drive
Woodbury, N.Y. 17797
516 921-8750

Basic Books
10 East 53d Street
New York, N.Y. 10022
212 593-7057

Baywood Publishing Co.
120 Marine Street
Farmingdale, N.Y. 11735
516 293-7130

Beacon Press
25 Beacon Street
Boston, Mass. 02108
617 942-2110

M. Bender & Co.
235 East 45th Street
New York, N.Y. 10017
212 661-5050

Bobbs-Merrill Company
4300 West 62d Street
Indianapolis, Ind. 46206
317 291-3100

Bowker
1180 Avenue of the Americas
New York, N.Y. 10036
212 764-5100

Brazziler
1 Park Avenue
New York, N.Y. 10016
212 889-0909

W.C. Brown
2460 Kerper Boulevard
Dubuque, Iowa 52001
319 588-1451

Bureau of National Affairs
(BNA)
1231 25th Street, N.W.
Washington, D.C. 20037
202 223-3500

Butterworth
2265 Midland Avenue
Scarborough, Ontario
MIP 4S1 Canada
416 292-1421
Borough Green
Sevenoaks
Kent TN 15 8PH
England

Callaghan & Co.
6141 North Cicero Avenue
Chicago, Ill. 60646
312 566-6920

Cambridge University Press
32 East 57th Street
New York, N.Y. 10022
212 688-8885

Carswell Co.
2330 Midland Avenue
Agincourt, Ontario
MIS 1P7 Canada

Central Book Co.
(see Clark Boardman)

Charles B. Sears Law
Library
Amherst Campus
SUNY at Buffalo
Buffalo, N.Y. 14260
716 636-2045

Charterhouse
750 3rd Avenue
New York, N.Y. 10017
212 752-4664

Chelsea
70 West 40th Street
New York, N.Y. 10018
212 840-0200

Christian Science Monitor
Boston, Mass. 02115
617 262-2300

Claitor's Books
3165 South Acadian at 1-10
Box 239
Baton Rouge, La. 70821
504 344-7631

Clarendon Press
333 Hudson Street
New York, N.Y. 10013
212 675-0130

Clark Boardman Co.
435 Hudson Street
New York, N.Y. 10014
212 929-7500

Clio (American Bibliographic
Center)
Riviera Campus
2040 A.P.S. Box 4397
Santa Barbara, Calif. 93103
805 963-4221

Columbia University Press
562 West 113th Street
New York, N.Y. 10025
212 678-6777

Commerce Clearing House (CCH)
4025 Peterson Avenue
Chicago, Ill. 60646
312 689-5233

Commercial Law League of
America
222 West Adams Street
Chicago, Ill. 60606
312 236-4942

Congressional Information
Service (CIS)
7101 Wisconsin Avenue, N.W.
Washington, D.C. 20014
202 387-0638

Congressional Quarterly
1414 22d Street, N.W.
Washington, D.C. 20037
202 296-6800

Corporation Reorganization
Reporter
1156 15th Street, N.W. #724
Washington, D.C. 20005
202 659-1450

Corporation Service Company
(CSC)
1105 North Market Street
P.O. Box 552
Wilmington, De. 19899
302 652-5636

Council of New York Law
Associates
36 West 44th Street
New York, N.Y. 10036
212 972-9370

Council of State Governments
P.O. Box 11910
Lexington, Ky. 40511
606 252-2291

Council on Foreign Relations
58 East 68th Street
New York, N.Y. 10021
212 734-0400

Council on Legal Education for
Professional Responsibility
(CLEPR)
280 Park Avenue
New York, N.Y. 10017
212 697-6800

CT Corporation System
277 Park Avenue
New York, N.Y. 10017
212 826-1800

Defense L.J. (see Allen Smith)

Delaware Law School
Wilmington, Del. 19802
302 658-8531

Dennis & Co.
251 Main Street
Buffalo, N.Y. 14203
716 852-2309

Dickerson Publishing Co.
16250 Ventura Boulevard
Encino, Calif. 91436
213 783-2750

Directory of Graduate (Summer)
Law Programs
Gainesville, Fla. 32611

Dow Jones-Irwin
Homewood, Ill. 60430
312 798-6000

EBSCO Subscription Services
P.O. Box 2543
Birmingham, Ala. 35201
205 252-9010

Elsevier (see North-Holland)

Empire State Report
P.O. Box 443
Fort Lee, N.J. 07024

Environment Index (EIC)
292 Madison Avenue
New York, N.Y. 10017
212 949-9494

Environmental Law Institute
1346 Connecticut Avenue, #620,
N.W.
Washington, D.C. 20036
202 452-9600

Equity Publishing Company
Orford, N.H. 03777
603 355-4375

Executive Enterprises
5811 La Jolla Corona Drive
Law Jolla, Calif. 92037
714 459-4901

Federal Bar Assocation
1815 H Street, N.W.
Washington, D.C. 20006
202 638-0252

Federal Judicial Center
Dolly Madison House
1520 H Street, N.W.
Washington, D.C. 20005
202 393-1640

Federal Publications
1725 K Street, N.W.
Washington, D.C. 20006
202 337-7000

Forster and Associates
Minneapolis, Minn.
612 871-1395

Foundation Press
170 Old Country Road
Mineola, N.Y. 11501
516 248-5580

Free Press
866 Third Avenue
New York, N.Y. 10022
212 935-2000

W.H. Freeman and Co.
660 Market Street
San Francisco, Calif. 94104
415 391-5870

Gale Research Co.
Book Tower
Detroit, Mich. 48226
303 961-2242

Wm. W. Gaunt and Sons
3011 Gulf Drive
Holmes Beach, Fla. 33510
813 778-5211

Glanville (see Oceana)

Greenwood Press
51 Riverside Avenue
Westport, Conn. 06880
203 226-3571

Grossman Publishers
c/o Viking Penguin
625 Madison Avenue
New York, N.Y. 10022
212 755-4330

Harper & Row
10 East 53rd Street
New York, N.Y. 10022
212 593-7000

Harrison Co.
178 Pryor Street, S.W.
Atlanta, Ga. 30303
404 447-9150

Harvard University Press
79 Garden Street
Cambridge, Mass. 01238
617 495-2600

Hawthorn Books
260 Madison Avenue
New York, N.Y. 10016
212 725-7776

Wm. S. Hein and Co.
1285 Main Street
Buffalo, N.Y. 14209
716 882-2600

Holt, Rinehard and Winston
383 Madison Avenue
New York, N.Y. 10017
212 688-9100

HMSO
(order from Pendragon)

Illinois Institute for Continuing Legal Education (ICLE)
2395 West Jefferson Street
Springfield, Ill. 62702
217 787-2080

Index to Foreign Legal Periodicals
Institute of Advanced Legal Studies
25 Russel Square
London, WC1B 5DR
England
(also, see, American Association of Law Librarians)

Information Handling Services
P.O. Box 1154 (15 Inverness Way East)
Englewood, Colo. 80110
303 771-2600
Toll free 1-800-821-3424, ext. 410

Institute for Business Planning (IBP)
IBP Plaza
Englewood Cliffs, N.J. 07632
(Distributed by Prentice-Hall)
201 592-2040

International Bar Association
Byron House
7-9 St. James Street
London, SW1A IEE
England

International Law Perspective
927 15th Street, N.W.
Washington, D.C. 20005
202 347-7928

International Universities Press
315 5th Avenue
New York, N.Y. 10016
212 684-7900

Jefferson
646 Main Street
P.O. Box 1936
Cincinnati, Ohio 45201
513 421-4142

Johns Hopkins University Press
Baltimore, Md. 21218
301 366-9600

Judge Advocate General (Army)
Charlottesville, Va. 22901

Jural
7122 North Clark Street
Chicago, Ill. 60626

Kimball-Clark
Barrister's Press
Box 4252
St. Paul, Minn. 55104

Kluwer Publishers
P.O. Box 23
Deventer
The Netherlands
15700-20511
(Publisher of Air Law)

Law Enforcement Assistance Administration
633 Indiana Avenue, N.W.
Washington, D.C. 20531
202 376-3604

Law Journal Press
233 Broadway
New York, N.Y. 10007
212 964-9400

Law Press
P.O. Box 760
Tiburon, Calif. 94920

Law Reprints
37 West 20th Street
New York, N.Y. 10011
212 242-5358

Lawyers Cooperative Publishing Co. (LCP)
Aqueduct Building
Rochester, N.Y. 14603
715 546-5530

LE Publishers
612 North Michigan Avenue
Chicago, Ill. 60611
312 944-1261

Legal-Medical Studies
Box 8219
John F. Kennedy Station
Boston, Mass. 02114

Lewis and Clark
Northwestern School of Law
Portland, Ore. 97219
503 244-1181

Lexington Books
125 Spring Street
Lexington, Mass. 02173
617 862-6650
212 924-6460
(Division of D.C. Heath and Co.)

Little, Brown and Co.
34 Beacon Street
Boston, Mass. 02106
617 227-0730

Lloyd's Maritime and Commercial Law Q.
Lloyd's of London Press
16-17 Bride Lane
London EC4Y 8EB

Lofit Publications
Box 297
Saugerties, N.Y. 12477

Lond Publications
Pomona, N.Y. 10970
914 354-3521

McGraw-Hill Book Co.
1221 Avenue of the Americas
New York, N.Y. 10036
212 997-2073

Macmillan Publishing Co.
866 Third Avenue
New York, N.Y. 10022
212 935-2000

Marquis
Who's Who Books
200 East Ohio Street
Chicago, Ill. 60611
312 787-20008

Martindale-Hubbell
1 Prospect Street
Summit, N.J. 07901
201 273-6060

MeadData Central
200 Park Avenue
New York, NY. 10017
212 883-8500

Meilen Press
443-445 Greenwich Avenue
New York, N.Y. 10013
212 966-4177

Methuen, Inc.
572 5th Avenue
New York, N.Y. 10036
212 869-9780

Michie Co.
P.O. Box 7587
Charlottesville, Va. 22906
703 295-6171

National Center for State Courts #200
1660 Lincoln Street
Denver, Colo.
80264

National Clearinghouse for Legal Services
500 North Michigan Avenue
Chicago, Ill. 60611
312 353-2566

National Conference of the Bar Examiners
1155 East 60th Street
Chicago, Ill. 60637
312 641-0963

National Institute of Municipal Law Officers
839 17th Street, N.W.
Washington, D.C. 20006
202 347-7996

National Lawyers Guild
853 Broadway
New York, N.Y.
212 260-1360

National League of Cities and U.S. Conference of Mayors
1620 Eye Street, N.W.
Washington, D.C. 20006
202 293-7310

New American Library
1301 Avenue of the Americas
New York, N.Y. 10019
212 956-3800

New York City Publications
Room 2213
Municipal Building
New York, N.Y. 10007
212 566-2616

New York Community Trust Fund
415 Madison Avenue
New York, N.Y. 10017
212 758-0100

New York Law Journal
233 Broadway
New York, N.Y. 10007
212 964-9400

New York Lawyers Diary and Manual
P.O. Box 1226
Newark, N.J. 07101
201 642-0355

New York State Association of Trial Lawyers
132 Nassau Street
New York, N.Y. 10013
212 349-5890

New York Times
229 West 43d Street
New York, N.Y. 10030
212 556-1234

New York University Press
21 West 4th Street
New York, N.Y. 10012
212 598-2886

New York University School of Law
Moot Court
249 Sullivan Street
New York, N.Y. 10012
212 598-3040

North-Holland Publishing Co. (American Elsevier Publishing Co.)
52 Vanderbilt Avenue
New York, N.Y. 10017
212 686-5277

Notre Dame Law School
Notre Dame, Ind. 46556
219 283-6626

Oceana Publications
Dobbs Ferry, N.Y. 10522
914 693-1320

Ohio State University Press
Hitchcock Hall, Room 316
2070 Neil Avenue
Columbus, Ohio 43210
614 422-6930

Oxford University Press
200 Madison Avenue
New York, N.Y. 10016
212 679-7300

Parker and Sons
6500 Flotilla Street
Los Angeles, Calif. 90022
213 724-6622

Pendragon
2595 E. Bayshone Road
Palo Alto, Calif. 94303
415 327-5631

Philgor
Denver, Colorado

Pike and Fischer
2000 L Street, N.W.
Washington, D.C. 20036
202 223-4880

Plenum Press
227 West 17th Street
New York, N.Y. 10011
212 255-0713

Practicing Law Institute (PLI)
810 Seventh Avenue
New York, N.Y. 10019
212 765-5700

Praeger
200 Park Avenue
New York, N.Y. 10017
212 949-8700

Predicasts, Inc.
11001 Cedar Avenue
200 University Circle Research Center
Cleveland, Ohio 44106
216 795-3000

Prentice-Hall
P.O. Box 21X
Englewood Cliffs, N.J. 07663
212 687-7660

Professional Books Service
Milton Trading Estate
Abingdon
Oxon. OX14 4SY
England
Steventon (STD 023584) 7221-2

Public Affairs Information
Service Bulletin
11 West 40th Street
New York, N.Y. 10018
212 736-6629

G.P. Putnam's Sons
200 Madison Avenue
New York, N.Y. 10016
212 576-8900

RADCO
14 Plaza Road
Greenvale, N.Y. 11548
516 921-6006

Rand McNally and Co.
P.O. Box 7600
Chicago, Ill. 60680
312 673-9100

Random House
201 East 50th Street
New York, N.Y. 10022
212 751-2600

Reader's Digest Press
10 East 53rd Street
New York, N.Y. 10022
212 972-4000

Reader's Guide to Periodical
Literature (see Wilson)

Research Group, Inc.
American Law Publishing Service
P.O. Box "U"
San Mateo, Calif. 94402

Ronald Press
79 Madison Avenue
New York, N.Y. 10016
212 683-9070

Fred B. Rothman and Co.
57 Leuning Street
South Hackensack, N.J. 07606
201 489-4646
212 244-6135

Rowman and Littlefield
81 Adams Drive, Box 327
Totawa, N.J. 07512
201 256-8600

Russell Sage
230 Park Avenue
New York, N.Y. 10017
212 689-6622

St. Martin's Press
175 Fifth Avenue
New York, N.Y. 10010
212 674-5151

Saturday Review
1290 Avenue of the Americas
New York, N.Y. 10019
212 246-9700

Sea Grant L.J.
New York Sea Grant Institute
State University of New York
Buffalo, N.Y. 14260
716 636-2060

Shepard's Citations
P.O. Box 1235
Colorado Springs, Colo. 80901
303 633-5521

Sijhoff
International Publishing Co.
Ash Street
Reading, Mass. 01867
617 944-7515

Simon and Schuster
1230 Avenue of the Americas
New York, N.Y. 10020
212 245-6400

Southern Methodist University
School of Law
Dallas, Texas 75275
214 692-2618

Standard and Poor
345 Hudson Street
New York, N.Y. 10014
212 924-6400

Stanford University Press
Stanford, Calif. 94305
415 323-9471

Stevens and Brown
Ardon House
Mill Lane
Godalming, Surrey
GU7 1HA
England

Supreme Court Historical Society
1511 K Street, N.W. #333
Washington, D.C. 20005
202 347-9888

Sweet and Maxwell Spon Ltd.
Northway
Andover, Hants SP10 5BE
England

Taplinger
200 Park Avenue South
New York, N.Y. 10003
212 553-6110

C.C. Thomas
301-327 East Lawrence Avenue
Springfield, Ill. 62717
217 789-8980

Time-Life
Time and Life Building
Rockefeller Center
New York, N.Y. 10020
202 586-1212

Uniform System of Citation
Harvard Law Review
Gannett House
Cambridge, Mass. 01238
(Note: available at all law school book stores)
617 495-7888

U.S. Corporation Co.
70 Pine Street
New York, N.Y. 10005
212 952-0400

U.S. Government Printing Office (GPO)
Washington, D.C. 20402
202 783-3238
or
Federal Plaza
New York, N.Y.
212 264-3826

U.S. Trademark Association
6 East 45th Street
New York, N.Y. 10017
212 986-5880

University Microfilm
300 North Zeeb Road
Ann Arbor, Mich. 48106
313 761-4100

University of Arizona Press
P.O. Box 3398
Tuscon, Ariz. 85722
602 844-1441

University of California School of Law
Berkeley, Cal. 94720
415 642-1741

University of Chicago Press
11030 South Langley Avenue
Chicago, Ill. 60628
312 753-3344

University of Louisville School of Law
Beklnap Campus
Louisville, Ky. 40208
502 588-6358

University of Nevada
Reno, Nev. 89507
702 784-6908

University of Texas School of Law
2500 Red River
Austin, Texas 78705
512 471-5151

University of Toledo College of Law
Toledo, Ohio 43606
419 537-2882

University of Washington School of Law
Condon Hall
Seattle, Washington 98105
206 543-4550

University of Windsor
Windsor, Ontario, Canada

University Press of Virginia
P.O. Box 3608
University Station
Charlottesville, Va. 22903
703 924-3468

University Publications
5630 Connecticut Avenue, N.W.
Washington, D.C. 20015
202 362-6201

Vantage Press
516 West 34th Street
New York, N.Y. 10001
212 736-2222

Volunteer Lawyers for the Arts
36 West 44th Street
New York, N.Y. 10036
212 575-1150

Warren, Gorham and Lamont
210 South Street
Boston, Mass. 02111
617 423-2020

Washington Book Publishing Co.
2518 Western Avenue
Seattle, Wash.
98121

West Publishing Co.
50 Kellogg Boulevard
St. Paul, Minn. 55102
612 228-2500

Westminster Press
Room 905
Witherspoon Building
Philadelphia, Penn. 19107
215 893-4400

Weybright and Talley
750 Third Avenue
New York, N.Y. 10022
212 490-1155

Wildy and Sons
Lincoln's Inn Archway
Carey Street
London, W.C. 2
01-242-5778
(new and secondhand books)

John Wiley and Sons
605 Third Avenue
New York, N.Y. 10016
212 867-9800

Williams and Wilkins
428 East Preston Street
Baltimore, Md. 21202
310 528-4000

Williams Press
Albany, N.Y. 12201
518 434-1141

H.W. Wilson
950 University Avenue
Bronx, N.Y. 10452
212 588-8400

World (New American Library)
1301 Avenue of the Americas
New York, N.Y. 10019
212 956-3800

World Peace Through Law
#800
1000 Connecticut Avenue, N.W.
Washington, D.C. 20036
202 466-5420

Yale University Press
302 Temple Street
New Haven, Conn. 06520
203 432-4969

QUOTATIONS (see LAW AND LITERATURE)

REGULATED INDUSTRIES (i.e., PUBLIC UTILITIES)

Course description: Substantive problems of business regulation in terms of natural monopolies, licensed industries, subsidized industries, and safety regulation. Typical problems raised include the role of intervenors, the impact of regulation upon management and market behavior, the uses and abuses of economic evidence, the role of agencies' staffs, interagency planning and regulation, and the effects of judicial and legislative review. Each student selects one industry and develops insight into economic regulation in terms of that industry's market structure, growth and development, trade associations, and regulatory agencies.

Bell J. of Economics and Management Science.
V. 8 published in 1977.
Federal Power Service. 3 v. (M. Bender).
Loose leaf. 1977 update.
National Association of Regulatory Utility Commissioners *Bulletin.*
V. 51-1977 published in 1977.
Priest. *Principles of Public Utility Regulation—Theory and Application.* 2 v. (Michie 1969).
Public Utilities Fortnightly.
V. 99 published in 1977.
Sichel. *Public Utility Regulation, Change and Scope* (Lexington 1975).

Transportation Law J. (University of Denver Law School).
V. 8 published in 1976.
Utilities Law Reporter. 3 v. (CCH).
Loose leaf.

For a bibliography, see Association of American Law Schools, *Law Books Recommended for Libraries,* No. 33: Regulated Industries (Rothman 1968; supp. 1974).

Checklist: 13 *C.J.S.* Carriers
73 *C.J.S.* Public Utilities
74, 75 *C.J.S.* Railroads
86 *C.J.S.* Telegraphs, Telephones, Radio and Television
13, 14 *Am. Jur. 2d* Carriers
26 *Am. Jur. 2d* Electricity, Gas, and Steam
61 *Am. Jur. 2d* Pipelines
64 *Am. Jur. 2d* Public Utilities
65 *Am. Jur. 2d* Railroads
78 *Am. Jur. 2d* Waterworks and Water Companies
7 *N.Y. Jur.* Carriers
19 *N.Y. Jur.* Electricity, Gas, and Steam
39 *N.Y. Jur.* Motor Transportation
45A *N.Y. Jur.* Pipelines
48 *N.Y. Jur.* Public Utilities
49 *N.Y. Jur.* Railroads
West Digest key number topics: Carriers, Public Services, Railroads

REMEDIES (see also DAMAGES)

Course description: The interplay and choice of possible recoveries in property, personal, and business interest situations. Damages: object of an award in contract and tort; limitations on recovery, elements of damage. Equity: specific relief, injunctions. The place and scope of restitution in the remedial structure. Theories of recovery in basic contract and tort situations including vendor and vendee relationships, conversion, personal injury, defamation, privacy, and unfair competition. Employer-employee relationships. Use of legal and equitable remedies in modern codes.

American Law Institute. *Restatement of the Law of Restitution: Quasi Contracts and Constructive Trusts.* (1937).

ROMAN LAW (see also CIVIL LAW, COMPARATIVE LAW)

Course description: A study of the history and system of Roman law as a foundation of modern civil law and as a basis for comparison with the Anglo-American legal system. A critical examination of the successive stages in the development of Roman law from early times down to the Justinian codification in order to explore the principles, techniques, and approaches developed by Roman jurists, which are of permanent value and which provide better appreciation of modern civil law.

Berger. *Encyclopedic Dictionary of Roman Law* (American Philosophical Soc. 1953).
Jolowicz and Nicholas. *Historical Introduction to the Study of Roman Law.* 3d ed. (Cambridge University Press 1972).
Lawson, ed. *The Roman Law Reader* (Oceana 1969).
Thomas. *Textbook of Roman Law* (North-Holland 1976).

For a bibliography, see Association of American Law Schools, *Law Books Recommended for Libraries,* No. 43: Roman Law (Rothman 1968; supp. 1974).

RULES OF COURT (see CIVIL PROCEDURE)

SALES (see COMMERCIAL LAW)

SECURITIES

Course descriptions (securities regulation): Federal and state regulations of business enterprise access to the financial markets; control of trading on the exchanges and in the over the counter market; disclosure and civil and criminal provisions; (purchasers and sellers of securities): Remedies under federal securities laws of defrauded purchasers and sellers of securities; the duty to disclose in connection with offers; purchases, and sales of securities. The subject matter includes Rule 10b-5 and Sections 13 and 14 of the Securities Exchange Act of 1934 and Sections 11, 12, and 17 of the Securities Act of 1933.

Bromberg. *Securities Law—Fraud—SEC Rule 10b-5.* 4v. (McGraw Hill).
Loose leaf. 1977 update.

Bureau of National Affairs. *Securities Regulation and Law Report.* 2 v.
Loose leaf. 1977 update.

Business Lawyer (ABA).
V. 33 published in 1976.

Commerce Clearing House. *Securities Law Reporter.* 5 v.
Loose leaf. Transfer binders for decisions affecting securities law. Also publishers of *Blue Sky Law Reporter* loose leaf service.

Fried. *Taxation of Securities Transactions.* (M. Bender).
Loose leaf. 1977 update. V. 11 series of Business Organizations.

Gadsby. *The Federal Securities Exchange Act of 1934.* 6 v. (M. Bender).
Loose leaf. 1977 update. V. 11 series of Business Organizations.

Jaffe. *Broker-Dealers and Securities Markets* (McGraw-Hill 1977).

Loss. *Securities Regulation.* 2d ed. and supp. 6 v. (Little, Brown 1961, 1969).

New York University. *Institute on Securities Laws and Regulations.* (M. Bender 1977).

Ratner. *Securities Regulation—Materials for a Basic Course* (West 1975).
Pp. 1–27 provide an understanding of the basic materials of securities law, including how to locate Rule 10b–5 (p. 21).

_____. *Security Regulation in a Nutshell* (West 1978).

Securities Law Review (Clark Boardman).
V. 9 published in 1977.

Securities Regulation Law J (Warren, Gorham and Lamont).
V. 4 published in 1977.

Sowards. *The Federal Securities Act: Analysis, Procedure, Forms.* 2 v. (M. Bender).
Loose leaf. 1977 update. V. 11 series of Business Organizations.

Sowards and Hirsch. *Blue Sky Regulation.* 2 v. (M. Bender).
Loose leaf. 1977 update. V. 11 series of Business Organizations.

Standard and Poor. *Review of Securities Regulation.*
1 volume loose leaf. Monthly.

Thomas and Shields. *Federal Securities Act Handbook.* 4th ed. (ALI-ABA 1977).

Wolfson, et al. *Regulation of Brokers, Dealers and Securities Markets* (Warrren, Gorham and Lamont 1977).

Checklist: 11 *C.J.S.* Bonds
79 Supp. *C.J.S.* Securities Regulation
12 *Am. Jur. 2d* Bonds
64 *Am. Jur. 2d* Public Securities and Obligations
6 *N.Y. Jur.* Bonds
48 *N.Y. Jur.* Public Securities and Obligations
54 *N.Y. Jur.* Securities Acts and Civil Frauds
West Digest key number topics: Bonds, Securities Regulation

SPACE LAW (see also AVIATION LAW for bibliography)

Checklists: 70 *Am. Jur. 2d* Space Law

TAXATION AND ESTATE PLANNING (see also TRUSTS)

Course descriptions (federal taxation of income): Basic concepts of federal income taxation of individuals: gross income, adjusted gross income, deductions, credits, gains and losses, income averaging, and certain nonrecognition transactions. (federal income tax I): Emphasis on rigorous analysis of statutory materials. Special attention to problems of individual taxpayers and basic concepts of gross income, adjusted gross income, deductions, exemptions, basis, and credit. (federal income tax II): Dispositions of property. Detailed treatment of capital gain provisions, including consideration of deferred payment sales, basis, nonrecognition exchanges, mortgages, and assignment of income principles. (advanced federal income tax II): Consideration of advanced problems of capital gains and losses including: stock options, mortgages, cancellation of indebtedness, deferred payment disposition, bootstrap acquisitions, patents, copyrights, know-how, and tax shelter techniques. (federal income tax III): Basic tax questions involved when operating in corporate form: organization, dividends, redemptions, liquidations, and Subchapter S corporations. (federal income tax IV): Income taxation of trusts and estates: grantor trusts, income in respect of a decedent, assignment of income, and the treatment of accumulation trusts under the throwback rules. (advanced foreign tax problems): Advanced treatment of problems of United States persons engaged in foreign trade and investment, with emphasis on planning aspects. Detailed consideration of United States taxation of controlled foreign corporations, including nature of Subpart F income, domestic international sales companies, special elections of individual shareholders, and other aspects of mitigating application. Also, analysis of foreign personal holding companies, foreign investment companies, and foreign trusts. (federal tax procedure): Study of procedural problems encountered at the administrative level: legal and practical aspects of Treasury regulations, administrative rulings, closing and compromise agreements, deficiency assessments, waivers, refund claims, and statutes of limitations. (federal tax procedure II): Procedural problems primarily centering on tax litigation: respective jurisdictions of the tax court, United States district courts, and the court of claims: problems peculiar to tax litigation in the pretrial, trial, and appellate processes; *res judicata* and related concepts, and the effect of state law; selected problems in tax collection, including preferential transfers, transferees, and the tax lien. (state and local taxation): The major issues arising under the principal forms of state and local taxation: corporate franchise and income taxation (with considerable emphasis on problems of apportionment), sales, use, gross receipts, property, personal income, and death taxes. Federal constitutional limitations of state taxation and congressional legislation affecting state taxation on interstate commerce. Each student selects the laws of the state of his or her choice for study throughout the term.

American Jurisprudence. Legal Forms 2d. *Federal Tax Guide to Legal Forms* (LCP 1971).

1977 pocket part.

Bittker and Eustice. *Federal Income Taxation of Corporations and Shareholders.* 3d ed. (Warren, Gorham and Lamont 1971).

1977 bound supplement.

Bureau of National Affairs. *Tax Management Portfolios.*

1977 monographs—location of portfolios by code section; estates, gifts, and trusts; foreign income, U.S. income; memorandum index, IRS forms, and so forth. BNA also publishes *Primary Sources* set (17 v. in 1977) that provides legislative history.

Casner. *Estate Planning.* 3d ed. 2 v. (Little, Brown 1961).

1977 bound supplement, 2 v.

Chirelstein. *Federal Income Taxation; A Law Students Guide to the Leading Cases and Concepts* (Foundation 1977).

Chommie. *Federal Income Taxation.* 2d ed. (West 1973).

Commerce Clearing House. *Standard Federal Tax Reports.* 9 v. plus citator and index volumes.

Loose leaf. The set is, to a great extent, replaced each year. Advance sheets of cases replaced by bound volumes, *United*

States Tax Cases (the tax court is treated separately). CCH also published a loose leaf *Federal Estate and Gift Tax*, a bound *Estate Planning Guide* (1977 ed.), and a bound guide to their tax set. CCH also issues a pamphlet that lists their loose leaf publications and shows how to use them.

Dukeminier and Johanson. *Family Wealth Transactions: Wills, Trusts, Future Interests, and Estate Planning—Cases and Materials* (Little, Brown 1972).

Bibliography, pp. li–lxxiii.

Federal Tax Locator. 4 v. (McGraw-Hill).

1977 pocket parts.

Folsom. *Legislative History*. . .(University Press of Virginia 1972).

Freeland et al. *Cases and Materials on Fundamentals of Federal Income Taxation* (Foundation 1977).

"Tax books are perishable" (p. xvii). Chapter I on orientation and Chapter II on tax practitioner's tools provide an excellent basis for research in the tax field. See also Kragen and McNulty's casebook (West 1974) for similar and complementary material (pp. 22–23). For researching tax material, see also the following, Folsom, *Legislative History* (University Press of Virginia 1972; p. 77 et seq.); Surrency, A Basic Survey of Research Sources and Tools in Taxation, 23 *J. of Taxation* 114 (1965); Rubenfeld and Albinger, The Basic Materials for Federal Tax Research, 19 *Practical Lawyer* 45 (November 1973); Golato, Internal Revenue Service Documents, 67 *Law Library J.* 466 (1974).

Freeland et al. *Federal Income Taxation of Estates and Beneficiaries* (Little, Brown 1970).

1976 pocket part.

Goldstein. *Index to Federal Tax Articles.* 3 v. (Warren, Gorham and Lamont).

1977 supplement. CCH also publishes *Federal Tax Articles.* 2 v. (1954–72). Loose leaf. 1977 update.

Harris. *Family Estate Planning Guide.* 2d ed. (LCP 1971).

1976 pocket parts.

J. of Taxation.

V. 46 published in 1977.

Law Reprints. *Tax Series.*

Briefs and records of current tax cases. V. 9 was published in 1976–77.

Los Angeles County Law Library. *Books and pamphlets on taxation. A Selective Bibliography.* Comp. by McCarthy (1974; 1977 supp).

Lowndes, Kramer, and McCord. *Federal Estate and Gift Taxes.* 3d ed. (West 1974).

Lynn. *An Introduction to Estate Planning* (West 1975).

Mertens. *The Law of Federal Gift and Estate Taxation* (Lofit).
2 loose leaf volumes; 1977 update, fifteen plus bound volumes.

______. *The Law of Federal Income Taxation* (Callaghan).
Loose leaf. Forty plus volumes of commentary, code, rules; 1977 supplementation.

Michie's Federal Tax Handbook. 2 v. (1974).

Morris. *Real Estate Tax Planning* (Little, Brown 1977).

Murphy's *Will Clauses—Annotations and Forms with Tax Effects.* 3 v. (M. Bender).
Loose leaf. 1977 update. N. Y. Notes section.

New York University. *Institute on Federal Taxation* (M. Bender).
V. 35 published in 1977.

Page on the Law of Wills. 8 v. (Anderson).
1975–76 pocket parts. Forms, taxation notes, and so forth.

Prentice-Hall. *Federal Taxes,* 9 v., Code v.; *AFTR 2d* (*American Federal Tax Reports 2d Series*); *Estate and Gift Taxes* 2 v. *Excise Taxes.*
Loose leaf. 1978 volumes substantially replace prior year's material. *AFTR 2d* (advance decisions) contains "How to Use Prentice-Hall's Federal Taxes Service." Bibliography of tax articles in v. 1, P-H, like CCH, issues committee reports and other government documents that are not filed into the loose leaf set but can be maintained chronologically by report number (check with the filer of the service). P-H also publishes *Federal Tax Handbook* 1978 and other publications on tax law.

Rabkin and Johnson. *Current Legal Forms with Tax Analysis.* 22 v. (M. Bender).
Loose leaf. 1977 update. Most form books have tax analysis. See also Part I: FORMS.

______. *Federal Income, Gift and Estate Taxation.* 11 v. (M. Bender).
Loose leaf. 1977 update.

Redman and Quiggle. *Procedure Before the Internal Revenue Service.* 5th ed. (ALI-ABA 1974).

Schwartz. *Future Interests and Estate Planning* (Anderson).
1977 pocket part.

Stephens et al. *Federal Estate and Gift Taxation.* 3d ed. (Warren, Gorham and Lamont).
Loose leaf. *Tax Reform Act Special Supplement* (1977).

Tax Law Review (Warren, Gorham and Lamont).
V. 31 published in 1976.
Tax Lawyer (ABA).
V. 31 published in 1977.
Taxes (CCH).
V. 55 published in 1977.
University of Southern California. *Major Tax Planning.*
V. 29 published in 1977.
U.S. Tax Week (M. Bender).
Weekly. 1978-1 published January 1978.
Willis. *Partnership Taxation.* 2d ed. 2 v. (McGraw-Hill 1976).
1977 pocket parts.

New York

Fingar et al. *New York Wills and Trusts—Law—Forms—Taxes.* 2 v. (M. Bender).
1977 update. Loose leaf.
Harris. *New York Estates Practice Guide.* 3d ed. 3 v. (LCP 1968).
1977 pocket parts.
New York Forms. Estates and Trusts, ch. 24-26 (LCP).
1977 pocket part. See also CCH and P-H services that cover New York tax law.

For an additional bibliography, see Association of American Law Schools, *Law Books Recommended for Libraries*, No. 35: Taxation (Rothman 1968; supp. 1974).

Checklists: 47 *C.J.S.* Internal Revenue
84, 85 *C.J.S.* Taxation
94-97 *C.J.S.* Wills
33, 34 *Am. Jur. 2d* Federal Taxation
68 *Am. Jur. 2d* Sales and Use Tax
71, 72 *Am. Jur. 2d* State and Local Taxation
74 *Am. Jur. 2d* Taxpayers' Actions
79, 80 *Am. Jur. 2d* Wills
20 *N.Y. Jur.* Estate Taxes and Gift Taxes
51 *N.Y. Jur.* Sales and Use Tax
58, 58A *N.Y. Jur.* Taxation
64, 65 *N.Y. Jur.* Wills
West Digest key number topics: Internal Revenue, Taxation, Wills

TORTS

Course description: Liability in damages arising from breaches of duties imposed by law. Torts involving both intentional and unintentional injury to persons, property, and mental tranquility; the fault theory of liability, strict products liability, and alternatives to fault in accident cases.

American Law Institute. Restatement of the Law, Second. *Torts 2d.* 3 v. Appendix 3 v.
Tentative drafts 1–23 (1957–1977).

American Trial Lawyers Association Law J.
V. 36 published in 1977. Covers tort law, workmen's compensation, labor law, criminal law, litigation, family law, railroad law, admiralty law, environmental law, aviation law.

Averbach. *Handling Accident Cases.* 9 v. (LCP).
1977 pocket parts.

Bureau of National Affairs. *Product Safety and Liability Reporter.* 3 v.
Loose leaf. 1977 update.

Commerce Clearing House. *Consumer Product Safety Guide.* 2 v.
Loose leaf. 1977 update.

______. *Products Liability Reporter.* 2 v.
Loose leaf. Transfer binder 1973–75.

Defense Law. J.
V. 26 published in 1977. Review of torts, trial practice, and so forth.

Dooley. *Modern Tort Law.* 3 v. (Callaghan 1977).

Harper and James. *The Law of Torts.* 3 v. (Little, Brown 1956).
1968 supplement to v. 2.

Heft and Heft. *Comparative Negligence Manual* (Callaghan).
Loose leaf. 1977 update.

Hursh and Bailey. *American Law of Products Liability.* 2d ed. 6 v. (LCP).
1976 supplement.

Jayson. *Handling Federal Tort Claims: Administrative and Judicial Remedies.* 2 v. (M. Bender).
Loose leaf. 1977 update.

Kimble. *Federal Consumer Product Safety Act* (West 1975).

Negligence and Compensation Cases Annotated (Callaghan).
A multivolume set containing leading cases and a digest of cases in point. V. 20, 4th series, published in 1977. "Common sense" index, pleadings index, instructions index, "notes"

(annotations) index, case table supplementing annotations.

Noel and Phillips. *Products Liability in a Nutshell* (West 1974).

Prosser on *Torts.* 4th ed. (West 1971).

Rheingold and Birnbaum. *Products Liability.* 2d ed. (PLI 1975).
Valuable compilation of leading law review articles.

Schwartz, V.E. *Comparative Negligence* (Allen Smith 1974; 1975 supp).

Schwartz and Jacoby. *Litigation with the Federal Government* (ALI-ABA 1970).
Attorney's fees, lobbying, conflict of interest, court of claims, GAO, Comptroller, federal Tort Claims Act.

Speiser. *Recovery for Wrongful Death.* 2d ed. 2 v. (LCP 1975).

_____. *Res Ipsa Loquitor.* 2 v. (LCP).
1975 pocket parts.

Trial (Ass'n. of Trial Lawyers of America).
V. 13 published in 1977.

New York Law

Warren and Markuson. *Negligence in the New York Courts.* 19 v. (M. Bender).
1977 supplement.

For a bibliography, see Association of American Law Schools, *Law Books Recommended for Libraries,* No. 36: Torts (Rothman 1968, 1974 supp.).

Checklists: 65, 65A *C.J.S.* Negligence
77 *C.J.S.* Right of Privacy
86 *C.J.S.* Torts
57, 58 *Am. Jur. 2d* Negligence
62 *Am. Jur. 2d* Privacy
74 *Am. Jur. 2d* Torts
41 *N.Y. Jur.* Negligence
47 *N.Y. Jur.* Privacy
59 *N.Y. Jur.* Torts
West Digest key number topics: Negligence, Torts

TRADEMARKS (see PATENTS, TRADEMARKS, AND COPYRIGHT)

TRADE REGULATION

Course descriptions (antitrust laws I): Legal protection of the competitive system under the Sherman Act, Clayton Act, Federal Trade

Commission Act, and related legislation. Consideration of problems relating to monopoly power, "horizontal" restraints on competition such as price fixing and concerted refusals to deal; "vertical" restraints such as resale price maintenance, tying and exclusive dealing arrangements; and limitations on permissible mergers and joint ventures. Economic as well as legal implications of legislation and court decisions are explored. (antitrust laws II): Competitive issues and competitive facts—the relations between economic concepts, economic facts, and antitrust case issues; analysis of methods of using and/or generating economic data, of analyzing economic concepts, and of preparing economic information for use in antitrust work. (advanced problems in monopolies and mergers seminar): Competition, concentration, and the structure of American industry: advanced problems in monopolies and mergers, including study of market definition, of concentration versus competition, and of judicial and legislative deconcentration remedies. Emphasis is placed on recent monopoly and merger cases and current government enforcement policy.

American Bar Association. Section of Antitrust Law. *Antitrust Civil Jury Instructions* (1972).
Loose leaf.
______. *Antitrust Consent Decree Manual* (1969).
Loose leaf.
______. *Antitrust Law Developments.*
1955-68—1 v.; 1975—1 v.; 1977 supp.
______. *Merger Case Digest* (1976).
______. *State Antitrust Laws* (1974).
Bureau of National Affairs. *Antitrust and Trade Regulation Report.* 2 v.
Loose leaf. 1977 update.
Callman. *The Law of Unfair Competition, Trade Marks and Monopolies.* 3d ed. 5 v. (Callaghan).
Loose leaf. 1977 update.
Commerce Clearing House. *Trade Regulation Reporter.* 5 v.
Loose leaf. 1977-1 is last bound volume of *Trade Cases.*
Fox and Fox. *Corporate Acquisitions and Mergers.* 3 v. (M. Bender 1968).
1977 update. Loose leaf. V. 13 series of Business Organizations.
Gellhorn. *Antitrust Law and Economics in a Nutshell* (West 1976).
Hills. *Antitrust Adviser.* 2 v. (McGraw-Hill 1971; 1974 supp.).
Kintner. *An Antitrust Primer. . .*2d ed. (Macmillan 1974).
______. *International Antitrust Primer* (Macmillan 1974).

Law Reprints. *Trade Regulation Series.*
U.S. Supreme Court briefs and records; v. 10 in 1977.

Lindstrom and Tighe. *Antitrust Consent Decrees.* 2 v. (LCP 1974; 1975 supp.).

Oppenheim and Weston. *Robinson-Patman Act Sourcebook.* 4 v. (Little, Brown 1971).

Stickells. *Federal Control of Business—Antitrust Laws* (LCP (1972).
1977 pocket parts.

Sullivan. *Handbook on the Law of Antitrust* (West 1977).

Toulmin. *A Treatise on the Antitrust Laws of the United States.* 7 v. (Anderson).
1977 pocket parts.

United States. *Report* of the Attorney General's National Committee to Study the Antitrust Laws (1955).

Van Cise. *Understanding the Antitrust Laws.* 7th ed. (PLI 1976).

Volz et al. *West's Federal Practice Manual*, v. 3. 1977 pocket parts.

Von Kalinowski. *Antitrust Laws and Trade Regulation.* 18 v. (M. Bender).
Also v. 18 series of Business Organization set. Loose leaf. 1977 update.

See also PATENTS, TRADEMARK, AND COPYRIGHT.

For a bibliography, see Association of American Law Schools, *Law Books Recommended for Libraries*, No. 37: Trade Regulation (Rothman 1968; 1974 supp.).

Checklists: 58 *C.J.S.* Monopolies
54, 55 *Am. Jur. 2d* Monopolies, Restraints of Trade, and Unfair Trade Practices
37 *N.Y. Jur.* Monopolies, Combinations, and Restraints of Trade
West Digest key number topic: Trade Regulation

TRIAL PRACTICE (see also CIVIL PROCEDURE, EVIDENCE, and specific subjects, such as CRIMINAL LAW)

Course descriptions (preparation for trial): Preparation for trial, including the gathering of evidence; interviewing witnesses; assembling of documentary evidence; preparing bills of particulars; demands for admissions; depositions and examinations before trial;

preparation of witnesses for direct and cross-examination; final trial preparation and trial memoranda. (New York practice): A comprehensive study of procedure and practice in New York under the Civil Practice Law and Rules. The main topics considered are the jurisdiction of New York courts, jurisdiction and service of process, venue, appearance, joinder of parties, pleading, motion practice, provisional remedies, pretrial devices, trial, judgment, and the doctrine of *res judicata.* (trial practice I): A seminar, with several small sections, primarily emphasizing the development of a trial lawyer's skills in civil and criminal cases. Among the topics to be considered and demonstrated by the students are: selection of a jury—conduct of *voir dire*, challenges; conducting the trial—opening statements, presenting the evidence, direct examination, introduction of exhibits, objections and motions during trial, strategy of cross-examination, examination and cross-examination of expert witnesses, redirect and re-cross-examination, impeachment of witnesses; closing statements—strategy and content; charge to jury—instructions, request to charge, exceptions to charge; verdict—proper and improper verdicts, post-trial motions. (trial practice II): A seminar, with several small sections, concerned with the conduct of civil litigation. Each student is required to prosecute or defend an assigned case from initial interview with the client through the process, pleading, pretrial, and trial stages of the action to final judgment. Strategy, tactics, and drafting of papers are all conducted by the students under the guidance and supervision of an experienced practicing attorney as instructor. (pretrial and discovery practice): An advanced course in the discovery and other pretrial aspects of civil procedure. Emphasis is placed on the conduct and use, both on trial and in the negotiation of settlements, of oral depositions, written interrogatories, production of documents, and other discovery and disclosure techniques in the federal, New York, and other courts. The theory of and techniques in pretrial hearings are also considered.

American J. of Trial Advocacy (Cumberland School of Law).
V. 1 published in 1977.

American Jurisprudence. *Proof of Facts* (LCP).
V. 14, 2d series, published in 1977. 1977 pocket parts.

______. *Trials* (LCP).
V. 24 published in 1977. 1977 pocket parts. See also *Federal Quick Index* volume (LCP) for references to LCP material including *Trials* and *Proof of Facts.*

Bender's *Forms of Discovery*. 20 v. (M. Bender).
Loose leaf. 1976 update. V. 1–10 interrogatories; v. 11–12A

discovery and inspection; v. 13 medical discovery; v. 13A criminal discovery; v. 14–16 admissions.

Bodin, ed. *Civil Litigation and Trial Techniques* (PLI 1976).
Marshaling the evidence, pleading and practice before trial, motion practice, depositions, final preparation for trial, selecting a jury, opening the trial, opening the court or jury, presenting the evidence, foundations for evidence, direct and cross-examination, rebuttal and surrebuttal, motions after evidence, final argument, instructions to jury, verdict, and motions after verdict.

Devitt and Blackmar. *Federal Jury Practice and Instructions—Civil and Criminal.* 3d ed. 2 v. (West 1977).
1977 pamphlet.

Figg et al. *Civil Trial Manual* (ALI-ABA 1974).
Loose leaf. Extensive bibliographies.

Goldstein and Lane. *Trial Technique.* 2d ed. 3 v. (Callaghan 1969).
Loose leaf. 1977 update.

Hunter. *Federal Trial Handbook* (LCP 1974).

Jeans. *Trial Advocacy* (West 1975).

Karlen. *Procedure Before Trial in a Nutshell* (West 1972).

Keeton. *Trial Tactics and Methods.* 2d ed. (Little, Brown 1973).

Levin et al. *Problems and Materials on Trial Advocacy* (Foundation 1968).
Bibliography following each section.

Litigation (ABA Section on Litigation).
V. 4, no. 1 (Fall 1977) has symposium on discovery.

Novok. *The Defense of Personal Injury Actions* (PLI 1972).

Practical Lawyer. *Manual of Trial and Appellate Practice No. 1* (ALI-ABA 1973).
Jury trial, direct and cross-examination, writing appellate briefs, oral argument.

Schweitzer. *Cyclopedia of Trial Practice.* 2d ed. 10 v. (LCP).
1976 supplement. Proof of specific facts, dollar verdicts—abdomen to wrist; proof of traumatic injuries—abdomen to x-rays.

Trial Lawyers Guide (Callaghan).
V. 21 published in 1977.

Trial Lawyers Q. (N. Y. State Association of Trial Lawyers).
V. 12 published in 1977.

New York Practice

Siegel. *New York Practice* (West 1978).

Checklist: 88, 89 *C.J.S.* Trial
4, 5 *Am. Jur. 2d* Appeal and Error
56 *Am. Jur. 2d* Motions, Rules, and Orders
61 *Am. Jur. 2d* Pretrial Conference and Procedure
75, 76 *Am. Jur. 2d* Trial
N.Y. Jur. (readers are referred to Carmody Wait 2d, *Cyclopedia of New York Practice*—1977 update)
West Digest key number topics: Appeal and Error, Motions, Pretrial Procedure, Trial

TRUSTS (see also TAXATION AND ESTATE PLANNING)

Course description (trusts and estates I): Gratuitous transfers: wills, intestate succession, gifts and trusts (including policy determinates), protection of the family, mental capacity, formalities of transfer; execution of wills, integration of wills and trusts, revival, revocation; creation of trusts, alienability of beneficiary's interest, termination of trusts, constructive and resulting trusts, charitable trusts; problems in the administration of trusts, deviation, trustee's duties and liabilities, investments, income and principal, accountability and liability of trustees. (trusts and estates II): Administration of decedents' estates, jurisdiction, elements of estate and gift taxation; classification of future interests, the rule against perpetuities, common pitfalls, salvage doctrines, powers of appointment. (estate planning): Intensive consideration of the marital deduction, lifetime gifts, the use of trusts, the selection of trustees, valuation problems, apportioning the tax burden, the charitable deduction, deferred compensation plans, and life insurance. (probate and fiduciary administration seminar): The administration of trusts and decedents' estates, with emphasis on problems raised by current cases and recent statutes, especially uniform laws. Problems considered include: procedure in the administration of decedents' estates; the appointment and qualification of fiduciaries; the powers and duties of fiduciaries, especially the duty of loyalty; trust investments; carrying on a decedent's business; allocation of benefits and burdens between life tenant and remaindermen; duties and liability of third parties. (problems in drafting wills and trusts seminar): An approach to estate planning through the drafting of wills and *inter vivos* trusts to meet specific but typical problems. A background of courses or experience in the law of wills, trusts, future interests, decedents' estates, and estate and gift taxation is desirable. Each student drafts instruments designed to cope with such matters as the rights of surviving spouses and infants, common disasters, perpetuities, powers of appointment, use of principal, incorporation by reference, the marital deduction and tax apportionment, and so forth.

American Law Institute. Restatement of the Law, Second: *Trusts 2d*. 3 v. (West 1959).

Bogert. *Handbook on the Law of Trusts.* 5th ed. (West 1973).

______. *Law of Trusts and Trustees.* 2d ed. 15 v. (West 1935).
1977 pocket parts.

Cohan and Hemmering. *Inter Vivos Trusts—Planning—Drafting—Taxation* (McGraw-Hill 1975).
1977 pocket part.

Comparative Probate Law Studies. . .(ALI-ABA 1976).
Includes comparisons of New York law with Uniform Probate Code.

Haskell. *Preface to the Law of Trusts* (Foundation 1975).

Hellmuth. *Modern Trust Forms* (Warren, Gorham and Lamont).
Loose leaf. 1978 update.

Nossaman and Wyatt. *Trust Adminstration and Taxation.* 2d ed. 4 v. (M. Bender 1956).
Loose leaf. 1975 update.

Prentice-Hall. *Estate Planning: Wills and Trusts.* 4 v.
Loose leaf. 1977 update. Also a forms volume.

Real Property, Probate and Trust J. (ABA Section on Real Property, etc.).
Also publisher of newsletter, *Probate and Property*; V. 6 in 1977.

Scott. The Law of Trusts. 3d ed. 6 v. (Little, Brown 1967).
1977 pocket parts.

Trusts and Estates.
V. 116 published in 1977.

Trusts in Midcentury—Transition, Taxation and Trends (ABA 1976).
Items selected from *Real Property, Probate and Trust J.*

Wellman, ed. *Uniform Probate Code Practice Manual*, 2d ed. 2 v. (ALI-ABA 1977).
Includes forms, bibliography.

For a bibliography, see Association of American Law Schools, *Law Books Recommended for Libraries*, No. 37A; (Rothman 1968; 1974 supp.).

Checklist: 90 *C.J.S.* Trusts

61 *Am. Jur. 2d* Trusts
14 *N.Y. Jur.* Decedents' Estates
45A *N.Y. Jur.* Powers
61 *N.Y. Jur.* Trusts
West Digest key number topic: Trusts

URBAN LAW (see also ENVIRONMENTAL LAW, LOCAL GOVERNMENT)

Course descriptions (the law of local government): A comprehensive study of the organization, structure, and functions of local units of government. Covers modern charter reforms; state-local and federal-city relations; the municipal decisionmaking process; and the related roles of the people, neighborhoods, officials, and courts: "home rule" in law and practice; scope and limits of municipal services and powers; citizen complaints; status and accountability of officers and employees; use and ownership of public property; tort liability; business and land use regulation; readjustment of municipal services and areas; and "model cities" programs. (government in urban areas): A study of the structure and operations of government in urban areas, including: (1) the distribution of power among city, state, and federal governments; (2) municipal programs and expenditures and sources of revenue; (3) legal and fiscal relations between cities and their suburbs, with emphasis on school financing and exclusionary zoning; and (4) decentralization of municipal government. (urban law seminar): Seminar forcuses on substantive and procedural issues related to juvenile justice, rights of youth, health and the law, drug abuse, and rehabilitation and on the professional role of the lawyer in dealing with major urban and poverty problems. The course also studies the relationship between governmental agencies, community-based service agencies, institutions, and individuals, and examines the role of the lawyer in advocating for indigent clients and in seeking to facilitate societal change.

Index to Current Urban Documents (Greenwood Press).
V. 6 published in 1977—includes N. Y. legislative documents and other New York material.

WILLS (see TAXATION AND ESTATE PLANNING)

WORKMEN'S COMPENSATION (see also ADMIRALTY, LABOR LAW)

Larson. *The Law of Workmen's Compensation.* 7 v. (M. Bender 1952).
Loose leaf. 1977 update.

______. *Workmen's Compensation for Occupational Injuries and Death.* 2 v. (M. Bender 1972).

Loose leaf. 1975 update. Condensation of above listing.

Schneider. *Workmen's Compensation.* 3d ed. 19 v. (Thomas 1939 to date).

See *American Trial Lawyer Association Law J.* and negligence publications in general for treatment of this topic.

Checklist: 99-101 *C.J.S.* Workmen's Compensation
81, 82 *Am. Jur. 2d* Workmen's Compensation
65, 66 *N.Y. Jur.* Workmen's Compensation
West Digest key number topic: Workmen's Compensation

ZONING (see PROPERTY)

Part III

Appendix

BOWLING v. SPERRY

The case reprinted below as it appears in the *Northeastern Reporter* is used to illustrate legal research in the following categories of Part I: ANNOTATIONS, DIGESTS, and REPORTS.

Larry BOWLING, by Norma Lemley, next friend, Appellant,

v.

Max SPERRY, d/b/a Sperry Ford Sales, Appellee.

No. 19501.

Appellate Court of Indiana,

Division No. 1.

Sept. 10, 1962.

Action to disaffirm and set aside the purchase of a used automobile on grounds of infancy of the buyer. The Circuit Court, Noble County, Lowell L. Pefley, Special Judge, rendered judgment for defendant, and plaintiff appealed. The Appellate Court, Myers, J., held, inter alia, that sixteen-year-old high school boy was entitled to disaffirm and set aside purchase of used automobile, though he was accompanied by grandmother and aunt at time of purchase and borrowed money from aunt to make final payment, and regardless of whether certificate of title was delivered in blank or bore buyer's name, and that the evidence was insufficient to meet seller's burden of showing that the automobile sold and delivered was a necessary within statute, Burns' Ann.St. § 58–102, requiring payment of reasonable price for necessaries sold and delivered to a minor.

Judgment reversed and cause remanded with directions.

1. Infants ⚿47

Contracts of minors are voidable and may be disaffirmed.

2. Infants ⚿58(2)

Other party to contract disaffirmed by minor need not be placed in statu quo and minor need not tender back money or property he has received before suing for value or possession of money or property given by him.

3. Infants ⚿58(1)

Voidable contracts of minor in regard to personalty may be avoided at any time during minority or upon attaining majority.

4. Infants ⚿58(1)

Minor was entitled to disaffirm purchase of used automobile and recover back purchase money paid therefor, even though he was accompanied by aunt and grandmother at time of purchase and borrowed money from aunt to make final payment, and regardless of whether certificate of title was delivered in blank or bore name of minor.

5. Infants ⚿58(1)

That burned-out bearing was caused by minor's operation of automobile and failure to put oil in crankcase would constitute no defense to action by minor to disaffirm and set aside purchase of used automobile.

6. Infants ⚿50

As used in statute requiring payment of reasonable price for "necessaries" sold and delivered to minor or other person incompetent to contract, quoted word means such things as are necessary to his support, use or comfort, including such personal comforts as comport with his condition and circumstances in life, provided he is in actual need of such things at time and obliged to procure them for himself. Burns' Ann.St. § 58–102.

See publication Words and Phrases for other judicial constructions and definitions.

7. Infants ⟹102

Whether goods are necessaries for which minor under statute may be required to pay reasonable price is a question of law, and if deemed necessaries, their quantity, quality and reasonable value are matters of fact. Burns' Ann.St. § 58–102

8. Infants ⟹98

Seller had burden of proving that used automobile sold and delivered to minor, seeking to disaffirm and set aside transaction, was a necessary for which under statute minor should be required to pay reasonable price. Burns' Ann.St. § 58–102.

9. Infants ⟹100

Evidence was insufficient to meet seller's burden of showing that used automobile sold and delivered to sixteen-year-old high school boy was a necessary for which under statute minor should be required to pay reasonable price. Burns' Ann. St. § 58–102.

John C. Hagen, Ligonier, for appellant.

Albert J. Kuster, Ligonier, for appellee.

MYERS, Judge.

This is an appeal from a judgment of the Noble Circuit Court in a civil action brought by appellant, Larry Bowling, by Norma Lemley as next friend, hereinafter referred to as Larry, against appellee, Max E. Sperry, d/b/a Sperry Ford Sales, to disaffirm and set aside a contract for the purchase of an automobile on the grounds of infancy.

Larry was a minor, sixteen years of age. On June 29, 1957, he purchased from appellee a 1947 Plymouth automobile for the sum of $140 cash. He paid $50 down on that day and returned on July 1, 1957, to pay the balance of $90 and take possession of the car. Appellee delivered to him a certificate of title and a written receipt. This receipt stated that as of June 29, 1957, Max Sperry Ford Sales sold to Larry Bowling a 1947 Plymouth for the amount of $140, cash, paid in full.

Larry drove the car several times during the following week and discovered that the main bearing was burned out. He had the car brought back to appellee's place of business where he was informed that it would cost him from $45 to $95 to make repairs. He declined to pay this amount and left the car on appellee's lot. Subsequently, he mailed a letter to appellee to the effect that he disaffirmed the contract of purchase and demanded the return of his money. Upon appellee's refusal to pay back the $140, this lawsuit followed.

Larry's complaint is based upon the fact that appellee sold him a car knowing that he was a minor; that he tendered back the car, rescinded the contract, and demanded the sum of $140. Appellee's answer was in two paragraphs, the first being in the nature of a general denial, pursuant to the provisions of Supreme Court Rule 1–3, and the second being an allegation that Larry was accompanied by his grandmother and aunt at the time of the purchase, and that the aunt paid appellee the sum of $90 of the purchase price. Upon trial of the case by the court, judgment was rendered in favor of appellee and against Larry.

[1–3] It has been the rule in Indiana for many years that the contracts of minors are voidable and may be disaffirmed. It is not necessary that the other party be placed in *statu quo*, nor is it necessary that the minor tender back the money or property he has received before suing for the value or possession of the money or property given by him to the adult. All such voidable contracts by a minor in regard to personal property may be avoided at any time during his minority or upon his arrival at full age.

Shipley v. Smith (1904), 162 Ind. 526, 70 N.E. 803; McKee v. Harwood Automotive Co. (1932), 204 Ind. 233, 183 N.E. 646; Wooldridge, by Next Friend, v. Hill (1953), 124 Ind.App. 11, 114 N.E.2d 646.

The evidence showed that Larry's grandmother and aunt accompanied him to appellee's used car lot on June 29, 1957, when he selected the automobile, and that his aunt drove the car around the lot at that time. Furthermore, it was revealed that his aunt had loaned him $90 in order to make final payment on the car and that he had commenced to pay this back at $10 a week thereafter.

[4] These facts, however, do not change the general rule. In so far as the agreement and sale is concerned, there was sufficient evidence to show that it was made between appellee and Larry, and no one else. It is of no consequence that his aunt and grandmother accompanied him at the time of purchase; and the fact that his aunt made payment of the $90 balance due could have no effect upon Larry's right to take advantage of his minority in an action to recover such payment. Story, etc., Piano Co. v. Davy (1918), 68 Ind.App. 150, 119 N.E. 177. Appellee was fully aware of Larry's age when the sale was negotiated. The written receipt was in Larry's name alone. This contract was squarely between an adult and a minor and falls within the rule pronounced above. Larry had every right to disaffirm it and set it aside.

Appellee claims there is doubt as to whether Larry received a certificate of title from appellee with his name on it. It is contended that the certificate was delivered in blank. As was said in the case of Wooldridge, by Next Friend, v. Hill, supra (at page 14 of 124 Ind.App., at page 648 of 114 N.E.2d): "It is of little consequence whether title to the property involved had passed to the infant or not." The certificate of title is only evidence of ownership, and in this case it would make no difference whether Larry had received a certificate in blank or with his name on it. Automobile Underwriters v. Tite (1949), 119 Ind.App. 251, 85 N.E.2d 365.

[5] Appellee argues that an inference may be drawn from the evidence to show that the burned-out bearing was caused by Larry's operation of the car and his failure to put oil in the crankcase. Even if this were true, it is no defense to this action. There is no requirement in Indiana that before a disaffirmance is effected the parties must be placed in *statu quo*. Story, etc., Piano Co. v. Davy, supra.

The question of whether or not the automobile was a necessary was injected into the trial of the case although appellee did not plead it as a defense. Some argument on this subject was made by the parties in the briefs. Section 58–102, Burns' Ind. Stat., 1961 Replacement, reads as follows:

> "Capacity to buy and sell is regulated by the general law concerning capacity to contract, and to transfer and acquire property.
>
> "Where necessaries are sold and delivered to an infant, or to a person who by reason of mental incapacity or drunkenness is incompetent to contract, he must pay a reasonable price therefor.
>
> "Necessaries in this section means goods suitable to the condition in life of such infant or other person, and to his actual requirements at the time of delivery."

[6] In the case of Price et al. v. Sanders et al. (1878), 60 Ind. 310, 314, the following is stated:

> " 'Necessaries,' in the technical sense, mean such things as are necessary to the support, use or comfort of the person of the minor, as food, raiment, lodging, medical attendance, and such personal comforts as comport with his condition and circumstances in life, including a common school education; but it has been pithily and happily said,

that necessaries do not include 'horses, saddles, bridles, liquors, pistols, powder, whips and fiddles.'"

[7] Whether the goods are necessaries is a question of law, and if they are deemed as such, their quantity, quality and reasonable value are matters of fact. Garr et al. v. Haskett et al. (1882), 86 Ind. 373.

It has been stated in 27 Am.Jur., Infants, § 17, pp. 760, 761, as follows:

> "Aside from such things as are obviously for maintenance of existence, what are or what are not necessaries for an infant depends on what is reasonably necessary for the proper and suitable maintenance of the infant in view of his social position and situation in life, the customs of the social circle in which he moves or is likely to move, and the fortune possessed by him and by his parents. It has been said that articles of mere luxury or adornment cannot be included, but that useful articles, although of an expensive and luxurious character, may be included if they are reasonable in view of the infant's circumstances. The necessities to be procured by the contract must be personal necessities, that is, for the living or personal well-being of the infant. * * *
>
> "What is furnished to the infant must be suitable, not only to his condition in life, but also to his actual requirements at the time—in other words, the infant must not have at the time of delivery an adequate supply from other sources. To be liable for articles as necessaries, an infant must be in actual need of them, and obliged to procure them for himself."

The evidence revealed that at the time of this transaction, Larry was living with his grandmother in Cromwell, Indiana, where he had lived for the past fifteen years; that his mother was dead and his father resided in Fort Wayne; that he was a student at Cromwell High School, but was on vacation; that he had a summer job working at a restaurant in the town of Syracuse, Indiana, which was eight or nine miles away from his home; that his usual means of transportation back and forth was with the cook; that on occasion he could "bum" rides with other people.

The acting manager for appellee, who had dealt with Larry, testified that when Larry's aunt and grandmother came to the sales lot on June 29, 1957, "they" said Larry needed something for him to get back and forth to work. He said it was his "understanding" that the car was needed for that purpose. Larry stated that during the short period of time he had possession of it, he only used it for pleasure, and did not drive it to work.

[8, 9] We are well aware of the overwhelming increase in the use and number of automobiles in this country since World War II. What once was a great luxury for only the wealthy has become a matter of common necessity for the ordinary workingman, farmer and businessman. The automobile is as important to the modern household as food, clothing and shelter. The problem here is whether the car in question was so needed by Larry, in view of his situation in life, his social status and his financial position, that he could not be maintained properly or suitably without it. The burden of showing this was upon appellee. Robertson v. King (1955), 225 Ark. 276, 280 S.W.2d 402, 52 A.L.R.2d 1108. From the evidence presented, we do not think appellee met this burden. While every high school boy today wants a car of his own, and many of them own automobiles which under given circumstances may be considered as necessaries, we do not consider the car in this case so vital to Larry's existence that it could be classified as a necessary.

Judgment reversed, and cause remanded with instructions that the trial court sustain appellant's motion for a new trial on the ground that the judgment is contrary to law.

COOPER, P. J., and AX and RYAN, JJ., concur.

LEGAL RESEARCH CHECK LIST

Project ____________________

DIGESTS
State and Federal
——Gen. Dig.
——8th Dec.
——7th Dec.
——6th Dec.
——5th Dec.
——4th Dec.
——3d Dec.
——2d Dec.
——Cent.
State
——Regional
——States
____
____

Federal
——Sup. Ct. (West)
——L. Ed.
——Fed. Dig. (to 1939)
——M.F.P. Dig. (to 1960)
——F. Prac. 2d (to date)
Misc.
——UCC Dig.
——NCCA
——USPQ
Descriptors used:
____
____

Key numbers checked:
____
____

Cases to be researched (use full citation):
____
____
____
____

RESTATEMENT
——1st
——2d
Topic and section checked: ____________
____
____

——Restatement in ct
——Shepard's
——Tentative Drafts

LOOSE LEAF SERVICES
——CCH
——P-H
——BNA
——Callaghan
——M. Bender
——P & F
——Other
____
____

TREATISES
____
____

ENC., DICT., etc.
——State enc. .
____

——Am Jur 2d
——Desk Book
——CJS
——Words & Phrases
——Black's Dict.
——Ballantine Dict.
——Proof of Facts
——Am Jur Trials
——USCS Guide. . .
Topics and titles checked: ____________
____
____
____

SHEPARD'S
——State
——Cases
——Statutes
——Federal
——U.S.
——F.S., etc.
——F.R., etc.
——Adm.
——Labor
——Copyright, etc.
——Restatement
——Criminal Just.
——Law Reviews
——Fed'l law
——Local Ordinances
——Popular Name Table
——Regional Rptrs
____
____
____

Cases checked:
____
____
____
____

Statutes checked:
____
____
____
____

FORMS
——Am Jur Forms
——Am Jur Pl & Pr
——Rabkin & J.
——Other
____
____
____

CARD CATALOG
Subjects and authors checked: ____________
____
____

STATUTES
State
——Annotated Code
——Official Code
——Session Laws
——Current Leg. Serv.
——Leg. History
——Adm. Code
——Court Rules
——Unif. Laws Ann (West)
——Model Codes
Federal
——USCA
——USCS
——Guide to ALR, L.ED., etc.
——S/L
——USCCAN
——Leg. Hist.
——FRCP/Cr.
——CFR
——Fed. Reg.
——Treaties in Force
Popular Name Tables
——USCA
——Shepard's
Comparative Law
——Martindale-Hubbell
——Am Jur Pl & Pr Forms
Index entries used and citations ____________
____
____

Statutes to be checked:
____
____

ANNOTATIONS
——ALR
——ALR 2d
——ALR 3d
——ALR Fed
Indexes
——ALR
——Quick Ind.
——Supp. Ser.
——ALR 2d
——Quick Ind.
——Late Case S.
——ALR 3d
——Quick Index
——P.P.
Shepard's
——Cases checked:
____
____

Words and phrases checked:
____
____

Annotations checked:
____
____

SHEPARD'S CITATIONS, SPECIMEN PAGES

SPECIMEN PAGE—Shepard's Massachusetts Citations, Case Edition, 1967

Vol. 193 **MASSACHUSETTS REPORTS**

317Mas[2]432
326Mas[2]147
184F[1]220
216F[1]507
248F[2]263
f258F[1]299
263F[2]1014
j39F2d540
6BUR234
8BUR151
8BUR210
11BUR142
24MQ(1)2
24MQ(4)9
59AR157n
–324–
(79NE734)
196Mas483
d197Mas [1]178
200Mas[1]35
206Mas[2]389
207Mas[1]501
d216Mas [1]322
216Mas[2]339
220Mas[1]30
220Mas[1]299
273Mas[2]29
273Mas[2]476
326Mas[1]795
–327–
(79NE818)
199Mas[1]11
202Mas[4]113
222Mas[5]261
266Mas[4]546
292Mas[4]550
299Mas[4]3
299Mas[5]4
321Mas[5]198
174FS[3]455
–331–
(79NE749)
194Mas[1]446
199Mas[1]541
220Mas[1]581
–332–
(79NE765)
(7Lns1076)
196Mas[2]31
199Mas[2]448
199Mas[2]475
201Mas[2]185
203Mas396
204Mas[2]68
206Mas[3]388
d207Mas[3]29
207Mas[3]448
217Mas[3]118
220Mas[3]31
220Mas[4]32
224Mas[2]407
241Mas[4]79
245Mas[4]121
246Mas[3]521
260Mas[1]337
263Mas[4]218
266Mas[4]543
267Mas[3]366
f269Mas[4]63
270Mas[4]266
276Mas[3]384
277Mas[2]365
279Mas[4]345

d283Mas[3]561
284Mas[4]607
297Mas[3]273
304Mas[2]642
d314Mas[2]682
322Mas[3]219
322Mas[3]227
328Mas[3]534
d339Mas[2]728
343Mas[3]779
182F[4]127
252F[3]516
245F2d[3]447
50AR1366n
–336–
(79NE771)
242Mas[1]392
282Mas376
101AR237n
–339–
(79NE733)
197Mas[1]292
d197Mas [1]422
201Mas[1]57
5A3815n
–341–
(79NE815)
(118AS516)
(7Lns729)
f194Mas[5]459
d195Mas [1]318
196Mas[1]71
201Mas[4]70
205Mas[1]3
d205Mas[2]36
206Mas486
207Mas[1]498
d207Mas [2]563
208Mas[3]447
210Mas[2]456
212Mas[2]309
213Mas[5]329
f213Mas[2]597
f217Mas[2]421
217Mas[1]517
223Mas[2]494
d227Mas [2]115
d229Mas[3]67
f232Mas[2]551
d233Mas [2]350
238Mas[2]231
239Mas[1]227
239Mas[1]567
244Mas[2]452
d245Mas [1]122
d248Mas [2]496
d250Mas [2]245
d251Mas[2]59
252Mas[1]274
d259Mas [3]328
264Mas[2]368
297Mas[1]195
303Mas[1]244
d316Mas[2]619
322Mas[5]294
338Mas[1]128

341Mas[1]642
269F[2]782
293F[2]406
32AR1316n
155AR643n
41A31304n
–351–
(79NE790)
cc222F349
203Mas[1]130
203Mas[2]424
241Mas[2]474
250Mas[2]314
281Mas[2]166
343Mas[1]371
343Mas[2]723
4BUR30
39BUR494
40BUR228
78AR1040n
45A3119n
45A3143n
45A3183n
45A3250n
46A3160n
46A3191n
46A3219n
46A3265n
46A3385n
–359–
(79NE742)
(9Lns874)
202Mas[1]495
207Mas[1]131
209Mas[1]88
214Mas[2]541
224Mas[2]360
245Mas[1]10
265Mas[3]412
272Mas[3]220
295Mas[2]55
339Mas[2]250
266F[2]198
28FS[2]157
46FS[1]957
46FS[2]958
41AR127n
44AR1068n
126AR1095n
126AR1097n
–364–
(79NE745)
(118AS523)
(23Lns1160)
a214US91
a53LE923
a29SC567
f193Mas[8]476
198Mas [11]256
200Mas[1]484
d203Mas[8]29
203Mas[7]155
206Mas[1]432
f206Mas[7]433
208Mas[1]622
208Mas[7]630
219Mas [11]197
220Mas[1]275
222Mas [11]580
225Mas [11]196
228Mas[8]374

230Mas[7]190
234Mas[2]602
234Mas[4]604
234Mas[5]609
241Mas[1]528
242Mas[3]32
f242Mas[6]34
245Mas8
f250Mas[5]60
250Mas[8]71
255Mas[7]171
257Mas[11]53
264Mas[1]87
270Mas[1]524
286Mas[1]618
286Mas[2]618
289Mas[4]185
315Mas[7]342
323Mas[1]650
323Mas[4]650
324Mas[10]448
328Mas[1]676
333Mas[4]778
339Mas208
f41F2d[1]938
6AG182
6AG440
7AG451
6BUR166
6BUR306
8BUR79
10BUR322
10BUR324
18BUR92
21BUR650
22BUR381
37HLR842
13MQ(6)72
43MQ(3)61
48MQ(4)492
34AR46n
8A3965n
58A31088n
–378–
(79NE777)
233Mas[1]253
32AR215n
–383–
(79NE737)
218Mas[1]191
260Mas[1]385
260Mas[1]397
312Mas[1]645
323Mas[1]567
f337Mas[1]30
339Mas[1]14
339Mas[1]16
4AG279
8AG474
3AR1456n
23AR249n
73AR825n
86A3675n

–392–
(79NE739)
(9Lns695)
201Mas[1]540
237Mas[2]398
280Mas[1]330
–400–
(79NE774)
203Mas[1]327
217Mas[1]32
244Mas[1]306
250Mas[1]87
256Mas[1]153
270Mas[1]39
284Mas[1]9
308Mas[1]405
–402–
(79NE776)
f195Mas[1]128
317Mas[1]566
74A3998n
74A31011n
315Mas[2]345
319Mas[2]674
7AG6
42AR1467n
–412–
285Mas[3]543
305Mas[4]440
–415–
(79NE821)
f196Mas[2]551
200Mas[2]193
200Mas[2]343
202Mas[3]224
204Mas[1]481
205Mas[2]179
205Mas[1]370
f212Mas[3]170
216Mas[3]498

219Mas[1]506
301Mas[3]327
167F[1]81
53AR145n
–419–
f208Mas[2]566
210Mas[1]552
213Mas[1]294
f236Mas[1]223
256Mas[2]56
257Mas150
262Mas[1]580
319Mas[2]314
319Mas[1]599
326Mas[1]460
335Mas[2]700
47ABA602
22AR578n
11A3434n
211Mas[1]485
(79NE748)
202Mas[2]204
201Mas[3]265
f202Mas[3]10
202Mas[1]65
204Mas[2]229
209Mas349
304Mas[1]222
304Mas[1]470
–444–
(79NE769)
204Mas[2]354
208Mas[2]403
224Mas[1]584
h234Mas[1]23
d239Mas [1]232
h247Mas [1]213
248Mas[1]289

264Mas[2]109
270Mas[1]173
312Mas[1]289
320Mas[1]626
321Mas[1]675
(79NE797)
(7Lns148)
197Mas[3]396
202Mas[2]446
205Mas[3]171
208Mas[3]157
215Mas[2]470
216Mas[3]180
d216Mas214
217Mas[3]95
223Mas[1]184
230Mas[2]391
236Mas[1]14
d236Mas[3]538
254Mas[1]189
d263Mas[1]75
327Mas[1]73
341Mas[1]699
48MQ(3)318
171AR369n
–453–
(79NE775)
–455–
(79NE770)
212Mas[2]109
227Mas[2]51
237Mas[2]507
274Mas[2]501
284Mas[2]506
292Mas[1]193
300Mas[2]88
309Mas[2]531
313Mas[2]416
337Mas[2]546
6MQ(2)27
16MQ(5)218
–458–
(79NE807)
216Mas[7]143
216Mas223
222Mas[5]82
236Mas[1]347
240Mas[7]370
256Mas[7]470
262Mas[1]53

311Mas[7]370
'03-22EC64
90AR755n
55A3224n
–464–
(79NE784)
195Mas[3]109
242Mas[1]534
250Mas[1]457
250Mas[1]535
319Mas[1]308
10BUR39
10BUR168
35AR963n
–470–
(79NE878)
247Mas[1]203
333Mas[1]777
34AR49n
8A3965n
–479–
(79NE787)
–482–
(79NE794)
284Mas[1]521
339Mas[1]710
–486–
(79NE763)
201Mas158
204Mas337
208Mas510
205Mas[1]461
221Mas[1]320
308Mas[1]545
–488–
(80NE583)
cc191Mas441
cc198Mas580
194Mas573
198Mas[1]582
276Mas[1]286
–495–
(79NE738)
198Mas[1]531
d203Mas[1]261
204Mas[1]201
205Mas[1]274
229Mas[1]44
335Mas[1]427
345Mas[1]41
–498–
(79NE796)
194Mas[3]575
1MQ311
–500–
(79NE781)
201Mas[2]607
205Mas[4]328
210Mas280
241Mas[3]544
254Mas[2]79
267Mas[4]101
30AR1164n
–507–
(79NE764)
195Mas[4]160
196Mas[1]128
196Mas[2]486
198Mas[2]571
200Mas[2]543
201Mas384
f203Mas[3]584
206Mas[4]545
208Mas[4]118
Continued

Followed with reference to paragraph six of syllabus

Cited by lower federal court

Cited in Boston University Law Review

Cited in Harvard Law Review

Cited in Massachusetts Law Quarterly

Cited in annotations of Annotated Reports System

Same case reported in Northeastern Reporter, American State Reports and Lawyers Reports Annotated, New Series

Affirmed by United States Supreme Court

Distinguished with reference to paragraph eight of syllabus

726

For later citations see any subsequent bound supplement or volume, the current issue of the periodically published paper-covered cumulative supplement and any current issue of the advance sheet

18

Source: *How to Use Shepard's Citations.* Colorado Springs, Shepard's Citations, 1971. Reprinted with permission.

STATE REPORTS

Illustration

Let us assume that, by reference to a digest, encyclopedia, text book, or other unit of legal research or the statute law of the state, you have located the case of *Welch v. Swasey*, reported in Volume 193, Massachusetts Reports, at page 364.

The specimen page (opposite) contains a reproduction of page 726 in the 1967 Case Edition of Shepard's Massachusetts Citations. Note the number of the volume of reports "Vol. 193" in the upper left corner of the page.

An examination of the bold face type numbers appearing in the column locates the page number "-364-" in the third column of citations. This is the initial page of the case under consideration. Following this page number you will find the citations "(79 NE 745)", "(118 AS 523)", "(23 Lns 1160)" indicating that the same case is also reported in 79 Northeastern Reporter 745, 118 American State Reports 523 and 23 Lawyers Reports Annotated, New Series 1160.

In obtaining the history of this case, you will observe that upon appeal to the United States Supreme Court it was affirmed ("a") in 214 United States Reports ["US"] 91, 53 Lawyers' Edition, United States Supreme Court Reports ["LE"] 923 and 29 Supreme Court Reporter ["SC"] 567.

It is also to be observed by examining the abbreviations preceding the citations that this case has been followed ("f") and distinguished ("d") in subsequent cases in the Massachusetts and federal courts.

In the citation "f 193 Mas^{8}476", the small superior figure $^{(``8")}$ in advance of the citing page number 476 indicates that the principle of law brought out in the eighth paragraph of the syllabus of 193 Mas 364 has been followed in 193 Mas 476.

You will note that other citations that contain the superior figure $^{(``8")}$ in advance of the citing page number and that deal with this point in particular are 203 Mas 29, 228 Mas 374 and 250 Mas 71.

In addition to the citations in point with paragraph eight of the syllabus, note the numerous citations in point with other paragraphs of the syllabus or other headnotes of this case by the Massachusetts and federal courts. The cases dealing with a point of law in any particular paragraph of the syllabus or headnote may thus be referred to instantly without examining every citing case listed.

This case has also been cited in the Harvard Law Review ("HLR"), Boston University Law Review ("BUR"), and Massachusetts Law Quarterly ("MQ").

The citations appearing in annotations of the Annotated Reports System are grouped together for convenience of use.

By examining this same volume and page number in any subsequent bound supplement or volume, the current issue of the periodically published paper-covered cumulative supplement, and any current issue of the advance sheet of Shepard's Massachusetts Citations, all subsequent citations to this case will be found.

In this instance, as in every instance, Shepard's Citations to cases will enable the lawyer in a very short time to collect the entire body of case law that revolves around and about a given case.

142NE[1]694
Ind
96NE[1]977
107AR23n
W Va
73SE268
–741–
(193Mas545)
–742–
Case 1
(193Mas398)
182NE[1]583
Iowa
179NW528
–742–
Case 2
(193Mas359)
89NE[1]133
92NE[1]1031
95NE[1]400
102NE[2]66
112NE[2]952
139NE[3]383
164NE376
172NE[1]215
3NE[4]27
266F[2]198
28FS[2]157
46FS[1]957
41AR127n
44AR1068n
126AR1095n
126AR1097n
Ala
70So728
169So719
Ark
65SW15
Calif
55P2d228
Ga
86SE328
Miss
80So282
Tenn
192SW169
–744–
(194Mas14)
121NE[1]31
158NE[1]799
Vt
13A2d208
Wyo
120P2d597
–745–
(193Mas364)
a214US91
a53LE923
a29SC567
f79NE[1]879
84NE[5]456
86NE[1]917
d89NE[1]146
89NE[3]180
92NE[1]708
f92NE[4]709
94NE[3]1045
95NE[3]932
106NE[5]853
107NE[3]79
111NE[5]412
114NE[5]289
117NE[2]589
119NE[3]689
127NE[1]527

127NE[4]528
135NE[3]876
136NE[2]339
136NE[4]339
139NE382
f145NE[2]264
145NE[2]268
150NE[4]897
153NE[5]356
161NE[1]899
170NE[1]391
191NE[1]35
193NE815
f41F2d[1]938
Ill
e94NE[4]924
133NE[5]270
149NE[1]789
180NE[1]773
193NE[1]134
Ind
d92NE[5]650
172NE[1]312
172NE[4]312
N Y
118NE[3]792
150NE[1]123
154S97
216S311
220S660
258S890
14S2d593
28S2d318
Ohio
149NE[4]33
34AR46n
Ala
52So945
Calif
134P973
Conn
111At357
111At902
162At29
165At605
179At200
Del
129At518
Fla
65So284
94So689
157So655
Iowa
126NW917
184NW830
273…
46P…
Ky
159SW975
Md
70At114
95At1063
Me
69At629
128At185
137At400
140At387
Minn
158…
25…
256SW491
N C
122SE472

161SE80
N H
141At145
Okla
192P353
So C
150SE275
Va
67SE376
134SE916
192SE888
Wis
147NW28
194NW161
196NW455
W Va
84SE107
94SE498
–748–
(193Mas431)
88NE[3]591
f116NE[1]899
56F2d[2]811
Ill
104NE[1]675
177IlA181
Ind
f104NE[1]61
N Y
119NE[1]558
217S59
Me
108At194
Mo
164SW641
–749–
Case 1
(193Mas331)
80NE[1]610
85NE[1]847
108NE[1]364
–749–
Case 2
(193Mas438)
79NE[1]751
87NE[1]475
f8…
98…
117NE[1]311
136NE[1]104
19AR1372n
…
Minn
…
85NE[1]573
93NE[1]840
95NE[1]752
120NE[1]591
142NE[1]904
…
97NE[2]103
100NE[2]545
e104NE[1]344

105NE[1]985
105NE[2]987
127NE[1]432
140NE[1]594
189NE[2]593
26…
j70…
164So569
Calif
258P139
Del
197At384
…
s92NE61
81NE[1]914
f83NE[1]1019
84NE[1]8
88NE[1]696
9…
(7…
–757–
(75OS355)
119NE[1]416
142NE[2]691
3NE[3]354
3OA496
9OA22
Ind
e89NE[1]517
e89NE[3]517
–762–
(193Mas556)
102NE[1]67
d155NE[1]443
165NE[1]513
j169NE[1]493
181NE[1]716
15NE[1]487
232F[2]559
296F[2]375
Ill
241IlA17
…
108AR411n
108AR419n
108AR421n
Ala…
…
101P2d715
Iowa
…
Kan
171P6
Md
96At518
Me
138At71
135SW73
N C
195SE808

N D
137NW416
Nebr
180NW560
N H
…
Okla
138P155
Ore
206P297
S D
…
Vt
130At767
Wis
196NW766
W Va
…
–763–
(193Mas486)
s87NE189
s90NE578
s94NE752
92NE[1]47
108NE[1]1086
33NE[1]269
–764–
(193Mas507)
80NE[1]508
80NE[1]697
81NE[2]888
82NE[1]497
84NE[1]842
86NE[2]936
87NE613
f89NE[1]1041
92NE[2]720
94NE[1]390
104NE[1]381
107NE450
…
–765–
(193Mas332)
81NE[1]895
85NE[1]571
…NE[1]573
…NE[1]490
…NE[2]564
90NE[1]534
90NE[1]548
…
107NE[1]377
112NE[1]1025
134NE[2]376
139NE[1]822
141NE[1]587
157NE652
…98
…59
…634
f168NE172
169NE[1]781
177NE[1]580

178NE[1]542
181NE[1]219
d186NE[1]671
188NE[1]391
…
252F[1]516
N Y
166NE[1]174
50AR1366n
Ark
…
20P2d752
Conn
85At636
Del
197At486
…
Minn
217NW375
Mo
236SW20
Okla
159P1013
Va
63SE448
86SE66
128SE541
162SE20
Wash
5P2d986
–766–
(193Mas419)
88NE[1]836
f93NE[1]605
f95NE[1]94
96NE[1]1095
100NE[1]557
f128NE[1]14
152NE[1]78
…69
…18
…
22AR578n
Ala
81So21
Ark
179SW818
Conn
181At209
Iowa
186NW442
…NW277
Ky
267SW228
N D
147NW785
R I
129At804
So C
76SE699
Wis
228NW507
–769–
(193Mas444)
90NE[1]590
94NE[1]466

113NE[1]202
h124NE431
d131NE[1]855
h142NE[1]90
142NE[1]799
…
186F[1]754
–770–
(193Mas455)
98NE[1]696
116NE[1]544
…NE[1]112
…NE[1]79
…NE[1]351
197NE[1]888
d14NE[1]154
36NE[1]413
48NE[1]44
–771–
(193Mas336)
…1190
…387
…237n
–772–
(193Mas551)
99NE[1]415
100NE[1]62
102NE[1]420
137NE[1]375
137NE[1]694
156NE[1]744
161NE[1]621
192NE[1]630
10NE[1]126
36FS[1]925
36FS[1]928
Ill
101NE[1]945
N Y
288S440
Ohio
142NE[1]896
Me
145At398
N J
8A2d569
–774–
(193Mas400)
89NE[1]546
104NE[1]450
138NE[1]551
145NE[1]54
152NE[1]229
169NE[1]517
187NE[1]107
32NE[1]271
–775–
Case 1
(193Mas453)
97NE[1]100
110NE[1]962
135NE[1]139
Utah
220P699
–775–
Case 2
(193Mas518)
f83NE[2]324
92NE506
94NE[2]266
97NE[1]921
190NE[2]737

–776–
(193Mas402)
f80NE[1]807
81NE[1]911
130NE[3]206
177NE[2]823
22NE[1]46
129AR13n
Conn
92At681
Idaho
26P2d122
Me
104At228
–777–
(193Mas378)
124NE[1]21
32AR215n
–779–
Case 1
(194Mas44)
104NE[1]467
107NE[2]58
165NE[2]903
167NE[1]679
197NE[2]103
N Y
38S2d300
Ga
23SE418
–779–
Case 2
(193Mas540)
s77NE762
21AR1445n
–780–
Case 1
(193Mas593)
106NE[2]852
138NE[2]7
138NE[1]816
144NE[2]764
196NE860
199NE[2]896
42NE[1]562
21AR1459n
60AR385n
Ala
161So551
Pa
162At344
Tex
252SW268
–780–
Case 2
(193Mas534)
106NE[1]633
108NE[1]471
127NE[1]517
137NE[1]295
144NE[1]404
146NE[1]687
177NE[1]270
e31NE[1]554
235F[1]653
65F2d[1]868
N Y
290S212
56AR65n
Vt
146At74
–781–
(193Mas500)
88NE[1]334
Continued

Cited in annotations of the American Law Reports

Followed with reference to paragraph one of syllabus

Cited by the lower federal courts

Cited in all units of the National Reporter System with state of citing case shown

Cross references to state reports

Affirmed "a" by the United States Supreme Court

Citations analyzed to paragraph of syllabus of cited case

For later citations see any subsequent bound supplement or volume, the current issue of the periodically published paper-covered cumulative supplement and any current issue of the advance sheet

NATIONAL REPORTER SYSTEM

Illustration

To illustrate the use of Shepard's National Reporter Citations, we will use the same case, *Welch v. Swasey*, that was selected to demonstrate the use of the state publication. This time we will make our search in terms of its Northeastern Reporter reference, 79 NE 745. The mechanics are the same as in the preceding illustration dealing with a state reports edition.

Let us further consider this reporter citator in light of its use as a case finder. By a check of the specimen page (opposite), we find every Massachusetts case that cites 79 NE 745 in terms of their Northeastern Reporter references, as well as cases from other states within the scope of the Northeastern Reporter, namely Illinois, Indiana, New York and Ohio. In addition, we find every other state citing reference to our case (nineteen states in addition to those within the Northeastern Reporter area). Add to this the references to annotations and you can see that exhaustive national research is instantly available, opening avenues of investigation that would have required countless hours of search using other methods.

The use of the Northeastern Reporter publication with respect to the evaluation of our material is also exactly the same as in the state reports example, as is the ability to pinpoint research by use of the small superior figures immediately to the left of the page reference.

When research in depth is desired, the careful investigator will use both the state and the reporter citation units in searching his problem. The state units, being intrastate in their orientation, will emphasize local citing references, including statutory material and law reviews. The reporter units, with their interstate frame of reference in addition to sate case coverage, also lead to regional and national citing refernces.

NOTE: To obtain regional and national citing references for cases reported prior to the first units of the *National Reporter System*, use your Shepard "state" edition.

AMERICAN LAW REPORTS ANNOTATED (ALR)

A Quick Command Of All Case Law In Point

With Additional References To Law Reviews And Other Legal Authority

LAW FINDERS	ALR Quick Index Alternates: Word Index – 4 vols. Digest – 12 vols. AmJur 2d	ALR 2d–3d Quick Index, Second Edition (Supplemented by Paperback for ALR 3d, vol. 51 –) Alternates: ALR 2d Word Index – 3 vols. ALR 2d Digest – 7 vols. AmJur 2d	Alternates: AmJur 2d	ALR Federal Quick Index, Second Edition Alternates: AmJur 2d U.S. Code Guide
THE LAW	ALR First Series 1919–1948 Vols. 1–175	ALR 2d Second Series 1948–1965 Vols. 1–100	ALR 3d Third Series 1965–Present Vols. 1–	ALR FED ALR Federal 1969–Present Vols. 1–
	AMERICAN LAW REPORTS ANNOTATED			
UPDATING TOOLS	Annotation History Table for ALR, ALR 2d, ALR 3d, ALR FED (located in the back of Quick Index for ALR 3d)			
	ALR Blue Book of Supplemental Decisions 5 Volumes plus Paperback Supp. published annually	ALR 2d Later Case Service 16 Volumes Supplemented on an annual basis by pocket parts	ALR 3d Pocket Part Supps. Published annually for each volume	ALR FED Pocket Part Supps. Published annually for each volume

LCP BWD
THE LAWYERS CO-OPERATIVE PUBLISHING CO.
Rochester, New York 14603
BANCROFT-WHITNEY CO.
San Francisco, California 94107

How to Find U.S. Statutes and U.S. Code Citations

PRINCIPAL FINDING AIDS*

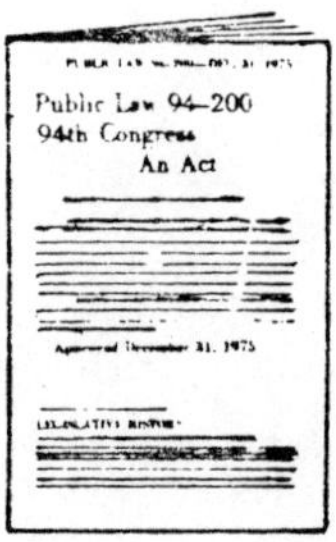

Slip Law

U.S. Statutes

U.S. Code

U.S. Code Supplement

*For description see "REFERENCES", below.

INTRODUCTION

This "How To Find" guide is designed to enable the user to obtain—quickly and easily—an up to date and accurate citation to the United States Statutes at Large and the United States Code.

In using the chart, the reader should read the items from left to right across the two pages.

The *first* column contains the typical references that require further citing, which are (1) Revised Statutes section, (2) date of law, (3) name of law, (4) number of law, (5) statutes citation, and (6) code citation; the *second*, *third*, and *fourth* columns point to the official published volumes in which the citations may be found and suggest logical sequences to follow in making the search; *column five* suggests additional finding aids, some of which are especially useful for citing current legislation; and the *last* column shows some examples of the citations resulting from following the steps in the chart.

The careful following of the steps set forth carries the assurance that each search will be complete and that all appropriate points will be covered.

Publications referred to in abbreviated form are identified and described in a convenient list in the "References" section.

HOW TO FIND CITATIONS TO THE UNITED STATES

IF YOU HAVE this reference	AND YOU USE THESE basic finding aids	
	U.S. STATUTES AT LARGE (new volume added each year)	U.S. CODE[1] (new edition every 6 years)
1. Revised Statutes Section..................... [e.g., Rev. Stat. 56]	[Revised Statutes, 1873, were published as pt. 1, vol. 18, U.S. Statutes at Large; 2d edition published in 1878.]	See U.S.C. tables volume to find U.S.C. section; verify text; then—
2. Date of Law:[2]		
(*a*) For any year *up to* and *through* year of last edition of U.S.C. [e.g., June 22, 1942];	Use statutes volume for that year to check the List of Public Laws; get law number and verify page number from list; then—	Use U.S.C. tables volume to find U.S.C. section; verify text; then—
(*b*) For any year *after* year of last edition of U.S.C. and *through* year of latest supplement;	Use statutes volume for that year to check the List of Public Laws; get law number and verify page number from list; then—	....
(*c*) For current year.......	....	....
3. Name of Law:		
(*a*) For any year *up to* and *through* year of last edition of U.S.C. [e.g., Consumer Credit Protection Act];	....	Use U.S.C. popular names index (preceding general index) to obtain Stat. and U.S.C. citations; verify both; then—
(*b*) For any year *after* year of last edition of U.S.C. and through year of latest supplement;	....	....
(c) For current year......	....	....

STATUTES AT LARGE AND THE UNITED STATES CODE

PLUS latest published U.S. CODE SUPPLEMENT (*all* changes since last edition)	AND/OR THESE additional finding aids (see "REFERENCES")	YOU SHOULD GET this citation
Check latest U.S.C. Supplement for recent changes; verify text.	Check Table 3 in latest U.S.C. Congressional and Administrative News for changes during current period; if code section is included, verify text in same publication or in slip law.	Rev. Stat. 56. 2 U.S.C. 64.
Check latest U.S.C. Supplement for recent changes; verify text.	Check Table 3 in latest U.S.C. Congresssional and Administrative News for changes during current period; if code section is included, verify text in same publication or in slip law.	56 Stat. 377. 36 U.S.C. 171–178.
Use tables volume in latest U.S.C. Supplement to find U.S.C. section; verify text.	Check Table 3 in latest U.S.C. Congressional and Administrative News for changes during current period; if code section is included, verify text in same publication or in slip law.	
....	Use slip law or U.S.C. Congressional and Administrative News *text* to get law number, statutes citation, and to verify subject matter; also use Table 2, U.S.C. Congressional Administrative News to find U.S.C. classification.	
Check latest U.S.C. Supplement for recent changes; verify text.	Check Table 3 in latest U.S.C. Congressional and Administrative News for changes during current period; verify any changes in same publication or in slip law.	82 Stat. 146. 15 U.S.C. 1601 note.
Use U.S.C. popular names index (preceding general index) to obtain Stat. and U.S.C. citation; verify both; then—	Other sources; Index of Popular Names in U.S. Statutes at Large *Laws Affected Tables, 1956–70;* Digest of U.S. Supreme Court Reports; Shepard's Acts and Cases by Popular Name; U.S.C.A. Popular Name Table; U.S.C.S. tables volume.	
....	Use House Calendar *index* and *numerical list* to get bill number, then law number (if assigned); of U.S.C. Congressional and Administrative News *index* or Table 10; use slip law or U.S.C. Congressional and Administrative News *text* to get statutes citation, and U.S.C. classification, and to verify date and subject matter; also, with law number, use Table 2, U.S.C. Congressional and Administrative News to find U.S.C. classification.	

IF YOU HAVE this reference	AND YOU USE THESE basic finding aids	
	U.S. STATUTES AT LARGE (new volume added each year)	U.S. CODE[1] (new edition every 6 years)
4. Number of Law:		
(*a*) For any year *up to* and *through* year of last edition of U.S.C. and the law—		
(1) *does not* have a numerical prefix [e.g., Public Law 702];	[You will need additional information, such as the Congress, the year, or the Stat. volume—year 1956 used here; then] use the Stat. volume to check the List of Public Laws; get and verify page number from list; then—	Use U.S.C. tables volume to find U.S.C. section; verify text; then—
(2) *does* have a numerical prefix [e.g., Public Law 85-227];	Use Stat. volume for the Congress indicated by the numerical prefix; check the List of Public Laws; get and verify page number from list; then—	Use U.S.C. tables volume to find U.S.C. section; verify text; then—
(*b*) For any year *after* last edition of U.S.C. and *through* year of latest Supplement [e.g., Public Law 92-513];	Use Stat. volume for the Congress indicated by the numerical prefix; check the List of Public Laws; get and verify page number from list; then—	....
(*c*) For current year......	....	....
5. Stat. Citation:[3]		
(*a*) For any year *up to* and *through* year of last edition of U.S.C. [e.g., 72 Stat. 997];	Use Stat. volume to get date and law number; verify subject matter; then—	Use U.S.C. tables volume to find U.S.C. section; verify text; then—
(*b*) For any year *after* year of last edition of U.S.C. and *through* year of latest supplement;	Use Stat. volume to get date and law number; verify subject matter; then—	....
(*c*) For current year.......	....	....

PLUS latest published U.S. CODE SUPPLEMENT (*all* changes since last edition)	AND/OR THESE additional finding aids (See "REFERENCES")	YOU SHOULD GET this citation
Check latest U.S.C. Supplement for recent changes; verify text.	Check Table 3 in latest U.S.C. Congressional and Administrative News for changes during current period; if code section is included, verify text in same publication or in slip law.	70 Stat. 531. 25 U.S.C. 304s.
Check latest U.S.C. Supplement recent changes; verify text.	Check Table 3 in latest U.S.C. Congressional and Administrative News for changes during current period; if code section is included, verify text in same publication or in slip law.	71 Strat. 512. 42 U.S.C. 418 and note.
Use tables volume in latest U.S.C. Supplement to find U.S.C., section; verify text.	Check Table 3 in latest U.S.C. Congressional and Administrative News for changes during current period; if code section is included, verify text in same publication or in slip law.	86 Stat. 047. 15 U.S.C. 1901 *et seq.*
....	Use slip law or U.S.C. Congressional and Administrative News *text* to get Stat. citation, U.S.C. classification, and to verify date and subject matter; also, with law number, use Table 2, U.S.C. Congressional and Administrative News to find U.S.C. classification.	
Check latest U.S.C. Supplement for recent changes; verify text; then—	Check Table 3 in latest U.S.C. Congressional and Administrative News for changes during current period; if code section is included, verify text in same publication or in slip law.	72 Stat. 997. 29 U.S.C. 301–309.
Use tables volume in latest U.S.C. Supplement to find U.S.C. section; verify text; then—	Check Table 3 in latest U.S.C. Congressional and Administrative News for changes during current period; if code section is included, verify text in same publication or in slip law.	
....	Use slip law or U.S.C. Congressional abd Administrative News *text* to verify subject matter, date, U.S.C. classification and law number. Table 2, U.S.C. Congressional and Administrative News also may be used to find U.S.C. classification.	

IF YOU HAVE this reference	AND YOU USE THESE basic finding aids	
	U.S. STATUTES AT LARGE (new volume added each year)	U.S. CODE[1] (new edition every 6 years)
6. U.S.C. Citation:		
(*a*) For any year *up to* and *through* year of last edition of U.S.C. [e.g., 7 U.S.C. 182];	....	Check section in U.S.C. to verify subject matter and determine appropriate Stat. citation; verify text against Stat. volume; then—
(*b*) For any year *after* year of last edition of U.S.C. and *through* year of latest supplement;	....	....
(*c*) For current year	....	....

[1] If U.S. Code is not available, use U.S.C.A., or U.S.C.S. and their supplements.
[2] You will need some knowledge of the subject matter if more than one law was signed on the same day.
[3] You will need some knowledge of the subject matter if more than one law appears on the same page.

PLUS latest published U.S. CODE SUPPLEMENT (*all* changes since last edition)	AND/OR THESE additional finding aids (see "REFERENCES") at end of pamphlet)	YOU SHOULD GET this citation
Check latest U.S.C. Supplement for recent changes; verify text; then—	Check Table 3 in latest U.S.C. Congressional and Administrative News for changes during current period; if code section is included, verify text in same publication or in slip law.	42 Stat. 159. 71 U.S.C. 182.
Check section in latest U.S.C. Supplement to verify subject matter and determine appropriate Stat. citation; verify text against Stat. volume; then—	Check Table 3 in latest U.S.C. Congressional and Administrative News for changes during current period, if code section is included, verify text in same publication or in slip law.	
....	Check Table 3 in latest U.S.C. Congressional and Administrative News; if code section is included, get page number on which text of law appears, get law number from that page (footnote should show code citation there), then get specific Stat. citation from slip law and verify subject matter.	

REFERENCES

Title	Description
Government Publications:	
A. Principal Finding Aids	
1. Slip law.......................	A pamphlet print of each public and private law enacted by Congress, issued a few days after a bill becomes law; public (but not private) slip laws carry the statutes' page numbers that will be their permanent citation in a future statutes volume, marginal notes and citations (including U.S. Code and D.C. Code classifications of current legislation), and a guide to legislative history (which also contains dates of related presidential statements); text of both public and private laws with annotations are later cumulated and bound as part of the Stat. volume.
2. Stat.............................	United States Statutes at Large; contains all public and private laws and concurrent resolutions enacted during a session of Congress, plus reorganization plans, proposed and ratified amendments to the Constitution, and proclamations by the president, with finding aids including legislative history and Laws Affected Tables; arrangement is chronological by approval date in each category; by law, these volumes are "legal evidence" (1 U.S.C. 112); only the general and permanent laws are codified (arranged by subject in titles) in the U.S.C.
3. U.S.C..........................	United States Code and its annual, cumulative supplements; published every six years; only the general and permanent laws of the United States are codified (arranged by subject in titles) in the U.S. Code; temporary, local, or private laws are not included; the code establishes "prima facie the laws of the United States" except "whenever titles of such Code shall have been enacted into positive law the text thereof shall be legal evidence" (1 U.S.C. 204(a)); to date, nineteen titles have been enacted into positive laws; contains list of acts by popular name, index, and tables.
4. U.S.C. Supplement.....	Annual, cumulative supplements to the United States Code; contains all changes in or additions to the general and permanent laws and Code ancillaries since the last edition of the Code.
B. Others	
5. Laws Affected Tables..	Published in each statutes volume since 1956, showing the prior laws affected by the public laws in each volume.
6. Laws Affected Tables for 1956–1970.	Fifteen-year cumulation, published separately; contains Index of Popular Name Acts Affected; a five-year cumulation for period 1971–1975, available 1977.
7. House Calendar...........	Calendars of the U. S. House of Representatives and History of Legislation (1 publication)—very useful for following day-to-day progress of legislation through both Houses of Congress; index, usually on Mondays; final edition covers the session (1st) or the Congress (end of 2d session).
8. Index Analysis of Federal Statutes, 1789–1893; Index to Federal Statutes, 1874–1931.	Subject index covering all general and permanent laws through 46 Stat. (March 4, 1931); useful for tracing early legislation.

REFERENCES (Cont.)

Title	Description
Nongovernment Publications:	
9. U.S.C. Cong. and Adm. News.	United States Code Congressional and Administrative News—published at least monthly during each session of Congress; monthly when Congress is not in session. Gives slip law information, including legislative history; has subject index, list of popular name acts, tables; material is currently supplemental to and annually codified in U.S.C.A.
10. U.S.C.A. and supplements.	United States Code Annotated—an annotated version of the U. S. Code with periodic supplements and annual, cumulative pocket parts.
11. U.S.C.S. and supplements.	United States Code Service; annotated version of U. S. Code with monthly advance service containing text of slip laws, proclamations, and so forth, and cumualtive tables and index; annual, cumulative pocket parts.
12. Shepard's Acts and Cases by Popular Names.	Bound volume of federal and state acts by popular name or short title with U. S. Code and U. S. Statutes at Large citations; cumulative supplements.

Index and Source Finder

(includes names, topics, titles of books and subjects)

About the Author

Edward J. Bander has had the rare experience of working in the largest law library in the world (Harvard) as well as in one of the smallest (U.S. Court of Appeals, Boston). A librarian and lawyer, he has served judges, lawyers, clients, professors, students, paralegals, and the public; taught legal research at New York University; edited and written six books (one a Lawyers Literary Club Selection); and been published in *Commentary*, ABA *Journal* and a number of law reviews and bar journals, as well as in the Boston *Globe* and the New York *Times.* His zest for making law intelligible began with an article published in the *New Jersey State Bar Journal*, "How to Practice Law Without a License." Mr. Bander is in *Who's Who in American Law*.